KERR AND HUNTER ON RECEIVERS AND ADMINISTRATORS

First Supplement to the Eighteenth Edition

AUSTRALIA
Law Book Co.
Sydney

CANADA and USA
Carswell
Toronto

HONG KONG
Sweet & Maxwell Asia

NEW ZEALAND
Brookers
Wellington

SINGAPORE and MALAYSIA
Sweet & Maxwell Asia
Singapore and Kuala Lumpur

KERR AND HUNTER
on
RECEIVERS AND ADMINISTRATORS

FIRST SUPPLEMENT TO THE
EIGHTEENTH EDITION

BY

Muir Hunter Q.C. M.A. (Oxon), LL.D (Hon), MRI

One of Her Majesty's Counsel and a
Bencher of Gray's Inn
Visiting Professor of Insolvency Law,
Bournemouth University and at Kingston University

Edited for Scotland by

David A. Bennett, M.A., LL.B. (Edin.) W.S.

Solicitor, Gillespie Macandrew LLP, W.S., Edinburgh
Visiting Professor of Company Law,
The University of Edinburgh

LONDON
SWEET & MAXWELL
2006

Published in 2006 by
Sweet & Maxwell Limited of
100 Avenue Road London NW3 3PF
http:/www/sweetandmaxwell.thomson.com
Typeset by J.P. Price, Chilcompton, Somerset
Printed and bound in Great Britain by
Athenaeum Press Ltd, Gateshead

A CIP catalogue record for this book is available from the British Library

ISBN Main Work 0–421–70540–X
ISBN Supplement–10 0–421–95590–2
ISBN Supplement–13 978–0–421–95590–5

No natural forests were destroyed to make this product, only farmed timber was used and re-planted.

PREFACE TO THE FIRST SUPPLEMENT TO THE EIGHTEENTH EDITION

Since the eighteenth edition of this work was published in January 2005, there have been many significant changes in the fields of insolvency procedure with which it deals.

The House of Lords, sitting as a bench of seven, reversed the decision of the Court of Appeal in *Re Spectrum Plus Ltd,* (*in liquidation*), *National Westminster Bank v Spectrum Plus Ltd,*[1] and restored the judgment of the Vice-Chancellor. The question was whether the standard banking form of bank charge over book debts constituted a floating charge, or, as the Bank contended, a fixed charge.The House's decision reversed the longstanding decision (at first instance) in *Siebe Gorman & Co Ltd v Barclays Bank Ltd,*[2] which the Court of Appeal had approved and followed. This decision, in theory at least, invalidates the dealing with and the enforcement of charges in the *Siebe Gorman* form as if they were fixed charges, rather than as floating charges, as they must now be regarded. It envisages the potential re-opening of many debenture-accounts, covering the last 27 years or more.

The Bank sought to rescue the position for the banking community by contending that the fact that charges in the *Siebe Gorman* form had been regarded universally, since the date of that decision, as fixed charges should justify the form being treated as having acquired a validity to that effect by time and commercial usage. This submission was rejected by the House, which pointed out that the decision had been at first instance only.[3] The Bank's second attempt to retrieve the situation was a plea that the judgment of the House should be declared to be only of prospective effect, and not—as judicially it must be—of retrospective effect. This plea was also rejected.[4] The Government has inserted into the Companies Bill, now before Parliament, a clause, reversing the House's decision.

Still in the field of charges, the Court of Appeal has adjudicated on the consequences of the invalid appointment under a debenture of a receiver, who took over and ran the company's premises, contracts and business.

This raised the problem of whether an actionable tort could be committed by the wrongful interference with a cause of action. The Court, by a reluctant majority, found that this was not possible, and limited the company to the recovery of very modest damages.[5]

An administrative receiver was held by the Court of Appeal to have committed wrongful acts, in extracting sensitive documents from the company, not for use in his receivership, but for the purpose of handing them to his debenture holder, to use in its other litigation. The company's

---

[1] [2005] UKHL 41; [2005] 2 B.C.L.C. 219, HL, reversing [2004] EWCA Civ 670; [2005] 2 B.C.L.C. 30, CA.
[2] [1979] 2 Lloyd's Rep. 142.
[3] See fn.1, per Lord Nicholls at [39]–[42], Lord Hope at [64].
[4] See fn.1, per Lord Nicholls at [43], Lord Hope at [71].
[5] *OBG Ltd v Allan* [2005] EWCA Civ 106; [2005] 1 B.C.L.C. 711, CA.

board were held entitled to sue the debenture holder and the receiver, on behalf of the company.[6]

More changes have been made in the field of administration, and much case law has developed, arising both from purely domestic cases, and also from multi-State cross-border cases, under the EC Regulation on Insolvency Proceedings. The policy of the Government, and the increasing practice of the courts, are to encourage the use of administration, in the place of liquidations.

On the procedural front, insolvent partnerships have now achieved parity with companies, in being authorised to enter administration by the appointment of an administrator, either by the holder of a qualifying agricultural charge, or by the members of the partnership.[7] The accidental imposition on insolvent partnerships of an obligation to pay "the prescribed part" of their assets to unsecured creditors has been corrected.[8]

The jurisdiction of the English courts to appoint administrators has been extended, by the EC Regulation on Insolvency Proceedings, to cover companies which, though registered, or even operating, abroad, are found to have their centre of main interests ("COMI") here. These appointments can lead to difficulties, such as where the administrators asked the court to make a declaration of the powers and duties of an English administrator for the information, and comfort, of foreign creditors, directors or shareholders of such companies.[9]

The field of directions, sought from the court by administrators, has been productive of many new cases, and some striking judgments.The court, while emphasising its unwillingness to answer abstract questions or to rule on academic propositions, has discovered that it possesses an overriding inherent jurisdiction, authorising it, by the giving of directions, to empower administrators, who are faced with serious administrative or legal problems, to take steps to solve them which prima facie lie outside their scope.[10] This power has been employed to briefly extend the duration of the appointment of an administrator after its expiry, notwithstanding the statutory prohibition.[11]

The one field in which there appears to have been as yet no case law to guide the litigant, is in the jurisdiction to apply to set aside the appointment of an administrator, where it was applied for, or made, "for an improper motive".[12] The problems presented to the practitioner by this obscure cause of action, which were extensively discussed in the main work in Chapter 17, remain unresolved and unilluminated.

---

[6] *Sutton v G E Capital Commercial Finance Ltd* [2004] EWCA Civ 315; [2004] 2 B.C.L.C. 612, CA.

[7] Insolvent Partnerships (Amendment) Order 2005 (SI 2005/1516).

[8] See fn.7, partly repealed by Insolvent Partnerships (Amendment) Order, 2006 (SI 2006/622).

[9] *Re MG Rover Espana SA & ors* [2005] B.P.I.R. 1162.

[10] *Re WBSL Realisations 1992 Ltd* [1995] 2 B.C.L.C. 576; *Re Mark One (Oxford Street) Plc* [1999] 1 W.L.R. 445.

[11] *Re T T Industries Ltd* [2006] B.P.I.R. 597 notwithstanding IA 1986, Sch.B1, para.77(1)(b).

[12] IA 1986, Sch.B1, para.81. But in an unreported case, an unjustified application for an administration order was rejected as presented for an "improper purpose"; *Re Doltable Ltd* [2005] EWHC 1804 (Ch); [2006] 1 B.C.L.C. 384.

In the field of the personal liability of administrative receivers (and, to a more limited extent, of administrators) for sums payable to the employees of companies whose contracts of employment they are deemed to have "adopted", attempts to extend the categories of such sums so as to include protective awards, payments for unfair dismissal, redundancy payments and money in lieu of notice, have been dismissed.[13]

The contentious subject, whether a liquidator can recover his costs of administration out of the assets of a company charged by a floating charge, has also been ruled upon by the House of Lords, which held that, in any liquidation, there are two distinct funds to meet charges and liabilities, the fund of assets bound by a floating charge (whether crystallised or not) for the charge-holder, and the fund of the company's other assets, for the liquidator and the creditors. Each fund is a trust, to be expended only to defray the liabilities for which it is constituted; however, where the liquidator has incurred expense in preserving or realising assets bound by a charge, he may apply for reimbursement of his expenses out of those assets.[14] But he cannot recover his costs of unsuccessful litigation from the assets.[15]

The field of administration law has developed much case law, and some striking rulings, and also some judicial dissent.The subject of "qualifying liabilities", referred to above, was the subject of dissent at first instance, which was resolved by the Court of Appeal.[16] Comparable dissent was manifested on the subject of whether an administrator, moving from administration to voluntary winding-up or dissolution, required an order of the court to authorise it.[17]

The remuneration and conditions, and the proper duration of appointment, of receivers of the High Court was extensively examined by the Court of Appeal, in a Criminal Justice Act 1988 case, where the remuneration of a receiver appointed in support of a restraint order was in issue.[18] The Court emphasised that the remuneration of all High Court receivers was now regulated by CPR Pt 69, but not their expenses, which fell within their accounting for assets recovered.[19]

The Court also emphasised that receivership must not be continued when it was no longer serving any valid purpose, and that close financial control must be maintained of all receiverships under the criminal confiscation

---

[13] *Re Huddersfield Fine Worsteds & ors* [2005] EWCA Civ 1072; [2005] 4 All E.R. 886, a.

[14] *Buchler v Talbot* [2003] UKHL 9; [2004] 1 B.C.L.C. 281, HL, disapproving of *Re Barleycorn Enterprises Ltd* [1970] Ch. 465, CA.

[15] *R B G Resources Ltd (in liquidation) v Rastogi* [2005] EWHC 199 (Ch); [2005] 2 B.C.L.C. 592.

[16] See fn.13.

[17] *Re Ballast Plc (in administration)* [2005] 1 B.C.L.C. 446; [2005] 1 W.L.R. 1928, per Blackburne, J; *per contra Re G H E Realisations Ltd* [2005] EWHC 2400 (Ch); per Rimer, J.

[18] *Capewell v Customs & Excise (No.1)* [2004] EWCA Civ 1628; *(No.2)* [2004] EWCA Civ 964; [2005] B.P.I.R. 1266, CA.

[19] See fn.18 (second hearing) at [25].

statutes. Guidelines proposed by counsel for the appointment and regulation of receivers under those statutes were commended by the Court.[20]

The law is stated generally as at April 1, 2006.

Introductory comments in Scotland and Scots law follow.

MUIR HUNTER
GRAY'S INN

MAY 2006

[20] See fn.18 (first hearing) at [66].

[*Delete Publisher's Note and substitute: page vii*]

SCOTLAND AND SCOTS LAW
INTRODUCTORY COMMENTS

The main body of the text of this work has been written from the point of view of English law and companies incorporated in England and Wales. Scots law and Scottish court procedure, which are applicable to companies incorporated in Scotland, differs from English law in many respects, the relevant differences being noted in the text of this Supplement.

Scots law relating to floating charges, receivers and administration is entirely statute based. Floating charges were introduced into Scots law by the Companies (Floating Charges) (Scotland) Act 1961, which also introduced to Scotland the system of registering all securities granted by companies incorporated in Scotland ("charges") at Companies House. Although integrated with Companies House for England and Wales in Cardiff, the Registrar of Companies maintains a separate office in Edinburgh. After amendment by subsequent legislation, Scots law on floating charges now appears as Chapter I of Part XVIII of the Companies Act 1985 (Sections 462 to 466) and the Scottish provisions on the registration of charges by companies incorporated in Scotland are now found in Chapter II in Part XII of the same Act (Sections 410 to 424).

Receivership was introduced into Scots law by the Companies (Floating Charges and Receivers) (Scotland) Act 1972, the current provisions of which appear as Chapters II of Part III of the Insolvency Act 1986 (Sections 50 to 71) together also with Chapters III and IV of the same Part III (Sections 72 to 72H). In Scots law only the holder of a floating charge is entitled to appoint a receiver (subject to the limitations on that power discussed in the main text) (see Chapter 30).

Administration was introduced in Scotland (along with England and Wales) by the Insolvency Act 1986 and the current statutory provisions which apply in both jurisdictions now appear (after revision by the Enterprise Act 2002) as Schedule B1 to the Insolvency Act 1986.

The establishment of the Scottish Parliament by the Scotland Act 1998

By this Act, the power to legislate with respect to Scots law has been delegated to the Scottish Parliament, except in those matters where legislative authority is reserved to the Westminster Parliament. In the context of this work, power to legislate in respect of floating charges and receivers has been delegated to the Scottish Parliament (other than the regulation of insolvency practitioners, the law of preferential debts and co-operation of insolvency courts). The supervision of the procedure in individual receiverships and the relative insolvency rules have also been delegated, along with the power to make rules of court in relation to all insolvency proceedings. Supervision of these delegated procedures is the responsibility of the Accountant in Bankruptcy ("A.I.B.") (a Scottish official). Consequently, statutory forms in relation to them are now lodged with the A.I.B. instead of (or in some cases as well as) the Registrar of Companies. Legislative power with respect to administration, however, is reserved to the Westminster Parliament. Subordinate legislation in Scotland following devolution is by way of Scottish Statutory Instrument (abbreviated as "SSI").

At the time of writing two major pieces of legislation are before the UK and Scottish Parliaments. The Companies Bill contains a power to effect changes in company law by way of statutory instrument, and it is understood that this will be used to amend the provisions of the Companies Act 1985 with respect to the registration of charges in both Scotland and England and Wales. A Bill currently before the Scottish Parliament entitled "The Bankruptcy and Diligence Etc (Scotland) Bill" includes in Part 2 revised provisions for the creation, effect and registration of floating charges in Scotland. Neither Bill directly affects receivership or administration.

So far as Scotland is concerned this Supplement endeavours to state the law as it stood on August 31, 2006.

David A Bennett, M.A., LL.B., W.S., Solicitor
Consultant, Gillespie Macandrew LLP, W.S., Edinburgh
Visiting Professor of Company Law, The University of Edinburgh

HOW TO USE THIS SUPPLEMENT

This is the First Supplement to the Eighteenth Edition of Kerr and Hunter on Receivers and Administrators.

Where a heading in the table of contents has been marked with the symbol ■, the material under that heading has been added to or amended in this First Supplement.

Within each chapter, updating information is referenced to the relevant paragraph in the main work.

It should be noted that there is no material for Chapters 8, 13 and 26.

CONTENTS

TABLE OF CASES

(All references are to paragraph number)

Thomas, Re; Thomas v Thompson [1930] 1 Ch. 194, Ch D 2–9
Thomas Montgomery & Sons v Wallace (1891) 28 S.L.R. 1R, CH 30–39
T[illegible] Inland Revenue Commissioners; sub nom. Inland Revenue Commissioners v [illegible]; Inland Revenue Commissioners v [illegible]; Inland Revenue Commissioners [2002] UKHL 8; [2002] 1 W.L.R. [illegible] [2002] [illegible]; [2002] S.T.C. [illegible]; [2002] B.T.C. [illegible]; [2002] [illegible] 2002 S.C. (H.L.) 59; 2002 S.L.T. [illegible]; (2002) 146 S.J.L.B. [illegible]; The Times, February 28, 2002, HL 34–11
Troy, Re v Wilson (1881) 8 R. (H.L.) 42; (1881) 18 S.L.R. [illegible] 30–18, 30–39

Trustees [illegible] and [illegible] Ltd [illegible] [2000] 1 W.L.R. [illegible]; [2000] [illegible] 15–57
Trustee of [illegible] (No.2) [illegible]; [2000] 1 W.L.R. [illegible]; The Times, April 25, 2000, Ch D 36–38
Trust of [illegible] v [illegible] [2009] EWCA Civ [illegible]; [2009] R.V.R. 157, The Times, March [illegible] 2009, CA 15–157
Turnbull v [illegible] of Scottish [illegible] 1929 S.C. [illegible] 1929 S.L.T. 589, [illegible] 30–36, 30–40

[illegible] Estates Ltd v [illegible] Estates [illegible] [1989] 1 W.L.R. [illegible]; [1989] [illegible] (Ch D) 30–62

WASH Nominees Pty Ltd, Re [illegible] [1995] [illegible] 2–13
W[illegible] v [illegible] [1973] [illegible] 30–58
Westminster [illegible] v [illegible] [1970] [illegible] R. 66 [illegible] 30–120
Wickham [illegible] 30–36
W[illegible] [2008] 2 B.C.L.C. [illegible] 30–55
[illegible] v [illegible] Co. Ltd [2001] [illegible] CA 30–4
W[illegible] [1952] 1 Ch. [illegible] Ch D 2–64

Y[illegible], Re [1935] Ch. [illegible] Ch D 30–3, 30–8
Young [illegible] [1965] Ch. [illegible] [1964] [illegible] 30–108
[illegible] CA 30–4

TABLE OF STATUTES

EUROPEAN AND INTERNATIONAL LEGISLATION

TABLE OF EUROPEAN AND INTERNATIONAL CONVENTION AND TREATIES

TABLE OF STATUTORY INSTRUMENTS

TABLE OF PRACTICE DIRECTIONS

TABLE OF CIVIL PROCEDURE RULES

Part I

The Appointment of Receivers by the Court

[*Amend Part I title to read: page* 1]
The Appointment of Receivers by the Court in English Law
(For Scotland see Part VII and Chapter 30 below)

CHAPTER 1

PRINCIPLES ON WHICH A RECEIVER IS APPOINTED BY THE COURT

Appointment to preserve property. **1–8**
[*Add to footnote 36–38, after "Homan* 1032": *page* 7]
, see at fn.30, above.

Pleading and practice. **1–13**
[*In the sixth line delete sentence beginning "References to writs and originating summonses . . ." and substitute: page* 9]
References to writs and originating summonses are now replaced by references to claim forms and, where appropriate, applications and application notices.

CHAPTER 2

IN WHAT CASES A RECEIVER WILL BE APPOINTED

SECTION 2—IN THE CASE OF EXECUTORS AND TRUSTEES

2–3 Misconduct, etc., a ground for a receiver.
[*In footnote 31, after "Sch.6 (as . . . " delete: page* 16]
to be

2–5 Poverty, etc., of trustee.
[*In the fifth line, after "spouse," add: page* 17]
or, now, civil partner.[42a]

[42a] Since the coming into force of the Civil Partnership Act 2004 on December 5, 2005.

2–9 Trust of land.
[*In paragraph cross-heading, add new text after "land.": page* 18]
The new law as to joint ownership.

[*Delete the first paragraph and substitute: page* 18]
Land can no longer be held in undivided shares, and the interests of tenants in common take effect behind what is now to be known as "a trust of land", replacing the former designation, "a trust for sale", enacted by the Trusts of Land and Appointment of Trustees Act 1996.[58]

That Act[59] substantially changed the law, where land is held by more than one person, and where the interest of one co-owner (or more than one, but not all) has been charged to an outside party.[60] The former rule[60a] that, save in exceptional circumstances, the wish of a trustee in bankruptcy or of a chargee of a co-owner to sell the property should prevail over the interests of the other co-owner or co-owners, or of their chargees,[60b] has been repealed, although it remains substantially in operation for trustees in bankruptcy.[60c]

On any application to the court by a chargee under the new Act, to deal with land subject to a trust of land, the court has to have regard to four matters: (a) the intentions of the creators of the trust, (b) the purposes for which the trust was created, (c) the welfare of minors occupying, or reasonably likely to occupy, the land, and finally (d) the interests of a secured creditor or of any beneficiary of the trust.[60d] The interests of any secured creditor is therefore now legislated for as being of no more importance than the other three potentially interested parties.

By contrast, the interest of a trustee in bankruptcy of a person holding an interest in land as a co-owner is excluded from the ambit of the Act,[60e] and is legislated for by a new section in the Insolvency Act 1986, s.335A. Any application by the trustee must be made to the Bankruptcy Court; but the interests of the bankrupt and his children and family are only entitled to be bracketed equally with those of the creditors for the twelve months after the first vesting of the land in a trustee in bankruptcy; after that period has expired, the court shall assume, unless the circumstances of the case are exceptional, that the interests of the creditors outweigh all other considerations.

It would therefore appear that, in view of the four matters to which the court is to have regard on an equal footing, that a chargee who seeks the appointment of a receiver over land of this status, can no longer expect to receive the instant satisfaction that he has enjoyed under previous legislation, but must seek to persuade the court that his application should be treated as paramount.

[58] Partition actions have been abolished, but, in addition to the trustees' power under L.P.A. s.28(2), exercisable where the shares have vested in trustees, whether or not subject to a further settlement (see *Re Brooker* [1934] Ch. 610, and *cf. Re Thomas* [1930] 1 Ch. 194), the court has jurisdiction to order partition or sale, but subject of course now to the provisions of the 1996 Act.

[59] The Trusts of Land and Appointment of Trustees Act 1996, came into force on January 1, 1997.

[60] *Mortgage Corporation v Shaire* [2001] Ch. 747; [2000] B.P.I.R. 483, where Neuberger, J. considered that the decisions in *Re Citro* [1991] Ch. 142, CA, and *Lloyd's Bank v Byrne & Byrne* [1993] 1 F.L.R. 369, CA, did not apply to the new Act, s.15 of which had changed the law, giving the court "greater flexibility". See the Civil Court Practice (2006) CPR 73.10(3).

[60a] Law of Property Act 1925, s.30 (repealed).

[60b] fn.58, s.15(4).

[60c] fn.58, s.15(1) and (2).

[60d] fn.58, s.15(1)(c).

[60e] See fn.60b.

SECTION 3—PENDING GRANT OF PROBATE OR LETTERS OF ADMINISTRATION

Pleading. 2–18

[*In the sixth line, delete "will" and substitute: page* 24]
bill

SECTION 4—IN CASES BETWEEN MORTGAGOR AND MORTGAGEE

Rentcharge. 2–23

[*In the second line of the second paragraph, delete "providing" and substitute: page* 27]
provided

Section 5—In Cases Between Debtor and Creditor

2–42 **Partnership Act 1890, section 23.**
[*Renumber footnote 67–68 as 67: page* 38]

[*Add footnote 68 to the end of paragraph 2–42: page* 38]

68 See also the Insolvent Partnerships (Amendment) Order, 2005 (SI 2005/1516) and para.14–13.

2–43 **Appointment of receiver over insolvent partnership.**
[*In footnote 75 delete text "(2004)" and substitute: page* 39]
(2006)

2–45 **Family proceedings.**
[*In footnote 82, delete text "Ivirney v Ivirney" and substitute: page* 39]
Ivimey v Ivimey

Section 8—Companies Incorporated under the Companies Acts

2–63 **Limited validity of debenture.**[3]
[*Delete paragraph cross-heading "Limited validity of debenture.*[3]*" and substitute: page* 52]
Former limited validity of debentures.[3]

3 See generally Palmer, *Company Precedents* (30th edn), Vol.III, Ch.5.

[*Delete both paragraphs and substitute: page* 52]
Before the amendments enacted by the Companies Act 1989, considered below[3a]; which took effect on February 3, 1991, the legal position as to the validity of a company's acts in issuing debentures was as stated in the next paragraph. That law, with respect to the powers of a limited company, express or implied, may conceivably still need to be considered, relating to the acts of a company done before that date.

Under the old law and commercial practice, the memorandum of association of a company almost invariably conferred an express power to mortgage the undertaking.[4] But, even in the absence of an express power, a commercial or trading company was regarded as having an implied power to borrow on security.[5] Such a power might also be implied in the case of other companies, as incidental to the purposes for which they were formed. But in the case of a non-commercial company, such as a members' club, it was held that even a power to create debentures did not necessarily imply a power to charge the assets;[6] notwithstanding the new provisions, this may still be the law. Uncalled capital could only be charged under an express power.[7]

[3a] See para.2–64, below.

[4] As to the possibility of borrowing, formally in order, but being in law ultra vires, see *Charterbridge Corporation Ltd v Lloyds Bank Ltd* [1970] Ch. 62; *Introductions Ltd v National Provincial Bank Ltd* (1970) Ch. 199, sub nom. *Re Introductions Ltd* [1969] 1 All E.R. 887, CA. The position in this latter case would not have been affected by a copy of the memorandum. See also *Rolled Steel Products (Holdings) Ltd v British Steel Corp* [1986] Ch. 246, CA, which suggests that, if the memorandum contains a power to borrow, no borrowing can be ultra vires, if it is made formally in accordance with that power, although of course such borrowing may be a misfeasance on the part of the directors. This conclusion appears to be based upon a misunderstanding of the *Introductions Ltd* decision, and is wholly at variance with the decision of the House of Lords in *Sinclair v Brougham* [1914] A.C. 398. Having regard to the new ss.35, 35A and 35B, inserted into the Companies Act 1985 by Companies Act 1989, s.108(1), such literalist reasoning can now have no practical consequences, save in relation to a transaction where the other party does not "deal with" the company, as for example in the case of a voluntary payment not made in the interests of the company (see *Re Lee Behrens & Co. Ltd* [1932] 2 Ch. D. 45); and see fn.6 below, and Ch.19, below.

[5] See *Re Badger* [1905] 1 Ch. 568, 573; *Re Patent File Co.* (1870) L.R. 6 Ch. 83. In the case of industrial assurance companies, the industrial assurance fund cannot be charged: see Industrial Assurance Act 1923, s.13.

[6] *Wylie v Carlyon* [1922] 1 Ch. 51; nor does the fact that the advance was employed in paying off a prior charge necessarily create a charge: *ibid*. See now the definition of "debenture" in Companies Act, s.744.

[7] *Re Pyle Works* (1890) 44 Ch. D. 534; *Newton v Debenture-Holders' Co.* [1895] A.C. 244.

Registration under Part XII of the Companies Act 1985, after amendment by the Companies Act 1989. 2–65

[*Delete paragraph and substitute: page* 53]

Part IV of the Companies Act 1989, which was enacted to reform the provisions of Part XII of the 1985 Act on the registration of charges, has never been brought into force, and is scheduled to be repealed by Sch.15 of the Companies Bill, currently before Parliament. Alternative provisions are in preparation, based on the 2005 proposals of the Law Commission.

Protection of charges taken in good faith and for value. 2–66

[*In the final line of footnote 25, delete text "negotiable" and substitute: page* 54]

registrable

[*Add new paragraph 2–66A: page* 55]

Conclusiveness of registration, even if mistakenly made. Where application is made for the registration of a debenture or other security out of time, and the court is satisfied with the explanation for the failure to register in time,[33a] the court will make an order, known as an "*In re Charles* order".[33b] The order gives leave to register out of time, but with leave to the company, its administrators and any unsecured creditors to apply, within 14 days, to set it aside. Where the registrar mistakenly issued a certificate of registration, before the expiry of the 14 days, the certificate was held to be conclusive and binding, in favour of the debenture-holder,[33c] and applications by the company and its administrators to set it aside were dismissed.[33d] 2–66A

[33a] Companies Act 1985, s.404.

[33b] From *In re Charles & Co. Ltd* [1935] W N 15.

[33c] Companies Act 1985, s.404(1)(b).

[33d] *Ali v Top Marques Car Rental Ltd and ors* (2006) *The Times,* February 10. For a case where the non-registration of a charge could not have caused any prejudice to any other person, and registration out of time was permitted, see *Confiance v Timespan Images & another* [2005] EWHC 1557 (Ch); [2005] 2 B.C.L.C. 693, applying *Re Braemar Investments Ltd* [1988] B.C.L.C. 566.

2–67 Subsequent invalidity of debentures.

[*In the first line of the final paragraph, delete sentence beginning "The time between the presentation of a petition for the making . . ." and substitute: page* 56]

The time between the making of any application for an administration order and the making of such an order, as is the time between the filing with the court of a copy of a notice of intention to appoint an administrator (under IA 1986, Sch.B1, para.14 or para.22), and the making of an appointment under one or other of those paragraphs, is in all cases a "relevant time".[40]

[40] Insolvency Act 1986, s.245(3)(c) (as amended by Enterprise Act 2002, Sch.13, para.31, with effect from September 15, 2003).

2–69 Onset of insolvency.

[*In the fifth line, after "petition" add: page* 57]

(now the making of an application)

[*Add to the end of footnote 50: page* 57]

See para.17–41.

2–71 Right to appointment.

[*In footnote 88, delete text "Ch.28" and substitute: page* 60]

Ch.27

2–72 Where receiver appointed by debenture holders.

[*In the seventh line, after "crystallised" add: page* 60]

by virtue of

Section 11—In Partnership Cases

2–92 Disputes referable to arbitration.

[*Add to the end of paragraph: page* 71]

An administrative receiver has the power, unless it is expressly excluded by the terms of the debenture, to refer to arbitration any question affecting the company.[94a]

[94a] See Insolvency Act 1986, s.42, and Sch.1, para.6.

Section 12—In Cases of Mental Disorder

2–98 [*Add to the end of paragraph: page* 73]

Legislation is now before Parliament which, if enacted, will considerably extend the jurisdiction of the Court of Protection.

Receivers under the Mental Health Act 1983. 2–99
[*Add to the end of footnote 30: page* 74]
See fn.34a.

[*Add new paragraph 2–100A: page* 74]
The Fee Structure. The fee structure controlling the fees chargeable for receiverships by receivers appointed under the Mental Health Act 1953, and the Court of Protection Rules 2001,[34a] has been substantially amended.[34b] 2–100A

[34a] The Court of Protection Rules 2001 (SI 2002/824), as amended by SI2002/833, SI 2003/1733, SI 2004/1291 and SI 2005/667.
[34b] The Court of Protection (Amendment) Rules 2006 (SI 2006/653), which came into force on April 1, 2006.

Dealing with patient's estate. 2–102
[*In the third line of the fourth paragraph, after "wife." add new footnote 46a: page* 75]
[46a] The provisions relating to wives and husbands must now be read, since the coming into force of the Civil Partnership Act 2004, as including civil partners.

Discharge of a receiver. 2–105
[*In footnote 60, delete text "para.2–00, above." and substitute: page* 77]
paras 2–98, above.

SECTION 13—IN THE CASE OF PERSONS IN POSSESSION OF REAL ESTATE UNDER A LEGAL TITLE

Practice of the Court of Chancery. 2–106
[*In the seventh line, after "fraud" add: page* 78]
or

SECTION 14—IN CASES BETWEEN LANDLORD AND TENANT

Historical development. 2–108
[*Add to the end of footnote 90: page* 80]
See also *Daiches v Bluelake Investments Ltd* [1985] 17 H.L.R. 543.

SECTION 16—IN OTHER CASES

Interpleader. 2–116
[*In the third line, after "sheriff" add: page* 89]
(now the High Court enforcement officer),

CHAPTER 3

OVER WHAT PROPERTY A RECEIVER MAY BE APPOINTED

3–3 Assignments contrary to public policy.
[*In footnote 11, delete text "Practice Direction" and substitute: page* 92]
Probate Division

3–22 Settled land.
[*In the third line, delete "property" and substitute: page* 103]
proper

3–24 Miscellaneous.
[*Add to the end of footnote 84: page* 104]
Now, made the subject of a third party debt order.

COMPANIES

3–28 [*Add to the end of footnote 3: page* 105]
See para.2–64, above.

CHAPTER 4

WHO MAY BE APPOINTED RECEIVER

Considerations looked at in making the appointment. **4–5**

[*In the second line of footnote 43, delete text "Tollefmache" and substitute: page* 111]

Tollemache

Chapter 5

MODES OF APPOINTING A RECEIVER OF THE COURT: THE NEW PROCEDURES

5–3 **The Practice Guides.**
[*In the first line delete "2004" and substitute: page* 119]
2006

[*In the sixth line delete "had not been published at the time of going to press.", and substitute: page* 119]
will not now be separately published.

5–6 **Receivership jurisdictions not covered by CPR r.69.**
[*In the second line, after "receivers," add: page* 119]
including receivers under the criminal confiscation statutes,[4a]

[4a] See Ch.27, paras 27–42—27–42A.

5–31 **Receiver by way of equitable execution: practice on application.**
[*In the first line of the third paragraph, delete "2004" and substitute: page* 126]
2006

[*In the second line of the third paragraph, delete "Ord.30;" and substitute: page* 126]
Ord.51, and see CPR QBG 11.7.2.;

Part II

The Structure of Court-appointed Receiverships

[*Amend Part II title to read: page* 135]
The Structure of Court-appointed Receiverships in England and Wales
(This part has no application in Scotland. For Scotland, see Part VII and Chapter 30 below)

Chapter 6

EFFECT OF APPOINTMENT AND POSSESSION OF A RECEIVER

Bankruptcy of the debtor. **6–23**
[*In the final line of footnote 4, delete text "act" and substitute: page* 146]
action

Sheriff may not disturb possession of a receiver. **6–50**
[*In the second line, delete "sheriff" and substitute: page* 160]
High Court enforcement officer (this should presumably include a county court bailiff)

[*Add to the end of paragraph: page* 160]
See Ch.28, below.

[*Add new paragraph 6–51B: page* 162]
Principles regulating transfer of English assets to a foreign liquidation. **6–51B**
Under a scheme of arrangement, liquidators of an Australian company applied for an order for the transfer of the company's English assets to them; it was held that there was no power to order such a transfer, as the Australian distribution scheme was not the same as the English one.[41a]

That case was followed, where the provisional liquidators of a Korean company applied to the English court for an order permitting the sending of the proceeds of sale of the company's English assets to a receiver appointed by the Korean court, and the following principles were stated:

(1) where there is a foreign principal liquidation and an ancillary English liquidation, the English court cannot order the transfer of the English assets, unless the foreign insolvency's distribution scheme is substantially the same as the English one;

(2) if there is no English liquidation, other than the appointment of provisional liquidators, the decision as to whether to order a transfer of assets is a matter for the court's discretion;

(3) if the provisional liquidation is likely to proceed to a full English winding-up, it would not be right to order a transfer of assets, unless the distribution schemes are substantially the same;

(4) if no liquidation is likely in England, there is no objection to a transfer, as the English scheme of distribution will never apply.

Nearly all the creditors would be held to be likely to be advantaged, with a better cash dividend under the Korean distribution scheme than in an English winding-up.But the order for the transfer would be deferred for two months, to enable buyers of the company's cars to claim for breach of warranty.[41b]

[41a] *Re H I H Casualty & General Insurance Ltd* [2005] EWHC 2125 (Ch), [2005] 2 All E.R. (D) 74 (Oct), Richards J.

[41b] *Re Daewoo Motor Co. Ltd* [2006] B.P.I.R. 415, applying *Re H I H Casualty & General Insurance Ltd*, fn.41a.

Companies

6–57 Nature of floating charge.

[*Delete the final paragraph and substitute: page* 166]

As to the law on the registration of charges, and its intended amendment, see para.2–65.

6–60 Effect of winding up.

[*In the second line, after "sheriff" add: page* 167]

, now retitled the High Court enforcement officer,[90a]

[90a] See the Courts Act 2003, s.99(2), Sch.7, para.2, with effect from April 1, 2004.

[*Then substitute "High Court enforcement officer" for "sheriff" throughout the remainder of paragraph 6–60: page* 167]

6–62 Nature of possession of a receiver and effect on contracts.

[*In the eighth line, after "prima facie" add: page* 169]

agent

Contracts of employment. **6–64**

[*Delete the final paragraph and substitute: page* 170]

For the special categories of personal liability for sums owed to former employees, which are imposed on administrative receivers (and also, to a lesser extent, on administrators), see para.23–11, below.

Third party insurance. **6–68**

[*Delete footnote 35 text and substitute: page* 172]

[35] Under the Third Party (Rights against Insurers) Act 1930: see *Re O.T. Computers Ltd* [2004] EWCA Civ 653; [2004] 2 B.C.L.C. 682; [2004] B.P.I.R. 195, CA, *reversing* [2003] All E.R. (D) 144, V.-C., and applying *Tarbuck v Avon Insurance Ltd* [2001] 2 All E.R. 503.

CHAPTER 7

POWERS AND DUTIES OF A RECEIVER

7–2 **Parties required to deliver up possession.**
[*Delete footnote 2 text and substitute: page* 174]
CPR Sch 1, RSC 45, r.7; for the former procedure, see *Savage v Bentley* [1904] WN 89; (1904) 90 LT 64.

7–18 **Mode in which proposals for leases are dealt with.**
[*In the eighth line, after "application" add: page* 185]
Notice

7–21A **Rent review notices.**
[*Add to the end of paragraph: page* 187]
See para.7–17, above, and see fn.2.

[*Add new paragraph 7–42B: page* 196]

7–42B **Receiver's duties regarding competing bids for property.** The following passage from a Canadian Court of Appeal judgment, which has been adopted by our courts, offers useful guidance on this subject:

> "On a motion to approve a sale by a receiver, the court should place a great deal of confidence in the receiver's expert commercial judgment, particularly where the assets are unusual, and the process needed to sell them is complex. In order to support the role of any receiver, and to avoid commercial chaos in receivership sales, it is extremely desirable that prospective participants in the sale process know that a court will not lightly interfere with a receiver's dealings to sell to the selected participant, and that [it] will have the confidence that it will not be back-doored in some way.
>
> Specifically, the court's duty is to consider (a) whether the receiver made a sufficient effort to obtain the best price, and did not act improvidently; (b) the interests of all parties; (c) the efficacy and integrity of the process by which the receiver obtained offers, and (d) whether the working out of the process was unfair. As to the providence of the sales, a receiver's conduct is to be reviewed in the light of the (objective) information which the receiver had, and not with the benefit of hindsight.[94a]
>
> A dissatisfied bidder on the sale by the receiver has no locus standi to sue the receiver on the basis of his failed bid."[94b]

[94a] *Skyepharma Plc v Hyal Pharmaceutical Corp* [2001] B.P.I.R. 163 (Ontario Court of Appeal), affirming Farley J, reported at [2001] B.P.I.R. 531, at pp.552–3, and applied in *McGowan v Chadwick and Grant* [2001] EWCA Civ 1758; [2003] B.P.I.R. 647, CA, at [84].
[94b] See fn.94a.

COMPANIES: ADMINISTRATIVE RECEIVERS

The Enterprise Act 2002. 7–48
[*In the fifth line, delete "it does not restrict the court's powers to make such an appointment", and substitute: page* 198]
other than in the case of companies falling within the excepted categories represented by the "special administration regimes".[14]

Generally. 7–50
[*Delete paragraph cross-heading "Generally." and substitute: page* 199]
Powers of administrative receivers.

[*Renumber footnote 22–23 as 22: page* 199]

[*Add new paragraph 7–50A: page* 199]
Limitations on receiver's power. The powers conferred on the administrative receiver, by the statutes and by the terms of the debenture, are extensive, but not unlimited. They may only be exercised strictly in the interests of the charge, and the charge-holder, as such. They are conferred for the protection of the assets subject to the charge. Their exercise, for example, to forward the interests of the charge-holder in other directions, such as to assist with his litigation with guarantors of the company's debts, is improper and will be restrained.[23] 7–50A

[23] *Sutton v G E Capital Commercial Finance Ltd, Anglo-Petroleum Ltd v GE Capital Commercial Finance Ltd* [2004] EWCA Civ 315; [2004] 2 B.C.L.C. 662, CA. See also para.23–12A, below.

Enforcement of duties. 7–52
[*In the first line, delete "filling" and substitute: page* 201]
filing

Preferential debts and costs of liquidation. 7–54
[*Add to the end of footnote 43: page* 202]
See para.7–57, below.

Fixed charges not subordinated to preferential debts. 7–54A
[*Add to the end of the seventh line, after footnote 52: page* 203]
But this is no longer the law.[52a]

[52a] See *Buchler v Talbot* [2004] UKHL 9; [2004] 1 B.C.L.C. 281, HL; reversing sub nom. *Re Leyland-Daf Ltd* [2000] EWCA Civ 228; [2002] 1 B.C.L.C. 571, and disapproving of *Re Barleycorn Enterprises Ltd* [1970] Ch. 465, CA; see also para.20–58, below. Legislation is reported to be in draft to reverse the House of Lords decision.

7–63 **Order of application of assets.**

[*In the second line, delete "is" and substitute: page* 207]
was until recently thought to be

[*In the seventh line, delete "is" and substitute: page* 207]
was

[*Add to the end of paragraph: page* 207]
But this construction has been overruled by the House of Lords.[89a]

[89a] See *Buchler v Talbot*, at para.7–54, fn.52a, above, and at para.20–34, below.

7–67 **Leaseholds.**

[*Add to the end of the final paragraph: page* 209]
Where the company's lease had been forfeited by the landlord on the ground that the company had gone into administrative receivership, the receivers applied for relief, to enable them to assign the lease for value. The lease required the company to enter, on any assignment, into an "authorised guarantee agreement", which the landlord required to be also signed by the receivers personally. The landlord's application to strike out the application for relief, on the grounds of the receivers' refusal to provide such an agreement, was dismissed; the issue, as to whether his demand for the personal guarantee was an unjustifiable condition for the grant of relief, should go to trial.[3a]

[3a] *Legends Surf Shop Plc v Sun Life Assurance Society Plc* [2005] EWHC 1438 (Ch); [2005] B.P.I.R. 1145.

[N.B. THERE ARE NO AMENDMENTS TO CHAPTER 8]

Chapter 9

MANAGERS

Lien of creditors. **9–15**

[*Add footnote 78 to the end of paragraph 9–15: page* 228]

[78] *London Flight Centre (Stansted) Ltd v Osprey Aviation Ltd* [2002] B.P.I.R. 1115, and see para.20–54, below.

Liability of managers. **9–16**

[*Renumber footnote 78–79 as 79: page* 228]

[*Add to the end of footnote 92–93: page* 229]

See, as to the management of the affairs of mental health patients, para.2–98, above.

CHAPTER 10

REMUNERATION AND EXPENSES OF A RECEIVER

10–1 **Introduction.**
[*Add to the end of footnote 3: page* 238]
and see para.10–6, below.

10–2A **General principles for calculating bases of remuneration.**
[*In the second line, delete "others" and substitute: page* 239]
otherwise

10–6 **The Civil Court Practice, 2004.**
[*In paragraph cross-heading, delete "2004" and substitute: page* 240]
2006

[*In the fourth line, delete "2004" and substitute: page* 240]
2006

[*In the sixth line, after "rr.3 and 5" add: page* 240]
and Ord.51.

[*Add new paragraph 10–6A: page* 240]

10–6A **Principles applicable to the assessment of receivers' remuneration.** The Court of Appeal has now held that the provisions of CPR 69 and CPR PD 69 (replacing the former provisions of the RSC Ords 3, 5 and 51) regulate the remuneration and the expense claims of all receivers appointed by the High Court, including receivers appointed under the Criminal Justice Act 1988 and the Proceeds of Crime Act 2002.[9a] The court examined in detail the dicta in the *Hughes*[9b] case and the *Andrews* case (both decided by the court under the Criminal Justice Act 1988).[9c]

The court adopted many of the dicta in *Hughes*, as to the proper approach to the assessment and incidence of the costs of a receiver appointed under the Criminal Justice Act 1988, before the coming into force of the provisions of CPR 69.

They adopted in particular the expression of the court's duty, when considering the receiver's costs and expenses under the confiscation statutes, to exercise "close control" over the financial burdens sought to be laid on and discharged out of the assets bound by orders made against defendants and other parties (possibly innocent) under those statutes: "statutory receivers are to be treated precisely as their common law counterparts, save to the extent that the legislation expressly provides otherwise".[9d]

The expenses incurred by a receiver are to be defrayed out of the realisations of assets in his charge, and are not a matter for assessment by the court.[9e] The judgments include counsel's suggested guidelines for the appointment of receivers in confiscation cases, which the court commended.[9f]

See also Ch.27, below, at paras 27–40—27–43.

It should be noted that the remuneration of all court-appointed, or court-regulated, appointees, other than receivers appointed by the High Court, are now regulated by the provisions of the *Practice Statement: The Fixing and Approval of the Remuneration of Appointees* (2004), dated July 15, 2004, which took effect from October 1, 2004: see Appendix A, and para.15–131, below.

[9a] *Capewell v Customs & Excise and anor (first hearing)* [2004] EWCA Civ 1268; *(second hearing)* [2005] EWCA Civ 964; [2005] B.P.I.R. 1266, CA, *(first hearing)* paras [36] to [39].
[9b] *Hughes & others v Customs & Excise and other cases* [2002] EWCA Civ 374; [2003] 1 W.L.R. 177; [2002] 4 All E.R. 633, CA.
[9c] *Re Andrews* [1999] 1 W.L.R. 1236; [1999] 2 All E.R. 751; [1999] 2 B.C.L.C. 442, CA.
[9d] See fn.9a, above, *(first hearing)* at para.[38], citing fn.9b, above, at para.[60].
[9e] See CPR (69), and fn.9a, at paras [24], [25].
[9f] See fn.9a, above, *(second hearing)* at para.[66].

THE CASE LAW

Right to salary and allowances. **10–7**
[*Add to the end of footnote 19: page* 241]
, and see fn.9f, above.

CHAPTER 11

RECEIVER'S ACCOUNTS

11–6 Verification and examination of accounts.

[*In the second line, delete "69.8" and substitute: page* 251]

69

Chapter 12

DISCHARGE OF A RECEIVER

Continuance becoming unnecessary. **12–5**

[*Add to the end of paragraph: page* 261]

When the receivership has ceased to serve any valid purpose, it should be discharged without delay.[25a]

[25a] See *Capewell v Customs & Excise* [2004] EWCA Civ 1628; [2005] B.P.I.R. 1266, CA; see also para.10–6, above, and paras 27–22 and 27–42, below.

Service and appearance. **12–11**

[*Add to the end of paragraph: page* 263]

Those parties who are required to be served with notice include all those parties who were required to be served with the order appointing the receiver, and include any new parties, who have been added to the proceedings since the date of the order.[45a]

[45a] CPR 69(10), applying CPR 69(4): see *Shalso v Russo*, noted in Civil Court News (2005) November, p.1.

[N.B. THERE ARE NO AMENDMENTS TO CHAPTER 13]

Part III

Administration: The New Procedures

III–2 **Textbook assistance with the Statutory Instruments.**
[*In the third line, delete "Second Revised 7th edition, March 2004," and substitute: page* 269]
8th edn, 2005/2006,

[*Add new paragraph III–5: page* 270]

III–5 **Scotland.**

The statutory provisions which are discussed in the main text, Insolvency Act 1986, Part II and Schedule B1 of that Act, introduced by the Enterprise Act 2002 apply in Scotland. The Insolvency Rules 1986, the Rules of Court which are referred to in the main text do not, however, apply in Scotland, and where the relevant procedures are regulated by Insolvency (Scotland) Rules 1986 (as amended by the Insolvency (Scotland) Amendment Rules 2003 (SI 2003/2111, effective September 15, 2003) and the Insolvency (Scotland) Amendment Rules 2006 (SI 2006/734, effective April 6, 2006), the Rules of the Court of Session and the Sheriff Court Rules. The main text has been annotated at the appropriate places where Scots law differs from that discussed in the main text.

CHAPTER 14

ADMINISTRATORS: JUDICIALLY AND EXTRA-JUDICIALLY APPOINTED

SECTION 1—INTRODUCTION

The new statutes and rules. 14–2

[*Add to the end of footnote 5: page* 272]

The Insolvency (Amendment) Rules referred to do not apply in Scotland. Relevant amendments to the Insolvency (Scotland) Rules 1986 were made by the Insolvency (Scotland) Amendment Rules 2003 (SI 2003/2111) and the Insolvency (Scotland) Amendment Rules 2006 (SI 2006/734, effective April 6, 2006).

SECTION 2—THE OLD RÉGIME

"The purposes of administration" under the old régime. 14–5

[*Add to the end of footnote 10: page* 272]

This does not apply in Scotland, where insolvent partnerships are dealt with under the Bankruptcy (Scotland) Act 1985.

[*Add new paragraph 14–8A: page* 274]

Extension of duration before expiry. The statute expressly limits the duration of an administrator's appointment, whether made judicially or extra-judicially, to twelve months.[21aa] This period may be extended by the court,[21ab] or by the consent of creditors,[21ac] but only before its expiry.[21ad] The court is not limited in its number of extensions; but the creditors can only consent to an extension once, and then only for a period of six months, and not at all, if the court has already granted an extension.[21ae] Consent may be given in writing, or at a creditors' meeting.[21af] Complex qualifications attach to the consent of creditors.[21ag] 14–8A

Although the statute prohibits the extension of the period after expiry, it has been so extended at least once, for good commercial reasons.[21ah]

21aa IA 1986, Sch.B1, para.76(1).
21ab *ibid.* paras 76(2), 77(1).
21ac *ibid.* para.78(4).

[21ad] *ibid*. para.78(4).
[21ae] *ibid*. paras 76(2)(b); 78(4)(a), (b).
[21af] *ibid*. para.78(3).
[21ag] *ibid*. para.78(1), (2).
[21ah] *Re TT Industries Ltd, Re Fibaflo Ltd* [2006] B.P.I.R. 597, HH Judge Norris, QC, Birmingham District Registry; the application to extend was made before, but could not be heard until after, the expiry; the judge gave useful directions for future applications. *Cf. Re Roches Leisure Services Ltd* [2005] EWHC 3148 (Ch); [2006] B.P.I.R. 453, Rimer J.; an old regime case, to which IR 1986, r.7.47(1) could be applied.

Section 3—The New Régime

14–9 **The "purpose of administration" under the new régime.**
[*Add to the end of paragraph: page* 275]
The purpose of the administration provisions is to create a more flexible, cheaper and comparatively informal alternative to liquidation.

14–10 **The new régime's restrictions on making an administration order.**
[*Add to the end of footnote 29: page* 275]
See para.14–16, below.

[*Add to the end of paragraph: page* 275]
For the meaning of "reasonably likely", see paragraph 14–10A, below.

[*Add new paragraph 14–10A: page* 275]
14–10A **Weighing up the probabilities: "reasonably likely".** Under the old régime, the tests to be applied by the court to the propriety of making, or of not making, an administration order, were focused on (1) *the test of insolvency*, that is, whether the company was, or was likely to become, unable to pay its debts, and (2) *the test of achievability*, that is, whether the making of an order, on the conditions and proposals put forward, would be likely to achieve one of the prescribed purposes.

Under the new régime, the test of insolvency is calibrated by the same crucial adjective, "likely"; but the test of achievability has been amended from "likely" to "reasonably likely". The meaning and force of these adjectives has been the subject of judicial debate. The present practice of construction appears to be that the applicant has to show that it is "more probable than not" that the company will be unable to pay its debts, and "a real prospect" that an administration order would achieve the purpose of a better result for the company's creditors than if it was wound up. "A real prospect" does not equate with 50 per cent probability.[31a]

[31a] *Re Trident Fashions Plc* (No.2) [2004] EWHC 293 (Ch); [2004] 2 B.C.L.C. 35, at [39], per Lawrence Collins J.

Relaxation of restrictions entering administration. **14–13**
[*In paragraph cross-heading, add new text after "restrictions": page* 276]
on

[*Add to the end of footnote 38: page* 277]
The Insolvent Partnerships Order 1994 does not apply in Scotland, where insolvent partnerships are dealt with under the Bankruptcy (Scotland) Act 1985. Administration is not available to a Scottish partnership.

[*Add to the end of paragraph: page* 277]
Access by insolvent partnerships to the benefits of administration has recently been widened, to equate them, *mutatis mutandis*, with the procedure in the case of companies. Members of an insolvent partnership can now appoint an administrator out of court, and so can the holder of a qualifying agricultural charge over a partnership's assets. But in the case of such appointments by or in respect of a partnership, the partnership must be proved to be actually unable to pay its debts, and not just reasonably likely to become so.[40a]

[40a] Insolvent Partnerships (Amendment) Order 2005 (SI 2005/1516), which came into force on July 1, 2005; see also the Insolvent Partnerships (Amendment) Order 2006 (SI 2006/622).

[*Add new paragraphs 14–14A, 14–14B and 14–14C: page* 277]
Withdrawal of extended jurisdiction. That definition considerably extended the jurisdiction over companies whose constitutions fell outside the previous statutory categories, such as companies incorporated under royal charter; see text to fn.48, below. Concern is reported to have been expressed across the European Union at the width of the jurisdiction, as so extended. As a result, the definition was rapidly amended, so as now to read: **14–14A**

"Paragraph 111(1A): in this Schedule, 'company' means (a) a company within the meaning of s.735 (1) of the Companies Act, 1985; (b) a company incorporated in an EEA State,[46a] other than the United Kingdom, or (c) a company not incorporated in an EEA State, but having its centre of main interests in a member State other than Denmark (hereinafter called the 'COMI')".[46b]

"Paragraph 111(1B): 'Centre of main interests', in the absence of evidence to the contrary, is presumed to be the place of its registered office".[46c]
The exclusion of Denmark is a consequence of their having opted out of the EC Regulation on Insolvency Proceedings: see the Preamble, para.33.

[46a] An "EEA State" means a State that is a contracting party to the Agreement on the European Economic Area signed at Oporto on May 2, 1992, as adjusted by the Protocol signed at Brussels on March 17, 1993: see the Insolvency Act, 1986 (Amendment) Regulations 2005 (SI 2005/879), with effect from April 3, 2005.
[46b] See the Regulations at fn.46a, regs 2(1), 4(a).
[46c] EC Regulation, Preamble, para.13, and para.75 of the Regulation.

14–14B **Ascertaining the location of the COMI.** "The concept of the 'centre of main interests' must be interpreted as the place where the debtor conducts the administration of his interests on a regular basis and is therefore ascertainable by third parties".[46d]

The ascertainment of the COMI is to be made on the basis of evidence, both as to its actual location, and as to the circumstances in which it was established there, or transferred there. Important factors are whether, and to what extent, the company's creditors were aware that that was the company's COMI, and dealt with the company there, and on what basis. Sworn evidence given by or on behalf of the company may need to be accepted, in the absence of cross-examination.

The location of the COMI at the claimed place must have "an air of permanence". It is open to a debtor company (or a debtor) to move its or his COMI to another State, before the commencement of the insolvency proceedings, for acceptable reasons, and such a change is binding on, or against, the creditors. But the court must look critically at all the relevant facts, and be alert to identify changes to the COMI capable of giving rise to a suspicion of an attempt to defeat creditors.[46e]

If the debtor's COMI is not in England, on the basis of which "main proceedings" under the regulation could be opened, the presence of an "establishment" in England will justify the opening of territorial proceedings.[46f]

[46d] EC Regulation, Preamble, para.13, and IA 1986, Sch.B1, para.111(1B).

[46e] *Shierson v Vlieland-Boddy* [2004] EWCA Civ 974; [2005] B.P.I.R. 1170, CA, reversing [2004] EWHC 2852 (Ch), Mann J. This was a bankruptcy petition; the bankruptcy order, originally made on the ground of the debtor's COMI being in England, was set aside, but made *de novo* on the basis of the debtor having had an establishment in England. The decision was followed in *Re Collins & Aikman Europe SA* (2005) July 15, Lawrence Collins, J. (unreported). See article by Gabriel Moss, QC: "Jurisdiction follows the sun: debtor moves his COMI to Spain", [2005] 18 Insolvency Intelligence, p.6.

[46f] *Shierson v Vlieland-Boddy*, see fn.46e.

14–14C **Time at which the location of the COMI is to be ascertained.** The time for the ascertainment of the location of the company's COMI is the date when it is intended to open insolvency proceedings, that is, to make an insolvency order against it, and not the date when the debt was incurred.[46g]

[46g] *Shierson v Vlieland-Boddy*, see fn.46e, followed in *Re Collins & Aikman Europe SA* (2005) July 15, Lawrence Collins, J. (unreported): see Gabriel Moss Q.C. 18 Insolvency Intelligence (2005) p.6.

Conferment of jurisdiction by EC Regulation 2000: instances. 14–15

[*Add to the end of footnote 48: page* 278]

The amendment of the Insolvency Act, 1986, Sch.B1, para.111(1), has repealed the extended jurisdiction, which briefly included companies incorporated under royal charter: see para.14–14A, above.

[*In the eighth line, delete sentence beginning "Although the administration prospects . . ." and substitute: page* 279]

Since the administration's prospects of success were not made out, the court refused an administration order and made a winding-up order.[52a]

[*Delete footnote 52e: page* 279]

[*Add to the end of paragraph: page* 279]

The decision went to appeal in Ireland, but was referred by the Irish Supreme Court to the European Court of Justice.[52c]

Where a company registered in the Cayman Islands applied for an administration order, it was proved that its head office was in London, where its bank accounts were maintained, on which basis the court found that its centre of main interests was in the UK, and an administration order was made.[52d]

[52c] The European Court of Justice has now delivered its judgment in *Re Eurofoods IFSC Ltd*; it is dated May 2, 2006, and is reported as Case C–341/04 at [2006] B.C.C. 397, ECtJ.: see para.14–15A.

[52d] *Re Sendo Ltd* [2005] All E.R. (D) 356 (Jun).

[*Add new paragraph 14–15A: page* 279]

The Court's ruling. The Court's ruling is as follows: 14–15A

> "(1) Where a debtor is a subsidiary company whose registered office and that of its parent company are situated in two different Member States, the presumption laid down in the second sentence of Article 3(1) of Council Regulation (EC) No.1346/2000 of May 29, 2000 on insolvency proceedings, whereby the centre of main interests of that subsidiary is situated in the Member State where its registered office is situated, can be rebutted only if factors which are both objective and ascertainable by third parties enable it to be established that an actual situation exists which is different from that which location at that registered office is deemed to reflect. That could be so in particular in the case of a company not carrying out any business in the territory of the Member State in which its registered office is situated. By contrast, where a company carries on its business in the territory of the Member State where its registered office is situated, the mere fact that its economic choices are or can be controlled by a parent company in another Member State is not enough to rebut the presumption laid down by that Regulation.

(2) On a proper interpretation of the first subparagraph of Article 16(1) of Regulation No 1346/2000, the main insolvency proceedings opened by a court of a Member State must be recognised by the courts of the other Member States, without the latter being able to review the jurisdiction of the court of the opening State.

(3) On the proper interpretation of the first subparagraph of Article 16(1) of the Regulation, a decision to open insolvency proceedings for the purposes of that provision is a decision handed down by a court of a Member State to which application for such a decision has been made, based on the debtor's insolvency and seeking the opening of proceedings referred to in Annex A to the Regulation, where that decision involves the divestment of the debtor and the appointment of a liquidator referred to in Annex C to the Regulation. Such divestment implied that the debtor loses the powers of management that he has over his assets.

(4) On a proper interpretation of Article 26 of the Regulation, a Member State may refuse to recognise insolvency proceedings opened in another Member State where the decision to open the proceedings was taken in flagrant breach of the fundamental right to be heard, which a person concerned by such proceedings enjoys."

14–17 Companies excluded from administration by reason of their insolvency status, conditions or characteristics.

[*Add to footnote 62, after "the Insolvency Act 1986, ss.238–40": page* 280]
, 242, 243

[*Add to the end of footnote 62: page* 280]
See *Re Chesterton International Ltd* [2005] March 8, HH Judge Weeks (unreported).

SECTION 5—PERSONS ENTITLED TO APPLY FOR ADMINISTRATION ORDER (NEW RÉGIME)

14–18 Meaning of "qualifying floating charge".

[*Add to the end of footnote 63: page* 280]
This paragraph (c) and s.29(2) do not apply in Scotland.

[*At the end of sub-paragraph (c), insert "or" and add new sub-paragraph: page* 280]

(d) purports to empower the holder of a floating charge in Scotland to appoint a receiver who on appointment would be an administrative receiver.[63a]

[63a] For the possible effect of this terminology in restricting the definition in Scotland, see para.30–7 below. For a definition of "administrative receiver" in Scotland, see Insolvency Act 1986 s.251.

The re-definition of "floating charge". 14–19A

[*Add to the end of second paragraph: page* 281]

The law discussed in this paragraph does not apply in Scotland. In Scots law, it is not competent to create a fixed charge over a book debt without formal assignation of the debtor's obligation intimated to the debtor. Accordingly, the question of whether such a charge is fixed or floating does not arise in Scots law.

[*In footnote 67, delete text "(1998), The Times, July 15, CA," and substitute: page* 281]

[1999] B.C.C. 441, CA,

[*Add new paragraph 14–19B: page* 281]

***Re Spectrum Plus Ltd*: the final decision.** The Court of Appeal's decision, 14–19B discussed above,[67a] has been reversed by the House of Lords.[67b] The House held that where a charge over present or future book debts was given to a lending bank, it remained a floating charge, whatever it was called, even where the chargor was required to place the proceeds of the debts into a designated account, but still remained free to draw on that account for its business purposes, up to an overdraft limit. Unrestricted drawings on such an account, where the assets it contains, which are subject to the charge, are not finally appropriated as a security for the payment of money, were inconsistent with a fixed charge.

The House declined to make its judgment prospective only, and not (as was judicially mandatory) retrospective.[67c]

The proposition that the fact that the form of charge here under consideration, as it was in *Siebe Gorman,*[67d] had been in commercial use for many years by the banking community, should justify its previously accepted (though erroneous) construction, was also rejected.[67e]

The Government is in the process of seeking to reverse this decision, by including a clause (Clause 868) in the Companies Acts Reform Bill, now before Parliament.

[67a] See fn.65a.
[67b] [2005] UKHL 41; [2005] 2 B.C.L.C. 269 HL, heard by a bench of seven law lords.
[67c] See fn.67b, per Lord Nicholls at [43], and Lord Hope at [71].
[67d] See fn.66, above.
[67e] See fn.67b, per Lord Nicholls at [39]–[42], and per Lord Hope at [74].

Company in insolvent winding up: administration application by floating charge-holder or by liquidator. 14–20

[*Add to the end of paragraph: page* 282]

The Insolvency (Amendment) Rules 2003 referred to in this paragraph do not apply in Scotland, where the form of petition to the court is governed by the Insolvency (Scotland) Rules 1986, Chapter 2 (SI 1986/1915) as substituted by the Insolvency (Scotland) Amendment Rules 2003 (SI

2003/2111) and as amended by the Insolvency (Scotland) Amendment Rules 2006 (SI 2006/734) and by the Rules of Court.

14–22 Powers to apply for appointment: who may apply to the court.
[*In the fourth line, after "régimes" delete: page* 282]
transitional provisions

14–23 Making of administration application to the court: statutory notices.
[*Add to the end of footnote 82: page* 282]
The rules and forms referred to apply in England and Wales only. For Scotland, see the Insolvency (Scotland) Rules 1986, Rule 2.2 and Form 2.1B (Scot).

[*Add to the end of footnote 83: page* 282]
or, in Scotland, the Insolvency (Scotland) Rules 1986, Rule 2.3, the Rules of Court and Form 2.2B (Scot).

[*Add to the end of footnote 84: page* 283]
The foregoing applies in England and Wales only. For Scotland see the Insolvency (Scotland) Rules 1986, Rule 2.3 and Form 2.2B (Scot).

[*Add to the end of footnote 86: page* 283]
This does not apply in Scotland where the general powers of the court would enable such orders to be made.

Section 6—Drafting the Application: Procedure

[*Read alongside Section 6 for the position in Scotland: page* 283]
The procedure discussed in this section does not apply in Scotland, where the procedure is governed by the Insolvency (Scotland) Rules 1986 (as amended), and by the Rules of the Court of Session and of the Sheriff Court, to which reference should be made for the detailed provisions. An application to the Court of Session is by petition under the Act of Sederunt (Rules of the Court of Session) 1994 (SI 1994/1443) as amended, Chapters 14 and 74, Parts I and III. In the Sheriff Court a petition for the appointment of an administrator is governed by the Act of Sederunt (Sheriff Court Company Insolvency Rules) 1986 (SI 1986/2297) as amended, Part II. There is no affidavit procedure in Scotland. The petition must contain averments in support of the application and appropriate documentation, including a statement by the proposed administrator in the Prescribed Form 2.1B (Scot) states (pursuant to Rule 2.2(2)) that he consents to accept appointment, giving details of any prior professional relationship with the company, and that in his opinion it is reasonably likely that the purpose of administration will be achieved. The petition must also state whether the administration will be "main proceedings" or "territorial proceedings", within the meaning of the EC Regulation on Insolvency Proceedings (discussed inter alia in Chapter 28 below). Schedule B1, paragraph 14 and 15 (discussed in paras 14–25 to 14–26A) apply in Scotland, subject to the Scottish Insolvency Rules and Rules of Court.

The detailed provisions of the Insolvency Rules discussed in Section 6 do not apply in Scotland, although the relevant Insolvency (Scotland) Rules 1986 (as amended) and Rules of Court make provision for the same matters under the appropriate Scottish procedure.

Procedure on application: drafting the application. 14–24

[*Renumber footnote 88-89 as 88: page* 283]

[*Add to the end of the second paragraph: page* 283]

The application for an administration order must be made to a judge.[89]

[89] See para.15–35A, below.

Statement by the proposed administrator. 14–27

[*Add to the end of the second paragraph after "interest": page* 285]

"The Protocol for the instruction of Experts to give evidence in civil claims", has replaced the former Code of Guidance.[1a]

[1a] See Civil Courts Practice (2006) CPR PRO Vol. 1, p.719.

Subsequent notice of any insolvency proceedings. 14–31

[*Renumber footnote 15-16 as 15: page* 287]

Notice to execution officers. 14–32

[*In sub-paragraph (a), delete "sheriff" and substitute: page* 287]

High Court enforcement officer, county bailiff or other officer.[16]

[16] See Courts Act, 2003, s.99(2), and Sch.16, para.2.

Section 7—The Hearing and the Order

[*Read alongside Section 7 for the position in Scotland: page* 288]

The court procedure discussed in Section 7 refers to England and Wales. For the court procedure on these matters in Scotland, reference should be made to the Insolvency (Scotland) Rules 1986 (as amended) and to the Rules of Court. The Insolvency (Scotland) Amendment Rules 2003 (SI 2003/2111), as amended by the Insolvency (Scotland) Amendment Rules 2006 (SI 2006/734, effective April 6, 2006), prescribe the relevant forms for use in administration proceedings in Scotland.

[*Add new paragraph 14–35A, in front of existing paragraph 14–35A (renumber existing paragraph as 14–35B): page* 289]

Applications which must be made before a judge. All applications for an administration order must be listed before a judge. Applications for directions or case management, after any proceedings have been referred to or adjourned to a judge, must also be listed before the judge, except where liberty to apply to the Registrar or District Judge has been given. 14–35A

All other applications relating to administration orders should be listed for initial hearing before a Registrar or District Judge. When deciding whether to hear the proceedings themselves, or to adjourn them to the judge, they should have regard to the following factors:

(1) the complexity of the proceedings;

(2) whether the proceedings raise new or controversial points of law;

(3) the likely date and length of the hearing;

(4) public interest in the proceedings; and

(5) the availability in the court which is likely to hear the proceedings of relevant specialist expertise.[27a]

[27a] *Practice Note on the Hearing of Insolvency Proceedings*, by the Vice-Chancellor, dated May 27, 2005, printed at [2005] B.P.I.R. 688. The Note supersedes all previous Practice Statements of the Bankruptcy Registrars, dealing with jurisdiction and work distribution, and the Guidelines issued by the Insolvency Court Users' Committee in November 1988. The Practice Note is printed in Appendix B.

14–35B The merits of the application.

[*Add to the end of renumbered paragraph 14–35B: page* 289]

But where the company opposed the appointment of an administrator by the debenture-holder, on the ground that it bona fide disputed the debenture-holder's claim, it was held that such a dispute does not remove the debenture-holder's right to appoint an administrator; the realisation of securities could be seriously impeded, if secured creditors could be held up by a disputed debt.[28aa]

[28aa] *BCPMS (Europe) Ltd v GMAC Commercial Finance Ltd*, [2006] All E.R. (D) 285 (Feb) Lewison, J., applying *Rushingdale Ltd v Byblos Bank Plc* [1986] 2 B.C.C. 99,509.

[*Add new paragraph 14–35C, after renumbered paragraph 14–35B: page* 289]

14–35C **Competition between nominees for appointment.** Where a company, after having been served with a winding-up petition, applied for an administration order, the petitioning creditor supported the application, but nominated its own single candidate for appointment. The company had proposed two administrators, from a large firm of insolvency accountants, who had already acquired some experience with the company's affairs and problems. The court made the order, appointing the company's nominees, as being the more suitable candidates; in such cases of competition between nominees, it was not appropriate to hold a head count of the creditors; it was for the court to choose the most suitable candidates.[28a]

[28a] *Re World Class Homes Ltd.* [2004] EWHC 2996 (Ch); [2005] 2 B.C.L.C. 1; see per Lindsay J, at [12], applying *Re Maxwell Communications Corp Plc* [1992] B.C.L.C. 465.

[Read alongside paragraphs 14–42 and 14–43 for the position in Scotland: page 291*]* **14–42—14–43**
The power to make interim orders under the old regime was interpreted by the Scottish courts as sanctioning the appointment of an "administrator ad interim". However, in The Secretary of State for Trade and Industry v Palmer 1995 S.L.T. 188 [1994] B.C.C. 990, it was held that such an order was incompetent and did not constitute an "administration order" within the meaning of the Act. The Scottish courts are still reluctant to appoint an administrator in the first order in the petition, i.e. on the ex parte application of the petitioner, although the court is usually prepared substantially to reduce the normal period of twenty-one days for parties to lodge answers to the petition. Instead, the court has developed the practice of appointing the proposed administrator (or administrators) "managers ad interim" and prohibiting the directors from acting without their consent. The status of such appointees is open to doubt. It is clear that they fall within the definition of "shadow directors" (the Insolvency Act 1986 s.251) and may therefore be exposed to responsibility for "wrongful trading" under s.214 of the Act, if they permit the directors to continue trading for a significant period before their appointment as administrators takes effect.

SECTION 8—THE EXTRA-JUDICIAL APPOINTMENTS

[Read alongside Section 8 for the position in Scotland: page 292*]*
The provisions of Sch.B1 referred to in this section apply in Scotland, subject to the substitution of para.15(3) of Sch.B1 for para.15(2). The insolvency rules referred to in this section, however, do not apply in Scotland, and reference should be made to the Insolvency (Scotland) Rules 1986, Chapter 3 (Rules 2.9 to 2.12) and relative forms prescribed by the Insolvency (Scotland) Amendment Rules 2003 (SI 2003/2111), as amended by the Insolvency (Scotland) Amendment Rules 2006 (SI 2006/734, effective April 6, 2006).

SECTION 9—PROCEDURES FOR MAKING EXTRA-JUDICIAL APPOINTMENTS

[Read alongside Section 9 for the position in Scotland: page 293*]*
The provisions of Sch.B1 referred to in this section apply in Scotland, subject to the substitution of para.15(3) of Sch.B1 for para.15(2). The insolvency rules referred to in this section, however, do not apply in Scotland, and reference should be made to the Insolvency (Scotland) Rules 1986, Chapter 3 (Rules 2.9 to 2.12) and relative forms prescribed by the Insolvency (Scotland) Amendment Rules 2003 (SI 2003/2111), as amended by the Insolvency (Scotland) Amendment Rules 2006 (SI 2006/734, effective April 6, 2006).

The detailed rules and forms referred to in this Section 9 are those applicable in England and Wales. For Scotland, see the relevant provisions of the Insolvency (Scotland) Rules 1986 (as amended), and the forms prescribed by the Insolvency (Scotland) Amendment Rules 2003, as amended by the Insolvency (Scotland) Amendment Rules 2006 (SI 2006/734, effective April 6, 2006).

14–47 **Appointment by qualifying floating charge-holder: duty to give notice of intention to appoint.**

[*Add to the end of footnote 57: page* 293]

In Scotland, the relevant form is Form 2.4D (Scot) and the rules are the Insolvency (Scotland) Rules 1986, Rule 2.9.

[*Add new paragraph 14–61A: page* 301]

14–61A **Modes of giving notice to creditors.** Notices to creditors must be sent by post; notices by e-mail are not permitted.[15a] But notifications to creditors have been allowed to be made by advertisements, instead of by circular.[15b]

[15a] *Re Sporting Options Plc (in administration)* [2004] EWHC 3128 (Ch); [2005] B.P.I.R. 435; [2004] All E.R. (D) 30 (Dec); see also article at 21 I L & P (2005), p.28.

[15b] *Re A Licence-Holder & ors, Savill v Gerard* [2004] EWHC (Ch); [2005] B.C.C. 433.

Chapter 14A

ADMINISTRATION IN SCOTLAND

[*Add new Chapter 14A*]

Section 1—Introduction

Part II of the Insolvency Act 1986 and, in particular, Schedule B1 to the Act, applies in Scotland with appropriate modifications, which are noted at the appropriate point in this Supplement. **14A–1**

Neither the insolvency rules nor the court procedures referred to in the main text apply in Scotland, where administration procedure is governed by the Insolvency (Scotland) Rules 1986 (SI 1986/1915), as substituted by the Insolvency (Scotland) Amendment Rules 2003 (SI 2003/2111), with effect September 15, 2003 and as amended by the Insolvency (Scotland) Amendment Rules 2006 (SI 2006/734, effective April 6, 2006). Applications to the court for the appointment of an administrator, and incidental applications in respect of that procedure, are governed by the Rules of Court. In the Court of Session, these are contained in the Act of Sederunt (Rules of the Court of Session) 1994 (SI 1994/1443) as amended, in particular Chapters 14 and 15 (which apply to petitions generally) and Chapter 74, Parts I and III which apply to administration. In the Sheriff Court, the procedure is governed by the Act of Sederunt (Sheriff Court Company Insolvency Rules) 1986 (SI 1986/2297) as amended, Rules 1 to 3 and 10 to 17.

The Insolvency (Scotland) Rules 1986 also prescribe the forms to be used in connection with administration procedure. These are set out in the Schedule to the Insolvency (Scotland) Amendment Rules 2003, Part 2 as amended, with effect April 6, 2006, by the Insolvency (Scotland) Amendment Rules 2006 (SI 2006/734).

Chapter 15

THE ADMINISTRATOR IN OFFICE: POWERS AND DUTIES

[*Read alongside Chapter 15 for the position in Scotland: page* 303]
The legislation (principally the Insolvency Act 1986, Sch.B1) applies in Scotland, but for the procedural rules and the prescribed forms, reference should be made to the Insolvency (Scotland) Rules 1986 (as amended).

In connection with meetings of creditors, Chapter 6 of the Insolvency (Scotland) Rules 1986 applies Chapter 1 of Part 7 of those Rules, subject to modification. Rule 7.9 applies the Scottish rules applicable to claims in bankruptcy and liquidation to determine a creditor's right to vote at any meeting in accordance with the value of his claim.

Section 1—Introduction

15–1 **Status, roles and duties of administrator.**
[*Add to the end of sub-paragraph (4): page* 303]
He is entitled to apply to the court for directions for the performance of his functions;[5a]

[5a] *ibid.,* para.63; see para.15–3A, below.

[*Add to the end of footnote 18: page* 304]
The administrator can only have been appointed either with the consent of the floating charge-holder, or on the basis that his security is impeachable: see IA 1986, Sch.B1, para.39.

[*Add to the end of footnote 20: page* 304]
See paras 15–81—15–83, below.

[*In sub-paragraph (18), delete "divided" and substitute: page* 305]
dividend

Section 2—Functions of the Administrator: Process of Administration

[*Add new paragraph 15–3A and 15–3B, in front of existing paragraph 15–3A (renumber existing paragraph as 15–3C): page* 307]
15–3A **The giving of directions.** The formal limits imposed by the Insolvency Act, 1986[53a] on the giving of directions by the court do not, in practice, deter the court from giving directions which go outside those limits, where the

circumstances of the case demand such an extension. The court has a duty to assist the administrator, with a view to the administration succeeding and not failing, and being able to provide a cheaper, more efficient and less formal alternative to winding-up.[53b]

[53a] IA 1986, s.14(3) (repealed); *ibid.* s.7(4) (supervisors); *ibid.* Sch.B1, para.63 (administrators).
[53b] *Re Transbus International Ltd* [2004] EWHC 932 (Ch); [2004] 2 B.C.L.C. 550, per Lawrence Collins J, [12]–[14]; the administrators were directed that they could sell assets before creditors approved proposals. See also *Re A A Mutual International Insurance Ltd* [2004] EWHC 2430 (Ch) [2005] 2 B.C.L.C. 8, Lewison J., and *Re T & D Industries Plc (in administration), Re T & D Automotive Ltd (in administration)* [2000] 1 W.L.R. 646; [2000] 1 B.C.L.C. 471.

General principles governing the giving of directions. The administrator must not abuse his right to apply for directions, nor must he ask abstract questions, or pose academic propositions.[53c] He must decide for himself questions of business, management and administration, being the person best qualified to decide them.[53d] Even in such major matters as deciding whether the company should move from administration into voluntary winding-up or into dissolution, he must, with such technical or legal advice as he feels that he needs, decide for himself, provided that the prescribed conditions are present.[53e] **15–3B**

The court is not disposed to receive objections from creditors or other parties, claiming to fault an administrator's decisions, unless they reflect a course of reasoning which no reasonable insolvency practitioner could entertain.[53f] Generally, the administrator should confine his applications for directions to serious legal or procedural problems,[53g] or to important points of principle or procedure, such as the nature and extent of an English administrator's powers,[53h] or the application of EC Regulation jurisdiction to English administrations.

Over and above its statutory powers, the court has an inherent overriding jurisdiction, enabling it to confer additional specific powers on an administrator, for the purpose of solving specific problems brought by him before the court,[53i] such as the power to make distributions to creditors, otherwise than in accordance with IA 1986, Sch.1, para.65.[53j]

The relevant case-law in this field is already extensive, and increasing; only a few examples can be given here.

[53c] *Re P N C Telecom (in administration)* [2003] EWHC 2230 (Ch); [2004] B.P.I.R. 314.
[53d] *Re Ballast Plc (in administration) and other companies* [2004] EWHC 2356 (Ch); [2005] 1 B.C.L.C. 446 at [15]. *Re PNC Telecom Ltd (in administration)* [2003] EWHC 2220 (Ch); [2004] B.P.I.R. 314.
[53e] *Re T & N Ltd & ors* [2005] EWHC 2870 (Ch); the administrators asked whom they should treat as creditors in a scheme under CA 1985, s.425, which included contingent claims.
[53f] *Re Trident Fashions Plc (No 2)* [2004] 2 B.C.L.C. 35 at [39].
[53g] *Re SSSL Realisations Ltd (in liquidation)* (2005) *The Times,* January 20, CA, *rvsg* [2005] 1 B.C.L.C. 1; set-off rules held not to apply, where rule in *Cherry v Boultbee* (1839) My Cr 442 applies, one debt being not provable because of rule against double proof; see also *Re Melton, Mill v Towers* [1918] 1 Ch. 37, and see *Re Mark One (Oxford Street) Plc* [1999] 1 W.L.R. 445, applied in *Re TXU Ltd* [2003] 2 B.C.L.C. 341.

[53h] *Re WBSL Realisations 1992 Ltd & anor* [1995] 2 B.C.L.C. 576; *Re MG Rover España SA & ors* [2005] B.P.I.R. 1162: overseas companies in English administration (COMIs in England) needed a supplemental order, defining the administrators' powers, to inform and to reassure foreign creditors, directors and members. See para.15–3C.

[53i] See fn.53h, and see also *Re Mark One (Oxford Street) Plc,* (see fn.53g).

[53j] *Re The Designer Room Ltd* [2004] EWHC 720 (Ch); [2005] 1 W.L.R. 1581; [2004] B.C.C. 904. *Cf. Re MG Rover Espana SA & ors*; in *Re WBSL Realisations 1992 Ltd* (see fn.53h), the permission to make the distribution was expressly given to achieve the purpose of the administration.

[*Add new paragraph 15–3D, after renumbered paragraph 15–3C: page* 308]

15–3D **Further case-law.** Administrators of a number of overseas sales companies of a UK-based manufacturing company (their parent) applied to the court to provide them with an outline of their powers as administrators for the information of overseas customers, employees and creditors, who were anxious at what had happened to the group. The companies had been collectively put into administration by administration orders, based on each of them having its centre of main interest in England.

Supplemental orders were made by the court, declaring the relevant responsibilities and powers of the administrators, and the material effect of the administration orders. The administrators were empowered to make payments to their local employees, over and above their entitlement under English law, where such payments would promote the purposes of the administration, and might avert the commencement locally of secondary insolvency proceedings in each national jurisdiction, where payments to such employees were generally higher than under the English jurisdiction; but whether they made such higher payments was left for their own commercial decision.[61a]

[61a] *Re M G Rover España SA & ors* [2005] B.P.I.R. 1162, HH Judge Norris; see also *Corporate Administrators and Rescue Procedures*, by Fletcher, Higham and Trower, (Lexis-Nexis, UK, 2nd edn, 2004), and article by Emily Springford in (2005) 21 IL & P at p. 91.

[*Add new paragraph 15–4A: page* 308]

15–4A **Jurisdiction to extend appointment after expiry.** Although Sch.B1[66a] expressly provides that when the administrator's period of appointment, whether original or as extended, has expired, it cannot be renewed, the court has jurisdiction, and a discretion, to construe that paragraph so as to permit such an extension. Such a renewal and extension may be obtainable on the following conditions: (1) that an application to extend, or to extend again, has been made to the court well before the expiry date, and (2) (if such be the case) that there is a real possibility that any delay in the hearing of the application is attributable to the fault of the court staff. The administrator should therefore make, in good time, a paper application to a judge of the Chancery Division, seeking a brief extension, pending the hearing of the full application for a substantial extension.[66b]

[66a] IA 1986, Sch.1, para.77 (1).

[66b] *Re TT Industries Ltd & anor* [2006] B.P.I.R. 597; *cf.* the dicta, regarding the extension of a period, declared to be non-extendible, in *Jacobs v Official Receiver* [1999] 1 W.L.R. 619; *Bagnall v Official Receiver* [2003] EWCA Civ 1925; [2004] 2 All E.R. 294; [2003] All E.R. (D) 14 Dec, CA, *affirming* [2003] B.P.I.R. 1080.

Permission for enforcement proceedings notwithstanding moratorium. **15–12**
[*Add to the end of footnote 88: page* 311]
See *Re Atlantic Computer Systems Plc (No 2)* [1992] Ch. 505, and see para.15–12A.

[*Add new paragraph 15–12A: page* 311]
Leave to mortgagees to appoint receiver. Under the old régime,[92a] the **15–12A**
administration order prohibited any actions or proceedings by creditors of the company to enforce their securities, or to recover their debts, without the permission of the court or the consent of the administrator. The exercise of the court's discretion was recognised as being "left at large", and "not to be confined in a straitjacket".[92b] Those principles are recognised as applying to cases under the new régime, where the principal prohibition has been compressed into a ban on any step to enforce security over the property of the company.[92c]

Under the new régime, where a company had given charges over its land to creditors, and, immediately before payment of the principal was due, obtained the appointment of an administrator, who contemplated attacking the validity of the charges, the chargees retaliated by applying to the court for permission to appoint a receiver. The court, applying the dicta in *Re Atlantic Computer Systems Plc (No 2)*,[92d] and balancing its discretion between the parties, gave the chargees permission to appoint a receiver, against their undertakings as to financing the development of the land, while visualising the possible setting aside of the charges, in the winding-up of the company, for which the administrator was directed to petition.[92e]

[92a] Insolvency Act 1986, s.11(3)(b) (repealed).
[92b] *Re Atlantic Computer Systems Plc (No.2)*, fn.88, above.
[92c] Insolvency Act 1986, Sch.B1, para.43(2).
[92d] See fn.88, above.
[92e] *Re Rosshill Properties Ltd (in administration), Sinai Securities v Hooper* [2003] EWHC 910 (Ch); [2004] 2 B.C.L.C. 575.

Initial duties of the administrator: notices. **15–13**
[*In sub-paragraph (c), delete "sheriff" and substitute: page* 311]
High Court enforcement officer

SECTION 3—PREPARING THE STATEMENT OF AFFAIRS

The expenses of the statement of affairs. **15–21**
[*Delete footnote 125 text and substitute: page* 315]

[125] *ibid.* r.2.30(9).

15–24 Challenge to withheld disclosure: change of circumstances.
[*In the first line of the second paragraph, delete "take" and substitute: page* 316]
make

[*Delete footnote 143 text and substitute: page* 316]
ibid. r.2.30(6).

SECTION 4—THE ADMINISTRATOR'S PROPOSALS

15–29 "The likelihood of achievement".
[*In the third line, delete " 'not merely possible, but more probable than not"*[15] *and substitute: page* 318]
if there is a real prospect that the administration order will achieve its purpose".[15] The test of there being "a real prospect of achieving its purpose", first formulated by Hoffman J., in *Re (Harris) Simons Construction Ltd,*[15a] seems to have been generally adopted for the construction of the relevant clause.[15b]

[15] Under the IA 1986, s.8(c); and see *Re Lomax Leisure Ltd* [1999] 3 W.L.R. 650.
[15a] [1989] B.C.L.C. 202; [1989] 1 W.L.R. 368.
[15b] Under IA 1986, Sch.1, para.11(b); see *Re AA Mutual International Insurance Ltd* [2005] EWHC 2430 (Ch); [2005] 2 B.C.L.C. 8, at para.[21], and see also para.14–10A.

[*Add new (and centre) heading immediately before paragraph 15–30: page* 318]
PROBABILITIES WHERE EXTRA-JUDICIAL APPOINTMENTS ARE MADE

SECTION 5—MEETINGS OF CREDITORS AND OF MEMBERS OF THE COMPANY IN ADMINISTRATION

15–36 General.
[*Add to the end of footnote 35: page* 321]
Order (SI 2003/2093).

[*Add new paragraph 15–45A: page* 324]
15–45A Procedure where proposals rejected. Where an administrator's proposals had been rejected, he applied to the court for an order that his appointment should cease,[57b] that he be discharged from liability[57c] and that remuneration be fixed and paid.[57d] In the absence of specific procedure for applications under paragraph 55, the court directed him to follow the procedure laid down for Paragraph 79, and the relevant rules,[57e] giving notice to the creditors, and informing them of their rights to petition for the company to be wound up.[57f]

57b Under para.55(1).
57c Under para.98(2)(c).
57d Under IR 1986 r.2.106 (6).
57e *ibid.* rr.2.106 and 2.114.
57f *Re ML Designer Group Ltd* [2006] All E.R. (D) 75 (Jan).

Section 8—Dealing with Property not belonging to the Company

[*Read alongside Section 8 for the position in Scotland: page* 334]
Sch.B1, paras 70 to 72, apply in Scotland, with the substitution of reference to a "ranking security" for "charge" (Sch.B1 para.112). Under para.113, where property in Scotland is disposed of under para.70 or 71 the administrator shall grant an appropriate document of transfer, and upon completion of the title of the disponee or transferee the property is freed from the security or incumbrance in question. Under para.114, where goods subject to a hire purchase agreement are disposed of under para.72, the disposal has the effect of extinguishing as against the disponee all rights of the owner of the goods under the agreement.

Section 9—Distribution by Administrator

[*Read alongside Section 9 for the position in Scotland: page* 337]
For the rules applicable in Scotland, see (where the company entered into administration before April 6, 2006) the Insolvency (Scotland) Rules 1986 (as amended), Chapter 9 (Rules 2.40 to 2.41) which apply, with adaptation, the rules in respect of distribution which apply to liquidations in Scotland (themselves adapted from the rules applicable in bankruptcy). In relation to later administrations, the position is regulated by amendments to Rule 2.41 and a new Rule 2.41A, made by the Insolvency (Scotland) Amendment Rules 2006 (SI 2006/734, effective April 6, 2006).

[*Add new paragraph 15–90A: page* 338]
New provisions for contingent debts, and liabilities in tort. New provisions have been made,[107a] regarding the meaning of "debts" and "liabilities" in administration (and also in winding-up), which came into force on June 1, 2006, (subject to transitional provisions for existing administrations),[107b] which may be summarised as follows: **15–90A**

(1) "debt", in relation to an administration, means any debt or liability to which the company is subject at the date when it enters administration, or to which, after that date, it becomes liable, by reason any obligation incurred before that date, and any interest specially provided for;[107c]

(2) A liability in tort is provable in the administration, if either (a) the cause of action has accrued at the date the company enters administration, or (b) all the elements necessary to establish the cause of action exist at that date, except for actionable damage;

(3) For the purposes of proof in an administration, it is immaterial whether the debt or liability is present or future, certain or contingent, fixed or liquidated, capable of being ascertained by fixed rules, or as a matter of opinion, and references to "owing a debt" are to be read accordingly;

(4) Unless the context of the provision otherwise requires, "liability" means (subject to (3) above) a liability to pay money or money's worth, including any liability under any enactment, any liability for breach of trust, any liability in contract, tort or bailment, and any liability arising out of an obligation to make restitution.

[107a] Insolvency (Amendment) Rules, 2006 (SI 2006/1272), which apply equally to winding-up, r.4, which revokes and replaces IR 1986. r.13.12.
[107b] I(A)R 2006, r.3.
[107c] See IR 1986. r.4.93(1).

15–108 **Revision of the law on mutual credit and set-off: *Re West End Networks Ltd.***
[*Add to footnote 161, after "UKHL 24": page* 343]
[2004] 2 A.C. 506, HL;

[*Add to the end of footnote 161: page* 343]
See also para.20–35, and para.20–55, below, and see article by Professor Ian Fletcher Q.C., "Crown Set-off and Contingent Liabilities" (2005) 18 Insolvency Intelligence, p. 6.

Section 10—The Carrying out of the Distribution

[*Read alongside Section 10 for the position in Scotland: page* 345]
For the rules applicable in Scotland, see (where the company entered into administration before April 6, 2006) the Insolvency (Scotland) Rules 1986 (as amended), Chapter 9 (Rules 2.40 to 2.41) which apply, with adaptation, the rules in respect of distribution which apply to liquidations in Scotland (themselves adapted from the rules applicable in bankruptcy). In relation to later administration, the position is regulated by amendments to Rule 2.41 and a new Rule 2.41A made by the Insolvency (Scotland) Amendment Rules 2006 (SI 2006/734, effective April 6, 2006).

Section 11—Remuneration of Administrator

[*Delete section heading* "Section 11—Remuneration of Administrator" *and substitute: page* 348]
Section 11—Remuneration of Appointees

[*Read alongside Section 11 for the position in Scotland: page* 348]
This section does not apply in Scotland where the position is governed by the Insolvency (Scotland) Rules 1986 (as amended), Rule 2.39, which in turn applies the rules in respect of remuneration of the office holder in liquidations in Scotland (themselves being an adaptation of the relevant rules in bankruptcy procedure). This Rule has, however, been superseded,

with effect April 6, 2006, by a new Rule 2.39 on the determination of the administrator's outlays and remuneration, and an additional Rule 2.39A governing appeals against such a determination. The former Rule 2.39 remains applicable where the company entered administration before April 6, 2006 (see the Insolvency (Scotland) Amendment Rules 2006, SI 2006/734).

General entitlement to remuneration. **15–124**

[*Add to the end of footnote 30: page* 348]

and see fn.32, below.

[*Add to the end of the second paragraph: page* 348]

But see Section 12, paras 15–132 *et seq.*, below.

[*Add new paragraph 15–125A: page* 349]

Treatment of receiver's expenses. The nature and amount of a receiver's **15–125A** expenses are not to be assessed by the court quâ remuneration; they are accounted for as part of his account for the assets he has recovered.[33a]

[33a] See CPR 69 PD, para.9(6) and para.10–6.

Costs of application to reduce remuneration. **15–131**

[*Add new (and centre) section heading after this paragraph: page* 350]

SECTION 12—NEW REMUNERATION DIRECTIONS

The New Practice Statement regarding remuneration of appointees. **15–132**

[*Delete footnote 49 text and substitute: page* 350]

Published in [2004] B.P.I.R. 953, and due to be published in the Civil Courts Practice. The publication of the Chief Registrar's Directions coincided with his extensive judgment, on the subject of administrators' remuneration, in a highly contentious dispute between the administrators and the creditors: see *Re Cabletel Installations Ltd* [2005] B.P.I.R. 28. The Chief Registrar's Statement is printed in full in Appendix A.

The intention and the extent of the new directions. **15–135**

[*Add to the end of footnote 50: page* 351]

See fn.49d, above.

[*Add new paragraph 15–137: page* 352]

The expenses of the administration, and the order of priority for their **15–137** payment out of the assets, are set out in the rules.[56] Unpaid non-domestic rates, incurred during the occupation of the company's premises for the purposes of the administration, may qualify for payment, either as expenses of the administration or as necessary disbursements.[57]

[56] IR 1986, r.2.67.

[57] *Re Trident Fashions Plc, Exeter City Council v Bairstow* [2006] EWCA Civ 203, CA, where the Court of Appeal examined the rules.

CHAPTER 16

CONVERSION FROM ADMINISTRATION INTO OTHER FORMS OF PROCEEDING

[*Read alongside Chapter 16 for the position in Scotland: page* 353]
The provisions of the Insolvency Act 1986 relating to company voluntary arrangements and the European Council Regulation on Insolvency Proceedings 2000 apply in Scotland, but Part VIII of the Act which deals with individual insolvency arrangements applies only in England and Wales. In Scotland, the insolvency or bankruptcy of an individual or a partnership is governed by the Bankruptcy (Scotland) Act 1985 (as amended). This includes provision for a bankrupt individual to grant a voluntary trust deed for behoof of his creditors, whose effect is approximately equivalent to an individual voluntary arrangement under English law. With the omission of comments relating to individual voluntary arrangements, however, the comments in this chapter on the legislation relating to company voluntary arrangements may be treated as relevant to Scotland.

The insolvency rules referred to in this chapter in relation to voluntary arrangements, and the conversion from administration to winding up and the conversion from administration to dissolution referred to in Sections 4 and 6, do not apply in Scotland where the position is governed by the Insolvency (Scotland) Rules 1986 (as amended). The Insolvency (Scotland) Rules 1986 in their unamended form remain applicable to proceedings which commenced on or before September 15, 2003 (as explained in para.16–7 below).

SECTION 2—COMPANY VOLUNTARY ARRANGEMENTS IN ADMINISTRATION

16–6 **Compliance with EC Regulation.**
[*In the fourth line, delete "Chap. 29," and substitute: page* 356]
Ch.28,

16–11 **Moratorium facilities for small companies: position of subsidiaries.**
[*In footnote 38 delete text "373" and substitute: page* 358]
325

[*In the fourth line, after "administrator.[38]" add: page* 358]
Where an application is made to sue a company in administration for a simple monetary debt, permission will only be given in exceptional circumstances; the administrator must be free to run the company, free from unnecessary litigation.[38a]

During the period when the stay of proceedings effected by the administration order was, (until the amended provisions came into force on September 15, 2003), limited to one year, that was an additional reason for refusing a creditor permission to continue proceedings against the company.[38b] This reason of course no longer applies.

Solicitors have been given permission to commence proceedings against a company in administration, seeking a declaration that they were entitled to a charge for their fees over a property recovered by them for the company.[38c]

[38a] See *A E S Barry Ltd v TXU Europe Energy Trading Ltd (in administration)* [2004] EWHC 1757 (Ch); [2005] 2 B.C.L.C. 22, at [24], applying the principles stated in *re Atlantic Computer Systems Plc (No 1)* [1992] Ch. 505, CA, at [15].

[38b] *Re Divine Solutions Ltd* [2003] EWHC 1931 (Ch); [2004] 1 B.C.L.C. 373; [2004] B.C.C. 325; see also *Enron Metals & Commodity Ltd v H I H Casualty & General Insurance Ltd (in provisional liquidation)* [2005] EWHC 485 (Ch) (unreported): the claim was held to have had no real prospects of success; permission was refused.

[38c] *Hammonds v Thomas Muckle & Sons (Builders) Ltd* [2006] B.P.I.R. 704, HH Judge Langan, Q.C., Leeds District Registry.

The company voluntary arrangement. 16–13

[*Add to the end of footnote 43: page* 359]

The Insolvent Partnerships Order 1994 does not apply in Scotland.

[*Read alongside paragraphs 16–14—16–54 for the position in Scotland: page* 359]

The procedural aspects of company voluntary arrangements in Scotland are dealt with in Part 1 of the Insolvency (Scotland) Rules 1986 (as amended).

Where administrator is not proposed as nominee. 16–17

[*Add to footnote 72, after "Sargent": page* 363]

[2003]

Decisions of meetings. 16–32

[*In the fourth line, delete "other" and substitute: page* 371]

another

[*In the fifth line, delete "other" and substitute: page* 371]

another

[*In the fifth line, delete "the" and substitute: page* 371]

they

Challenge to the decisions of the meetings. 16–38

[*Add to the end of footnote 6: page* 375]

See para.16–24, above.

16–48 **Matters arising during implementation.**
[*In the ninth line, delete "of" and substitute: page* 380]
on

16–49 **Production of accounts and records to the Secretary of State.**
[*In the second line, after "Secretary of State" add: page* 380]
may

SECTION 3—CONVERSION FROM ADMINISTRATION TO SCHEME OF ARRANGEMENT

[*Read alongside Section 3 for the position in Scotland: page* 382]
The Companies Act 1985, Section 425 applies in Scotland and the general principles applicable to the approval of a scheme of arrangement are the same as those applicable in England and Wales, discussed in the text. Court procedure, however, is governed by the relevant Scottish Rules of Court. In particular, the practice directions discussed in para.16–59 do not apply in Scotland.

[*Add new paragraph 16–58A: page* 384]
16–58A **Foreign companies.** The court can sanction a scheme of arrangement under s.425 of the Companies Act 1985 (as amended), submitted in the case of a foreign company, so long as the company is liable to be wound-up as an unregistered company;[85a] it need not be shown that at the date of the order, the court would actually have jurisdiction to wind up the company.[85b]

[85a] Under Insolvency Act 1986, s.221.
[85b] *Re D A P Holdings NV* (2005), September 26, Lewison J.

SECTION 4—CONVERSION FROM ADMINISTRATION TO WINDING-UP (NEW RÉGIME)

[*Read alongside Section 4 for the position in Scotland: page* 385]
This section applies in Scotland subject to substitution of reference to the Insolvency (Scotland) Rules 1986 in place of the rules referred to in the text, for procedural aspects.

16–64 **On the application of the supervisor.**
[*Add to the end of paragraph: page* 386]
Where the directors of a company, which was subject to a voluntary arrangement, petitioned for and obtained an order for its winding-up, this was held not to terminate the arrangement, or the interests of the creditors who had approved it.[99a]

[99a] *Re Excalibur Airways Ltd* [1998] 1 B.C.L.C. 436; [1998] B.P.I.R. 598, distinguishing *Re Arthur Rathbone Kitchens Ltd*; see fn.96, above.

SECTION 5—WINDING-UP PROCEDURES IN PRE-COMMENCEMENT CASES

[*Read alongside Section 5 for the position in Scotland: page* 388]
This section may be read as applicable in Scotland.

Under the old régime. **16–67**

[*In the final line of the second paragraph, delete text "logged" and substitute: page* 389]
lodged

[*In footnote 39 delete text "n.33," and substitute: page* 389]
fn.36,

[*Add to the end of paragraph: page* 389]
For the position and rights of bond-holders of a company, which was proposing a scheme for the transfer of the company's shareholding to a new company, the great majority of whose share-capital would be issued to the company's creditors.[40a]

[40a] *In the matter of Mytravel Group Ltd* [2004] EWHC 409 (Ch); [2005] 2 B.C.L.C. 125, CA.

SECTION 6—CONVERSION FROM ADMINISTRATION INTO DISSOLUTION

[*Read alongside Section 6 for the position in Scotland: page* 389]
The relevant insolvency rules applicable in Scotland are the Insolvency (Scotland) Rules 1986, Rule 2.48 together with the relative prescribed forms contained in the Insolvency (Scotland) Amendment Rules 2003.

CHAPTER 17

THE CESSATION OF THE EFFECT OF THE ADMINISTRATOR'S APPOINTMENT AND THE TERMINATION OF ADMINISTRATION

SECTION 1—REVIEW OF THE OLD AND THE NEW RÉGIMES

[*Read alongside Section 1 for the position in Scotland: page* 392]
This section may be read as applicable to Scotland.

SECTION 2—THE REMEDIES FOR UNSATISFACTORY APPOINTMENTS

[*Read alongside Section 2 for the position in Scotland: page* 393]
This section does not directly apply in Scotland, since Rule 7.47 which is discussed applies only in England and Wales. While there is no equivalent to Rule 7.47 in Scotland, the Court of Session has inherent jurisdiction under its *nobile officium* to grant a remedy in the circumstances discussed.

17–5 The remedy of judicial review: the *Cornhill Insurance* decision.
[*In footnote 23 delete text "[1990] B.C.C. 977 at 107–8." and substitute: page* 395]
[1990] B.C.C. 97, at 107–8; [1990] B.C.L.C. 1.

SECTION 3—REMEDIES UNDER THE NEW RÉGIME

[*Read alongside Section 3 for the position in Scotland: page* 396]
Paras. 74, 75 and 81 of Schedule B1 to the Insolvency Act 1986, which deal respectively with a challenge to the administrator's conduct, alleged misfeasance by an administrator and an application by a creditor for a court order ending administration, all apply in Scotland. If there is an existing court process, i.e. if the administrator was appointed by the court, any such application would be made by note in the process; if there is no existing process, such an application would be made by separate petition (Rules of the Court of Session 1994, Rule 74.15; Sheriff Court Company Insolvency Rules, Rule 12). Further procedural provisions including the prescribed forms are contained in the Insolvency (Scotland) Rules 1986, as amended by the Insolvency (Scotland) Amendment Rules 2003, Rule 2.56 and Sch.5.

The problems of the interpretation of the relevant provisions of Schedule B1 which are discussed in the main text would also be pertinent in Scotland.

Possible analogous constructions with the law of voidable preference. 17–13
[*In footnote 40, delete text "(Issue 35)" and substitute: page* 398]
(Issue 38)

[*Read alongside paragraphs 17–22A—17–23 for the position in Scotland: page* 402]
The discussion in paras 17–22A and 17–23 is equally relevant in Scotland.

[*Add new paragraph 17–23A: page* 403]
The question then arises, whether a defect in the completion of the giving 17–23A
of the statutory notices, which are requisite for the administrator's appointment to take effect, constitutes a "defect in his appointment", which will come within, and will be cured by, the protective provisions of the Insolvency Act 1986, Sch.B1, para.104.

[*Read alongside paragraph 17–24 for the position in Scotland: page* 403]
Out of hours appointment is dealt with in Scotland by the Insolvency (Scotland) Rules 1986 (as amended), Rule 2.12.

[*Read alongside paragraphs 17–25—17–32A for the position in Scotland: page* 404]
The discussion in paras 17–25—17–32A is relevant in Scotland subject to substitution of reference to the Insolvency (Scotland) Rules 1986 for the Insolvency Rules 1986.

Revocation of approval on grounds of invalidity. 17–32A
[*Add to the end of footnote 83: page* 408]
See para.16–40A, above.

Section 4—Contentious and Non-contentious Procedures

[*Read alongside Section 4 for the position in Scotland: page* 408]
This section may be read as applicable to Scotland substituting reference to the Insolvency (Scotland) Rules 1986 (as amended) for reference to the Insolvency Rules 1986.

(A) Non-contentious Procedures

[*Add new paragraph 17–41A, immediately after the end of the second paragraph of 17–41: page* 414]
Whether order of court is required. It has been held that it is not necessary 17–41A
for an administrator appointed by an administration order, who wishes to move the company in administration into a creditors' voluntary winding-up, to obtain an order from the court under the provisions of para.70 of Sch.B1; that paragraph provides that the court may, on the administrator's application, provide that the appointment of an administrator shall cease to have effect at a specified time. The employment of the procedures under

para.83 (or under para.84, which permit the company to be moved straight to a dissolution), are matters entirely for the administrator's discretion and decision, and not for the court.[23a] Those dicta have however been in part dissented from.[23b]

But although Blackburne J. ruled that the administrator did not need an order of the court to authorise him to move the administration into another mode, by virtue of which the appointment of the administrator would cease, *ipso jure*, to have effect, the administrator would still need an order of the court to discharge him from personal liability.[23c]

Where an administrator wished to make a distribution to non-preferential unsecured creditors, he was directed not to do so, unless his proposals had included a proposed distribution, and he had enough funds to cover it, and on terms that he does not propose to exit from the administration into creditors' voluntary liquidation,[23d] and that the proposed distribution was consistent with his functions and his proposals.[23e]

[23a] *Re Ballast Plc (in administration) and other companies* [2003] EWHC 2356 (Ch); [2005] 1 B.C.L.C. 446, per Blackburne, J.
[23b] See fn.23e.
[23c] See fn.23a at [17].
[23d] Under IA 1986, Sch.1, para.83.
[23e] See *Re G H D Realisations Ltd* [2005] EWHC 2400 (Ch), per Rimer, J., dissenting from the decision at fn.23a.

[*Immediately before the third paragraph of existing 17–41, add paragraph number and cross-heading: page* 414]

17–41B **Procedure.**

17–43 **Administration moving to dissolution (new régime) (paragraph 84).**
[*Add to the end of the first paragraph: page* 416]
For the exit from administration of court-appointed administrators, see article at (2005) 21 I L & P 1.

[*Add new paragraph 17–43A: page* 416]

17–43A **Administrator's duties after dissolution of company.** In the case of a company which went into administration on or after 15 September 2003, its last administrator may, after the expiry of one year from its dissolution, destroy all books, papers and records of the company. If the Secretary of State requests him to give particulars of any money in his hands or under his control, or dividends or other sums of money due to any person or member or former member of the company, he must supply these particulars within 14 days.[45a]

[45a] Insolvency (Amendment) Regulations 2005 (SI 2005/512) art. 6, inserting new art. 3A, and art. 8, inserting new art 36A, in the Insolvency Regulations, 1994 (SI 1994/2507).

Section 5—Appointments Ceasing to have effect and the end of Appointments of Administrators

[*Read alongside Section 5 for the position in Scotland: page* 420]

This section applies in Scotland, substituting reference to the Insolvency (Scotland) Rules 1986 for references to the Insolvency Rules 1986. The forms for use in these circumstances are prescribed by the Insolvency (Scotland) Amendment Rules 2003.

Part IV

Receivers Appointed out of Court

[*Read alongside Part IV for the position in Scotland: page* 427]
Part IV (Chapters 18 to 20) does not apply in Scotland. For receivership in Scotland, see Chapter 30 below.

Chapter 18

GENERAL PRINCIPLES GOVERNING APPOINTMENT

Section 1—the Old Régime

18–4 Duties of a receiver appointed out of court.
[*Add to the end of sub-paragraph (a): page* 430]
and if it is a registrable charge, that it has been duly registered; if it has not been duly registered, application should be made to the court without delay to obtain permission to register it out of time.[9a]

[9a] See para.2–66A, above.

18–7 Appointments by agreement.
[*Add to the end of footnote 23: page* 432]
Paras 10–6, 10–6A.

18–10 Property to which appointment extends.
[*Add to the end of footnote 30: page* 432]
See para.2–65, above.

18–27 Exceptions to the prohibition on the future appointment of administrative receivers.
[*In the third line, after "subject", add: page* 439]
to exceptions,

CHAPTER 19

APPOINTMENTS UNDER STATUTORY POWERS

Appointment of receiver by mortgagee. **19–2**
[*Delete footnote 9 text and substitute: page* 440]
See para.19–31, below.

Mode of appointment. **19–8**
[*Delete footnote 37 text and substitute: page* 444]
See para.21–18, below.

Receiver's liability to the mortgagor. **19–13**
[*In the ninth line, delete ", in failing to obtain proper commercial discounts off the cost of cattle-feed purchased for the feeding of the livestock.[72a]": page* 448]

[*Add new paragraph 19–13A: page* 448]
Receiver's duties when trading. There, the mortgagor, under agricultural charges, of a substantial farming trading business, who under the receivership had paid off the charges, claimed damages from the receivers for their negligent administration. His claim was principally founded on their alleged failure to obtain the substantial discounts obtainable on feed supplies, purchased for the feeding of the livestock. On a preliminary issue, the Court of Appeal held that a receiver and manager, managing mortgaged property in the form of a business, owes duties to the mortgagor, or to third parties interested in the equity of redemption. These duties are not limited to a duty of good faith, the extent and scope of the duties depending on the facts of the case. Subject to his primary duty to obtain payment in full of the mortgage debt and interest, he must manage the property with due diligence, which includes the taking of reasonable steps to do so profitably.[74a] **19–13A**

[74a] *Medforth v Blake* [2000] Ch. 86, CA. See also para.19–14A, below.

[*Add new paragraph 19–14A, in front of existing paragraph 19–14A (renumber existing paragraph as 19–14B): page* 449]
Receiver's duties to mortgagor in equity. In *Palk v Mortgage Services & Funding Plc*,[76aa] the Court of Appeal declared, *obiter*, that a mortgagee is not entitled, while preserving his own interest, to conduct himself in a way which unfairly prejudices the mortgagor, such as by taking possession of the mortgaged premises, but keeping them empty, hoping that the market will **19–14A**

improve. He must not sell hastily, nor at a knock-down price only sufficient to satisfy his own debt.In the instant case, however, the mortgagee was not held to be in breach of any duty of care to the mortgagor, by leasing the mortgaged property instead of selling it.

The court differed from the decision in *Re B. Johnson & Co. (Builders) Ltd*,[76ab] and did not follow the Privy Council decision in *Downsview Nominees Ltd v First City Corp Ltd*[76ac]

The judgment concludes with a judicial summary of a receiver's duties.[76ad]

[76aa] [1993] Ch. 330, CA; see also para.19–13A, above.
[76ab] [1955] Ch. 634, CA.
[76ac] *Orws First City Corp Ltd v Downsview Nominees Ltd* [1993] A.C. 295, PC (on appeal from New Zealand).
[76ad] fn.76a, at [21].

19–14B [*In footnote 76a of renumbered paragraph 19–14B, delete text "1409" and substitute: page* 449]
1429

[*In the first line of the third paragraph of renumbered 19–14B, delete "not" and substitute: page* 449]
nor

[*Add to the end of footnote 76b of renumbered paragraph 19–14B: page* 449]
See para.19–13A, above.

Chapter 20

APPOINTMENTS OVER THE PROPERTY OF A COMPANY

Exceptions to the prohibition on the appointment of administrative receivers. **20–5**

[*Add to the end of paragraph: page* 464]

The somewhat obscure meanings of the classifications of these excepted categories of companies were considered in *Cabvision Ltd v Levy*;[27a] there, the court had to decide whether complex business arrangements between the parties, in the course of which one company had appointed an administrative receiver over the assets of the other, constituted the latter a "project company", the subject of "project finance", and providing "step-in rights", over whose assets an administrative receiver could lawfully be appointed, under a debenture created after September 15, 2003. It was held that it was not such an excepted company, and that the appointment of the receiver was invalid."

[27a] *Cabvision Ltd v Feetum, otherwise Feetum v Levy* [2005] EWCA Civ 1601; [2006] B.P.I.R. 379, CA, *affirming* [2005] EWHC 349 (Ch); [2005] 1 W.L.R. 2576, the case involved the construction and application of Insolvency Act 1986, new s.72E.

Power of appointment: legal mortgages. **20–9**

[*Add to the end of paragraph: page* 466]

The certificate of registration of the charge out of time is conclusive, where it has been issued pursuant to a valid order, even where it was issued by mistake.[42a]

[42a] See para.2-66A, above.

Time allowed for payment. **20–14**

[*In the sixth line, delete "sign" and substitute: page* 468]

sight

[*Add new paragraph 20–18A: page* 472]

Invalid appointment of receiver: nature of potential damage. In *OBG Ltd v* **20–18A**
Allan,[93a] a purported debenture-holder appointed receivers over the undertaking of a construction company, who took possession of the company's premises and plant, and control over its workforce. They proceeded to complete or to close down the company's constructional activities carried on under contract, and terminated its business activities.

The appointment of the receivers was agreed by the purported debenture-holder and the receivers to have been invalid, due to a misconception of the nature and extent of the security held. The company sued the receivers and their solicitors for a declaration of invalidity, and for very substantial damages for the wrongful activities of the receivers, which they pleaded as the tort of tortious interference with the company's contractual relations, analogous to the tort of the conversion of chattels.

At first instance, the judge found in the company's favour that there had been wrongful interference with its contractual activities, but rejected the analogy with the tort of the conversion of chattels, while awarding the company a modest amount in damages.

The defendants appealed, and the company cross-appealed. Before the Court of Appeal, the issues were whether the receivers had committed the tort of wrongful interference with contractual relations, or a tort in the nature of conversion in relation to the company's contractual rights, and as to the nature and extent of the damages awarded, or being claimed, or capable of being claimed.

By a majority,[93b] the Court held, dismissing the defendants' appeal in part, and the cross-appeal, that the tort of interference with contractual rights did not cover interference by a third party with the contracting party's right to perform his contracts, no breach of contract having occurred. The receivers had not interfered with the company's contractual relations at all; nor could there be, in law, any conversion of a chose in action; the defendants' attempt to rely on s.232 of the Insolvency Act 1986, was rejected. The modest amount of damages awarded was confirmed.[93c]

[93a] [2005] EWCA Civ 106; [2005] 1 B.C.L.C. 711, CA, *reversing in part* HH Judge Maddocks, (2005) March 24.

[93b] Per Peter Gibson (with considerable regret) and Carnwath LL J.J.; Mance L.J. delivered a powerful dissenting judgment. The judgments suggest that the case was not very adequately presented, but for which the result might have been different.

[93c] The section reads: "The acts of an administrative receiver, a liquidator or a provisional liquidator of a company are valid, notwithstanding any defect in his appointment, nomination or qualifications."

20–24 Appointments over foreign-registered companies and industrial and provident companies.

[*In the fourth line, after "held" add: page* 475]
probably erroneously

[*In footnote 23, delete text "(1998) The Times, July 15, CA;" and substitute: page* 475]
[1999] B.C.C. 441, CA: see also para.14–14A, above.

[*Add to the end of paragraph: page* 475]
The judgment in *Re Devon and Somerset Farmers Ltd* throws doubt on the correctness of the decision in *Re International Bulk Commodities Ltd*.[25a] In

Re Dallhold Estates (UK) Pty Ltd,[25b] the court held that it could appoint an administrator over an Australian-registered company; but this was in response to a request from the Australian court, seeking an order in aid.

[25a] See also the comments of Rattee, J., in *Re Bank of Credit & Commerce International SA* [1993] B.C.C. 787.
[25b] [1992] B.C.L.C. 621; [1992] B.C.C. 394.

[*In footnote 25, delete ", where the decision at n.22 was doubted.": page* 475]

Regularity of appointment. **20–30**
[*Add to the end of footnote 54: page* 478]
And see para.20–19A, above.

Relationship with board of directors. **20–31**
[*In footnote 66–67, delete text ", below." and substitute: page* 479]
, above.

Preferential debts. **20–34**
[*Add to the end of footnote 74: page* 480]
Re Barleycorn Enterprises Ltd was disapproved in *Buchler v Talbot* [2003] UKHL 9; [2004] 1 B.C.L.C. 281, HL: see paras 7–54 and 20–58.

Other statutory obligations. **20–40**
[*In the fourth line of footnote 2, delete text "p.208, above," and substitute: page* 483]
para.8–1, above,

[*Add new paragraph 20–46A: page* 488]
Liability of invalidly appointed receiver. For the liability (or the absence of liability) of an invalidly appointed receiver, arising from his interference with the company's production contracts and work-force, see *OBG Allan Ltd* [2005] EWCA Civ 106; [2005] 1 B.C.L.C. 711, CA, examined at para.20–18A, above. **20–46A**

Contractual liens. **20–54**
[*In footnote 86, delete text "(Standard)" and substitute: page* 492]
(Stansted)

Contracts: set-off. **20–55**
[*Delete footnote 92a text, and substitute: page* 493]

[92a] See Paragraph 15–108, and article by Professor Ian Fletcher, QC, "Crown Set-Off and Contingent Liabilities", in (2005) 18 Insolvency Intelligence, p.6.

Set-off under different contracts. **20–56**
[*Add to the end of footnote 93: page* 493]
See also para.15–108, and article by Professor Ian Fletcher QC, "Crown Set-off and Contingent Liabilities", in (2005) 18 Insolvency Intelligence, p.6.

20–58 **Extent of receiver's indemnity.**
[*In footnote 3 delete text "Mond v Suddards" and substitute: page* 494]
Mond v Hammond Suddards (No. 2)

[*Delete the final sentence of footnote 3 "See now Buchler v Talbot . . . ": page* 494]

[*In the tenth line, delete sentence beginning "He can apply to enforce his rights of indemnity . . ." (including footnote) and substitute: page* 494]
The receiver can apply to enforce his indemnity by means of an application for directions.[4]

The expenses of a liquidator in winding-up an insolvent company are not payable out of the assets comprised in a crystallised floating charge, in priority to the charge-holder. It must be borne in mind that there are two separate funds under consideration: the fund represented by the assets subject to the charge, which are to be employed in satisfying the charge-holder, and the fund represented by the other assets in the company, which are to be employed in discharging the costs of the liquidation.[4a]

[4] *Re Therm-a-Stor Ltd* [1996] 1 W.L.R. 1338.
[4a] *Buchler v Talbot* [2003] UKHL 9, [2004] 1 B.C.L.C. 281, reversing sub nom. *Re Leyland-Daf Ltd* [2002] 2 B.C.L.C. 571, CA, and disapproving of *Re Barleycorn Enterprises Ltd, Mathias & Davies (a firm) v Down* [1970] Ch. 464, CA. *Cf. Mond v Hammond Suddards (No. 2)* sub nom. *Re R.S.M. Engineering Co. Ltd* [2002] Ch. 40, CA, where a liquidator attempted unsuccessfully to recover the costs of his unsuccessful litigation out of the assets subject to the charge.

20–64 **Power to carry on business.**
[*In the third line, after "his powers are" add: page* 496]
no longer

[*In the first line, add footnote 25a after "association.": page* 497]

[25a] Since the enlargement of a company's powers by the CA 1989: see para.2–63, above.

Part V

Administrative Receivers

[*Read alongside Part V for the position in Scotland: page* 501]
This part, (Chapters 21 to 26) does not apply in Scotland. For administrative receivers in Scotland, see Chapter 30.

Chapter 21

STATUS AND POWERS OF AN ADMINISTRATIVE RECEIVER

"The special administration regimes". 21–2
[*Add to the end of footnote 11: page* 504]
For a case where a prima facie invalid appointment of an administrative receiver, in contravention of the Enterprise Act 2002, s.72E, which has prohibited the appointment of administrative receivers under any instrument executed on or after September 15, 2003, was sought to be justified by bringing the company in question within the Exceptions to that prohibition, see *Cabvision Ltd v Feetum, otherwise Feetum v Levy*, [2005] EWCA Civ 1601; [2006] B.P.I.R. 379, CA, *affirming* [2005] EWHC 2576 (Ch): [2005] 1 W.L.R. 2576. See para.20–5, above.

The office holder. 21–4
[*In paragraph 21–4, read "an administrative receiver" for "he": page* 505]

Provisions of general application. 21–5
[*Add to the end of footnote 33: page* 506]
The form of order is Form 7.20.

21–9 Powers and privileges.
[*In sub-paragraph (1), delete "p.393, below." and substitute: page* 509]
para.21–10, below.

[*Add new paragraph 21–10A: page* 511]

21–10A Limitations on use of company documents. An administrative receiver is entitled to require the company to hand over any of its documents; but this power is exercisable solely for the purposes of his functions as receiver. He cannot, for example, obtain from the company confidential and sensitive documents, not for the purpose of using them as receiver, but of passing them to the debenture-holder, for use in its litigation against the company's guarantors.[80a] The company's sole director was held to be entitled to sue the debenture-holder, without the leave of the receiver, for the return of the documents to the receiver.[80b]

For a fuller examination of the administrative receiver's powers, see Chapters 22 and 23, below.

[80a] *Sutton v G E Capital Commercial Finance Ltd, Anglo-Petroleum Ltd v G E Capital Commercial Finance Ltd* [2004] 2 B.C.L.C. 662, CA; see also para.23–12A, below.
[80b] See fn.80a, above, applying *Newhart Developments Ltd v Co-operative Commercial Bank Ltd* [1987] Q.B. 814, CA.

21–13 Power to dispose of charged property.
[*In the third line, delete "ranking after" and substitute: page* 512]
ranking in priority to

21–15 Overriding provision.
[*Add to the end of paragraph: page* 513]
The effect of this section would seem to be that the acts of an invalidly-appointed administrative receiver may bind the company and its creditors, leaving them to their only remedy of proceeding personally against the invalidly-appointed office-holder.[3a]

[3a] *OBG v Allan* [2005] EWCA Civ 106; [2005] 1 B.C.L.C. 711, CA, otherwise *OBG Ltd & OBG (Plant & Transport) Ltd v Allan Stevenson & another* [2005] B.P.I.R. 928, CA, *reversing in part* [2001] B.P.I.R. 1111, HH Judge Maddocks.

Chapter 22

ADMINISTRATIVE RECEIVER'S RELATIONSHIP WITH THE UNSECURED CREDITORS

Section 1—The Meeting of Unsecured Creditors

Voting rights. **22–6**

[*In footnote 30, delete text "n.9", and substitute: page* 528]
fn.29

Section 2—The Creditors' Committee

Functions and meetings of the committee. **22–14**

[*In the final line, delete "him." and substitute: page* 532]
them.

CHAPTER 23

ADMINISTRATIVE RECEIVER'S RELATIONSHIP WITH THE COMPANY AND ITS STAFF: CONTRACTS OF EMPLOYMENT; RESIDUAL POWERS OF THE DIRECTORS

SECTION 1—CONTRACTS OF EMPLOYMENT OF EMPLOYEES GENERALLY

23–7 ***Powdrill v Watson*: its extent.**
[*In the fourth line, delete "contacts" and substitute: page* 539]
contracts

[*Add new paragraph 23–11A: page* 542]
23–11A **Liabilities held not to be "qualifying".** Sums due to employees, or former employees, of the company in respect of statutory liabilities for payments on account of redundancy, or by way of compensation for unfair dismissal, are not "wages or salary" within the Schedule,[32i] and are therefore not qualifying liabilities, entitled to preferential payment, in priority to the administrator;[32j] nor are they "expenses" or "necessary disbursements", ranking for preferential payment under those heads.[32k]

Administrators have similarly been held not to be liable to employees, or former employees, for sums due in respect of "protective awards",[32l] or in respect of awards of pay in lieu of notice. Judges at first instance had differed on the issue of liability:[32m] the Court of Appeal ruled that there was no liability under either head,[32n] except in respect of payments by way of "garden leave".[32o]

[32i] Under para.99.

[32j] *Re Allders Department Stores Ltd (in administration)* [2005] EWHC 172 (Ch); [2005] 2 All E.R. 122; [2005] B.C.C. 289. The dicta in *re Toshoku Finance UK Plc (in liquidation)* [2002] UKHL 6; [2002] 3 All E.R. 961; [2002] B.C.C. 110, HL, have no application to administrations.

[32k] See IR 1986, r.2.67.

[32l] Under the Trade Union and Labour Relations Act 1992, s.189.

[32m] In *Huddersfield Fine Worsteds Ltd and Re Globe Worsteds Ltd* [2005], All E.R. (D) 387 (Jul); Peter Smith J. had decided in favour of liability; in *Re Ferrotech Ltd and Re Granville Technology Ltd* [2005] All E.R. (D) 45 (Aug), Etherton, J. had decided against liability.

[32n] The four cases cited in fn.32m were decided by the Court of Appeal under those titles in [2005] EWCA Civ 1072; [2005] 4 All E.R. 886, CA, reversing Peter Smith, J. and affirming Etherton, J. The expression "a period" in IA 1986, Sch.B1, para.99(6), must be construed as "such period". For a discussion of the judgments, see also *Krasner v McMath and other cases* [2005] *The Times,* September 26, CA, reversing [2005] EWHC 1682 (Ch); and see case-notes in 21 I L & P (2005) 135 and 175, and article by Laura Fairley, *ibid.,* in 22 I L & P. (2005) pp.137, 175.

[32o] Applying the dicta of Lord Browne-Wilkinson in *Delaney v Staples* [1992] 1 A.C. 687, HL.

Section 2—The Management of the Company: Position of Officers

[*Add new paragraph 23–12A: page* 543]

Limitations on the powers of administrative receivers. The extent of, and the limitations on, the powers of an administrative receiver were further examined and defined in a case where an administrative receiver, in office, had required the company to deliver up to him important and sensitive documents, which he had then passed to the debenture-holder's solicitors. This he had done, not in the exercise of his functions as receiver, but for the purpose of assisting the debenture-holder in its other proceedings against the guarantors of the company's indebtedness. The company applied for an injunction to restrain this course of action. **23–12A**

The Court of Appeal held that the receiver had improperly exercised his powers, and had infringed the company's right to privacy and its legal professional privilege. It was ordered that the documents be returned to the receiver, to be held by him for the sole purpose of use in his functions of getting in, protecting and realising the assets comprised in the charge.

The company, by its sole director, had brought the proceedings for the injunction. The receiver had contended that the proceedings were invalid, as not having been authorised by him. But the Court of Appeal held that the directors of a company under administrative receivership were entitled, without the authority of the receiver, to bring any proceedings, which did not threaten the interests of the debenture-holder.[36a]

[36a] *Sutton v G E Capital Commercial Finance Ltd, Anglo-Petroleum Ltd v G E Capital Commercial Finance Ltd* [2004] EWCA 316; [2004] 2 B.C.L.C. 662, CA, applying *Newhart Developments Ltd v Co-operative Commercial Bank Ltd* [1978] Q.B. 814; see also fn.35, above, and para.21–10A, above.

"Deemed insolvency" for benefit of employees. **23–13A**

[*Delete footnote 40 text, and substitute: page* 544]

See para.6–65, above.

[*In footnote 41, delete text "para.00–00" and substitute: page* 544]

See para.20–43, above.

CHAPTER 24

EXTRA-TERRITORIAL EXTENT OF FLOATING CHARGES AND OF RECEIVERSHIPS

[*Add new paragraphs 24–9A and 24–9B: page* 557]

24–9A **The adoption of the UNCITRAL Model Law.** Great Britain has now adopted the UNCITRAL Model Law, by virtue of the enactment of the Cross-Border Regulations, 2006,[21a] which came into force on April 4, 2006.

The Model Law is defined as "the Model Law on cross-border insolvency, as adopted by the UNCITRAL Committee of the United Nations on May 30, 1997".[21b] It is to have the force of law in Great Britain in the form set out in Schedule 1 to the Regulations (which contains the law with modifications to adapt it for application to Great Britain).[21c]

The Regulations include a list of documents which may be considered in ascertaining the meaning or effect of any of its provisions.[21d]

[21a] SI 2006/1272, made under the Insolvency Act 2000, s.14.
[21b] Reg.1(2).
[21c] Reg.2(1).
[21d] Reg.2(2).

24–9B **Brief procedural guide to the Regulations.** British insolvency law,[21e] with such modifications as the context require, shall apply for the purposes of giving effect to the Regulations.[21f] In the case of any conflict between any provision of British insolvency law or of IA 1986, Part 3, and the provisions of the Regulations, the Regulations shall prevail.[21g]

Procedural matters are provided for by Schedules 2 and 3 of the Regulations (relating respectively to England and Wales and to Scotland). Sch.4 makes provision for the giving of "Model Law notices" to the registrars of companies in England and Wales and in Scotland. Sch.5 prescribes the forms to be used in proceedings under the Regulations.

The provisions of IA 1986, regulating the activities and functions of insolvency practitioners,[21h] do not apply to anything done by a "foreign representative".[21i] A foreign representative is defined as "a person or body, including one appointed on an interim basis, authorised in a foreign proceeding to administer the reorganisation or the liquidation of the debtor's assets or affairs, or to act as a representative in the foreign proceeding".[21j]

"A foreign proceeding" is defined as "a collective judicial or administrative proceeding in a foreign State, including an interim proceeding, pursuant to a law relating to insolvency, in which proceeding the assets and affairs of the debtor are subject to control or supervision by a foreign court, for the purpose of reorganisation or liquidation".[21k]

For a useful summary of the Model Law, see article by Professor Ian Fletcher, QC in (2006) *Insolvency Intelligence* 86, "Better Late than Never: the UNCITRAL Model Law enters into force in Great Britain".

[21e] As defined in Sch.1, art.2(a).
[21f] Reg.3(1).
[21g] Reg.3(2).
[21h] See IA 1986, s.388.
[21i] Reg.8.
[21j] Defined at Sch.1, art.2(j).
[21k] Defined at Sch.1, art.2(i).

Chapter 25

EFFECTS OF LIQUIDATION ON ADMINSTRATIVE RECEIVERSHIP

25–12 Incident of costs of litigation.
[*In paragraph cross-heading, delete "Incident" and substitute: page* 567]
Incidence

[N.B. THERE ARE NO AMENDMENTS TO CHAPTER 26]

Part VI

Other New Procedures

CHAPTER 27

THE PROCEEDS OF CRIME ACT 2002: RECEIVERS UNDER CRIMINAL CONFISCATION STATUTES

[*Read alongside Chapter 27 for the position in Scotland: page* 579]
Part 1 (Sections 1 to 5) of the Proceeds of Crime Act 2002 ("the Act"), which establishes the Assets Recovery Agency, applies in Scotland. Part 2 of the Act, which is referred to in detail in the main text, contains the provisions for Confiscation Orders in England and Wales. Equivalent provision is made for courts in Scotland (the High Court of Justiciary or the Sheriff Court).

Since the Act is concerned with the recovery of property from individuals who have benefited from criminal activity, and a receiver or administrator can only be appointed to a corporate body in Scotland, the Act is of limited impact on receivership and administration in Scotland.

Section 430 of the Act, however, restricts the power of a receiver in Scotland to deal with property held by the company which has been made the subject of a restraint order under Section 41 (England and Wales) or 190 (Northern Ireland) of the Act, or where there has been appointed in respect of such property an enforcement receiver or a director's receiver under Sections 50 or 52 (England and Wales) or 198 or 200 (Northern Ireland), or an enforcement administrator under Section 128(3)(Scotland) of the Act. Under Section 430(3), however, a restraint order which applies to heritable property in Scotland is effective only if the order has been recorded in the General Register of Sasines or the Land Register before the appointment of the receiver.

If a receiver has already been appointed, a restraint order cannot be granted in respect of property attached by the charge, nor can any receiver or administrator appointed pursuant to the Act exercise his powers in relation to such property (Section 430(4) of the Act). Moreover, under Section 430(5) and (6), the court's power to grant restraint orders or to appoint a receiver or administrator pursuant to the Act must not be exercised so as to prevent the receiver from exercising his functions for the purpose of distributing the property of the company to the creditors or the payment of his remuneration and other expenses.

The Act has no impact on administration procedure in relation to a Scottish company.

Section 2—Civil Recovery by Proceedings in the High Court

27–13 **Protection of the rights of interested parties to make representations.**
[*Add new paragraph, immediately after the end of the second paragraph of 27–13: page* 584]
Where a company was subject to an interim receiving order,[47a] parties claiming restitutionary relief against it applied for an administration order. The court accepted that the company must be presumed to be insolvent, and eligible to enter administration; but since all its assets were likely to be held to be recoverable property, there would be no assets available for administration.[47b]

[47a] Under *ibid.* s.246.
[47b] *Re Q3 Media Ltd* [2006] All E.R. (D) 307 (May) Ch D, Rimer J.

[*Add new paragraph 27–13A: page* 584]
27–13A **Confiscation orders and the matrimonial home.** Where the defendant owns a share in a matrimonial home, or a civil partnership home, the value of that share must be taken into account, when computing the value of the defendant's property to satisfy a confiscation order, taking into consideration that the home would be likely to be sold, irrespective of whether that might prejudice the interests of the wife, husband or civil partner.

However, if the court is later asked to make an order of sale to realise the defendant's share, it would have to consider whether or not it would be proportionate to so order.[48a] If the defendant was an undischarged bankrupt, the court would presumably have to take into consideration whether refusing to order a sale would merely be increasing the assets available to the creditors in the bankruptcy.

Where a confiscation order was quashed on appeal, the question arose whether civil proceedings could be taken for a recovery order, involving the danger of "double recovery".[48b]

[48a] *R. v Ahmed, R. v Qureshi* [2004] EWCA (Crim); [2005] 1 W.L.R. 122, CA (Crim).
[48b] *Director of Assets Recovery Agency v Singh* [2005] 1 W.L.R. 3747, CA.

SECTION 4—THE CIVIL JURISDICTION

The functions of the trustee for civil recovery. 27–25
[*Add to the end of paragraph: page* 590]
An important rule governing the recovery proceedings initiated by the Assets Recovery Agency has recently been formulated: when embarking on claims to recover property alleged to be the produce of a "criminal lifestyle",[83a] the Agency must produce evidence of what is alleged to be the "unlawful conduct" relied upon, not just allegations based on the respondents' lack of identifiable income to support his lifestyle".[83b]

[83a] See Proceeds of Crime Act 2002, Part 5, ss 240–316.
[83b] *R. (Director of Assets Recovery Agency) v Green* (2005) *The Times,* February 27, per Sullivan, J.

[*Add new paragraph 27–36A: page* 594]
Receiver not liable to pay capital gains tax or income tax. A receiver appointed under the Criminal Justice Act 1988 in a confiscation case was held to be not liable personally to pay either capital gains tax, or income tax, on the property and income of a defendant passing through his hands, nor are sums assessed under those taxes part of the receiver's expenses: liability for those taxes falls on the defendant.[10a] 27–36A

[10a] *Re Inland Revenue Commissioners and Piacentini, Re Criminal Justice Act 1988* (2003) *The Times,* February 10: see Proceeds of Crime Act 2002, s.448, Sch.10.

Analogy between receivers under the Act and receives under other Jurisdictions. 27–42
[*In paragraph cross-heading, delete "receives": page* 596]

[*Add new paragraph 27–42A: page* 596]
Case-law on remuneration of statutory receivers. Where a receiver, who had been appointed on the application of the Customs and Excise, under the Criminal Justice Act 1988, was discharged, it was held that he should have been discharged at an earlier date (thereby reducing his charges); the Court of Appeal, having discharged the receiver, ordered the Customs and Excise to pay him his remuneration in respect of the later period, and his costs of the discharge proceedings: but not the receiver's expenses.[16a] The terms of CPR 69 made it clear that the liability to pay the remuneration of the receiver and his expenses were distinct: it was not possible for the court to order another party to pay the receiver's expenses, which must be met out of the realisable assets in the receiver's charge.[16b] 27–42A

The judgments provide important guidance on the location of the liability for a receiver's remuneration and expenses, and the need to show that the receivership was, throughout the period in respect of which his remuneration was sought to be recovered, serving a valid purpose.

The judgments contain guidelines, proposed by counsel and commended by the court, for the appointment of receivers under the confiscation statutes.[16c]

See also para.10–6, above.

[16a] *Capewell v Customs & Excise (No. 1)* [2004] EWCA Civ 1628; (No. 2) [2004] EWCA Civ 964; reported together at [2005] B.P.I.R. 1266, CA, reviewing *Re Andrews* [1999] 1 W.L.R. 1236, CA, and *Hughes v Customs & Excise* and other cases, [2002] EWCA Civ 734; [2003] 1 W.L.R. 177, CA, both cases being decided under the Criminal Justice Act 1988, s.48, RSC Ord.30, r.3, and Ord.115, now replaced by CPR 69.7(2).
[16b] See fn.16a (second hearing) at [25].
[16c] See fn.16a (first hearing) at [66].

CHAPTER 28

THE EUROPEAN COUNCIL REGULATION ON INSOLVENCY PROCEEDINGS

[*Read alongside Chapter 28 for the position in Scotland: page* 598]
The EC Regulation on Insolvency Proceedings and the discussion of its effect in this Chapter apply in Scotland. The Insolvency Rules of 1986 referred to in the text do not, however, apply in Scotland.

In any insolvency proceedings in Scotland, a "member state liquidator" is deemed to be a creditor (Insolvency (Scotland) Rules 1986 (as amended) Rule 2.60). "Member state liquidator" is defined as a person within the definition of "liquidator" in Article 2(b) of the EC Regulation, appointed in proceedings to which it applies in a member state other than the United Kingdom, as listed in Annex A to the EC Regulation (Insolvency (Scotland) Rules 1986 (as amended) Rule 0.2(1)).

The procedure for an application by a member state liquidator to obtain a court order converting an administration of a Scottish company into a winding-up is governed by the Insolvency (Scotland) Rules 1986 (as amended) Rules 2.57 to 2.59. If there is an existing court process upon which the administration order was granted, the application is by way of note in that process; if there is no such process, the application is by way of petition to the relevant court (Act of Sederunt (Rules of the Court of Session 1994) 1994 Rule 7.15; Act of Sederunt (Sheriff Court Company Insolvency Rules) 1986 Rule 12).

The geographical and jurisdictional extents of the Regulation. 28–3
[*Add to the end of footnote 7: page* 599]
See *Re The Arena Corporation Ltd* [2003] EWHC 3032 (Ch): [2004] B.P.I.R. 375, where a winding-up order was made against a Danish company.

The debtor's centre of main interests. 28–6
[*Add to the end of footnote 10: page* 599]
As substituted by the Insolvency (Amendment) Rules, 2003 (SI 2002/1307), para.10 with effect from May 31, 2002. Other substitutions, and amendments in and to IA 1986, r.13.13, were made by those Rules, with effect from September 13, 2003.

The IA 1986 (Amendment) (No. 2) Regulations, 2002, (SI 2002/1240), the Insolvency (Amendment) Order, 2002 SI 2002/1308, the AIEO 2002, (2002/1309).

28–7 Meaning of a debtor's "establishment".

[*Add to the end of footnote 11: page* 600]

The premises of a subsidiary company in one Member State of a parent company, established in another Member State, do not constitute an "establishment" of the parent company in the first Member State; see *Telia AB v Hillcourt (Docklands) Ltd* [2002] 3277 (Ch); [2003] B.C.C. 886 (a Swedish case)' see also article by Gabriel Moss, QC, in 19 Insolvency Intelligence (2005) at p.20.

28–10 Conditions required to be present for the opening of secondary proceedings.

[*In the twelfth line, delete "conferred" and substitute: page* 601]

confirmed

28–11 The titles of national insolvency proceedings and national insolvency administrators.

[*In paragraph cross-heading, add new text after "administrators": page* 601]

and of their administrations.

[*In the eighth line, after "languages." add: page* 601]

After the enlargement of the European Union by the admission of ten further Member States, the Annexes have been amended by the addition of the national names of the insolvency proceedings, and of the titles of the insolvency administrators in each new Member State.[18a]

[18a] See the Treaty and Act of Accession, dated April 16, 2003, Annex 2, published in [2005] O.J. L236 (711) and see para.28–2, above; it was given effect to by the EC Regulation No. 603 of 2005, published in [2005] O J L 100/1, and came into force on April 21, 2005.

28–12 Meaning of "a court" and "a judgment" within the Regulation's ambit.

[*Add to the end of paragraph: page* 602]

e.g. including a qualified floating charge-holder, or a company or its directors.

28–14 The position and powers of the Member-State liquidator.

[*In the second line, after "attend" add: page* 603]

and participate in, as a creditor

[*Read alongside paragraphs 28–15—28–17 for the position in Scotland: page* 603]

The procedure for the liquidator of a Scottish company which is in creditors' voluntary winding-up to apply to the court for an order confirming the creditors' voluntary winding-up for the purposes of the EC Regulation is governed by the Insolvency (Scotland) Rules 1986 (as amended) Rules 4.84 and 4.85.

Confirmation of liquidator's appointment in creditors' winding up. **28–16**
[*Add to the end of footnote 33: page* 603]
The form of order is Form 7.20.

[*In the third line, delete "conversation" and substitute: page* 604]
conversion

[*Add to the end of paragraph: page* 604]
The court may require the validity of the administrator's voluntary resolutions to be confirmed.[40a] It may also require an undertaking from the liquidator that the foreign creditors will be fairly treated.[40b]

[40a] *Re TXU Europe German Finance BV, and Re TXU Europe Ireland Ltd* [2004] B.P.I.R. 209, Chief Registrar Baister, following *Re BRAC Rent-a-Car International Inc.* [2003] EWHC 128 (Ch); [2003] 1 W.L.R. 1421.
[40b] See fn.40a.

[*Read alongside paragraph 28–18 for the position in Scotland: page* 604]
In relation to Scotland, the right of a member state liquidator to receive notices, etc, is defined in the Insolvency (Scotland) Rules 1986, Rule 4.83.

Insolvency jurisdiction extended by the Regulation. **28–21**
[*In the first line of the final paragraph, delete "defines" and substitute: page* 605]
originally defined

[*Add to the end of the final paragraph: page* 605]
But, as described in para.14–14A, above, that definition has been repealed, and a narrower definition has been substituted.[54a]

[54a] See the Insolvency Act 1986 (Amendment) Regulations, 2005 (SI 2005/979), with effect from April 3, 2005. See also para.14–14A, above.

Cases of non-acceptance of the Regulation's jurisdictional rules. **28–22**
[*Delete the second paragraph, "In one recent case, a multi-State group . . . " (but retain footnote 55) and substitute: page* 606]
Another recent case concerned an Italian company, registered in Eire, where it also had its centre of main interests. The company was a subsidiary of a much larger company, registered in Italy, and already in liquidation in the Italian courts. The Eire company was made the subject of a winding-up petition in the Irish court, which appointed a provisional liquidator. That step was taken to prevent the Italian parent company from moving the company's centre of main interests out of Eire. That appointment was held by the Irish court to constitute, within the terms of the EC Regulation on Insolvency Proceedings, "an insolvency proceeding", marking the opening of main proceedings. Subsequently insolvency proceedings, not purporting to be territorial or secondary proceedings, were opened in French and German insolvency courts, with respect to French and German members of the group, in defiance of the existing main proceedings in England.[55]

[*Add to footnote 56, after "IFSC Ltd,": page* 606]
[2004] B.C.C. 383 (Irish High Court)

[*Add to the end of footnote 56: page* 606]
See also para.14–15, above.

[*Add to the end of the final paragraph: page* 606]
The European Court delivered judgment on May 2, 2006, which has been reported;[56a] its ruling is printed at para.14–15B.

[56a] *Case No C 341/04* [2006] B.C.C. 297 ECtJ.

[*Read alongside paragraphs 28–26—28–27 for the position in Scotland: page* 607]
The insolvency rules applicable in Scotland are the Insolvency (Scotland) Rules 1986 (as amended) Rules 4.84 and 4.85.

Chapter 29

THE FUND FOR UNSECURED CREDITORS: THE "PRESCRIBED PART"

[*Read alongside Chapter 29 for the position in Scotland: page* 609]
The Insolvency Act 1986, Section 176A, applies in Scotland. The insolvency rules referred to in the text apply to England and Wales. An application to the court to dis-apply Section 176A in respect of a company incorporated in Scotland is governed by the Insolvency (Scotland) Rules 1986, Rule 7.13A and 7.13B (inserted by the Enterprise Act 2002 (Consequential Amendments) (Prescribed Part) (Scotland) Order 2003 (SI 2003/2108), effective September 15, 2003. There are provisions elsewhere in the Insolvency (Scotland) Rules 1986, equivalent to the insolvency rules discussed in this chapter, requiring the relevant office holder to give information about the Prescribed Part in his accounts and report to creditors.

The new provisions under the Insolvency Act 1986, s.176A. **29–2**
[*In the third line, delete "charge" and substitute: page* 609]
change

[*Add new paragraph 29–2A: page* 610]
Insolvent partnerships. When the enactment of the provisions for the "Prescribed Part" was undertaken, those provisions were erroneously applied to the liquidation and administration of insolvent partnerships.[10a] This error has now been corrected, by excluding those provisions from the distribution of the assets of insolvent partnerships.[10b] **29–2A**

[10a] Insolvent Partnerships Order 1994 (SI 1994/2421).
[10b] Insolvent Partnerships (Amendment) Order, 2006 (SI 2006/622), which came into force on April 6, 2006.

Part VII

Receivership in Scotland

[Add new Chapter 30]

CHAPTER 30

THE RECEIVER IN SCOTLAND*

A. BACKGROUND

30–1 **Statutory references and other abbreviations.** In this Chapter, unless otherwise stated, the statutory references are to the Insolvency Act 1986, references to the Rules are to the Insolvency (Scotland) Rules 1986 (SI 1986/1915), and references to the Regulations are to the Receivers (Scotland) Regulations 1986 (SI 1986/1947) (as amended, in each case). References to the 1961 Act are to the Companies (Floating Charges) (Scotland) Act 1961, and references to the 1972 Act are to the Companies (Floating Charges and Receivers) (Scotland) Act 1972. References to the Companies Act are to the Companies Act 1985.

References to the Cork Report are to the Report of the Insolvency Law Review Committee, "Insolvency Law and Practice" (June 1982; Cmnd. 8558).

References to the Scottish Law Commission Report are to the Scottish Law Commission Report on Bankruptcy and Related Aspects of Insolvency and Liquidation (February 25, 1982; Scots. Law Com. No. 68).

---

* This Chapter has been contributed by David A. Bennett, M.A., LL.B., W.S., Solicitor, Gillespie Macandrew, W.S., Edinburgh, Visiting Professor of Company Law, The University of Edinburgh.

Distinction from English law. In contrast to the position in English law, the office of receiver is a modern introduction to the law of Scotland. The main differences from receivership in England are: **30–2**

(i) only the holder of a floating charge granted by a company (itself a modern novelty in Scotland) can appoint or procure the appointment of a receiver;

(ii) express power to appoint a receiver need not be reserved in the instrument of charge;

(iii) while there is power for the court to appoint a receiver, in practice this is almost invariably effected by the charge-holder;

(iv) the office is a creature of statute;

(v) there is no "official receiver" in Scotland;

(vi) there is no distinction between a "receiver" and a "receiver and manager" (the office of receiver in Scotland approximating to the functions of the latter);

(vii) there is no significant difference between a receiver appointed by the court and one appointed by the charge-holder ("out of court", in the English sense).

Historical development: the floating charge in Scotland. Prior to 1961, the law of Scotland did not permit the granting of security by way of floating charge. All securities had to be constituted as fixed securities (although the amount secured could fluctuate), by one of the methods recognised by long established principles of Scots property law.[1] Scots law declined to give effect to any form of "floating charge", even where it was granted by a company incorporated in England and valid in English law. The commercial and banking community saw this as a severe limitation on the Scottish economy and, as a result of a recommendation by the then Law Reform Committee for Scotland,[2] by the Companies (Floating Charges) (Scotland) Act 1961 (effective October 27, 1961) the facility of granting a floating charge was made available to Scottish companies. At the same time, arrangements were made for the registration of all floating and most fixed charges by companies in Scotland, and the recognition by Scots law of floating charges created by English and overseas companies. **30–3**

Introduction of receivership to Scotland. The 1961 Act did not provide the holder of a floating charge with an effective remedy to realise his security. His only recourse was to petition for the winding up of the company, on grounds similar to those available to all creditors, but with the additional possibility of securing an order on the ground that his security was in **30–4**

---

[1] *Carse v Coppen* 1951 S.C. 233; 1951 S.L.T. 145; *Re Anchor Line (Henderson Bros.) Ltd.* [19371 Ch. 483.

[2] Eighth Report of the Law Reform Committee for Scotland: "The Constitution of Security over Moveable Property; and Floating Charges" (1960 Cmnd. 1017).

jeopardy. It was accepted in a Scottish Law Commission Report[3] that the charge-holder required a method of directly intervening in the affairs of the company to realise his security, which would not necessarily entail the full consequences of liquidation. The solution adopted, and enacted by the Companies (Floating Charges and Receivers) (Scotland) Act 1972 (effective November 17, 1972), was to allow the charge-holder to appoint a receiver, with power to displace the directors and realise the assets or manage the company for the purposes of satisfying its debt to the charge-holder.

The concepts of the floating charge and receivership in Scotland are inextricably linked. They are also inconsistent with the traditional approach of Scottish security law.[4] This has led to some difficulty in applying the legislation, and also to the suggestion that the basis on which the floating charge was introduced was misconceived, and that its objectives could have been achieved by traditional security law. It is clear, however, that the floating charge and the office of receiver are now an established part of Scots law. The Scottish Law Commission, in a Consultative Memorandum (No.72, October 1986) on Floating Charges and Receivers, discussing possible reform or clarification of that law, comments (para.1.3) that:

> "receivership has become the dominant procedure for the conduct of the affairs of insolvent companies".[5]

Nevertheless it is not, in principle, an insolvency process, but a procedure for the realisation of a security. Some of the difficulties which have arisen in practice, and the criticism of receivership in Scotland generally, undoubtedly derive from the tension between these concepts, compounded by the grafting of an English Equity Law procedure onto the uncongenial host of the Scots law of security rights.

30–5 **Statutory reforms 1985/1986.** Two important Reports were published in 1982, inter alia dealing with the working of the 1972 Act, the Report of the Cork Committee on Insolvency Law, and the Scottish Law Commission Report (No.68) on Bankruptcy Law, etc. (February 25, 1982). These led to wide-ranging reforms in insolvency law, which were enacted in the Insolvency Act 1985. In 1985, also, the existing Companies Acts 1948–1983 were consolidated, mainly into the Companies Act 1985. Although some of the provisions of the Insolvency Act 1985 were brought into force earlier in 1986, the effective date for most of the Act was delayed until December 29, 1986, when the consolidating Insolvency Act 1986 (and related legislation),

---

[3] "Report on the Companies (Floating Charges) (Scotland) Act 1961" (January 1970; Cmnd. 4336).

[4] See G. L. Gretton "What went wrong with Floating Charges," 1984 S.L.T. (News) 172, and "Should Floating Charges and Receivership be Abolished?" 1986 S.L.T. (News) 325. See also the comments of Lord President Hope in *Sharp v Thomson*, 1995 S.L.T. 837, 854 (reversed 1997 S.L.T. 636 (HL). This case is discussed in para.30–29, below).

[5] The restrictions on the appointment of an administrative receiver in force since September 15, 2003 (discussed in para.30–7, below) may have rendered this statement historical.

along with relative Rules and Regulations, came into effect. The 1986 Act superseded the relevant parts of the Companies Act 1985, as well as the Insolvency Act 1985. Accordingly the reforms of the Insolvency Act 1985 now appear in the Insolvency Act 1986 (effective December 29, 1986), which (unless otherwise stated) is the legislation discussed in this chapter. The 1986 Act has itself been substantially amended, notably by the Insolvency Act 1994, the Scotland Act 1998, the Insolvency Act 2000 and the Enterprise Act 2002.

Transitional arrangements. Schedule 11, para.3, to the Insolvency Act 1986 provides that "the new law" does not apply to any receiver appointed under s.467 of the Companies Act (or its predecessor, s.11 of the 1972 Act) before "the appointed day", which was December 29, 1986. "The new law" is defined as, in effect, those changes which are embodied in the Insolvency Act 1986, together with the Receivers (Scotland) Regulations 1986 and the Insolvency (Scotland) Rules 1986 (as amended). Schedule 11, para.3(3), envisages the making of rules to apply the 1986 Rules to receivers appointed before December 29, 1986, but this has not been done (see r.0.3). **30–6**

Under "the former law" (i.e. ss.467–485 of the Companies Act 1985, without amendment) on the death, resignation or removal of a receiver, the holder of the charge (or the court) had to make a new appointment (s.478(6)). If, therefore, a receiver appointed under the former law ceases to hold office after December 29, 1986, any receiver appointed to succeed him (and those dealing with him) will be governed by "the new law".

The former law was unclear on the position where joint receivers were appointed, and one of them ceased to act. Section 467(6) merely provided that a joint appointment was competent, and s.472(3) provided that joint receivers must act jointly, unless the instrument of appointment provides otherwise. Presumably, if one of the joint receivers who must act jointly ceased to hold office, the appointment as a whole would fall, but if they could act separately, it would not do so. It is suggested that, in the latter case, if a successor to one of several joint receivers is appointed (and nothing in "the former law" indicates that this would be incompetent), he and his colleagues will continue to be governed by the pre-1986 provisions, and this will remain the position, even if as a result of successive retirals, etc. all the joint receivers in office were appointed after December 29, 1986.

The Enterprise Act 2002 and Restrictions on the appointment of an Administrative Receiver. The Enterprise Act 2002, s.250, which became effective September 15, 2003,[6] inserted ss.72A–72GA and Sch.2A into the Insolvency Act 1986. Section 72A(2) provides that, "In Scotland, the holder of a qualifying floating charge in respect of a company's property may not appoint or apply to the court for the appointment of a receiver who, on **30–7**

[6] The Enterprise Act 2002 (Commencement No.4 and Transitional Provisions and Savings) Order 2003 (SI 2003/2093), together with the Insolvency Act 1986 (Amendment) (Administrative Receivership and Urban Regeneration, etc.) Order 2003 (SI 2003/1832).

appointment, would be an administrative receiver of property of the company". Exceptions from this general prohibition are set out in ss.72B–72GA together with Sch.2A.[7]

The prohibition on the appointment of an administrative receiver applies only in respect of a floating charge created on or after September 15, 2003.[8] "Qualifying Floating Charge" is defined[9] as a floating charge "created by an instrument which:

(a) states that (para.14) applies to the floating charge,

(b) purports to empower the holder of a floating charge to appoint an administrator of the company,

(c) . . .[10] or

(d) purports to empower the holder of a floating charge in Scotland to appoint a receiver who, on appointment, would be an administrative receiver".

With respect to this definition it should be noted that the holder of a floating charge in Scotland may still appoint a receiver, notwithstanding s.72A, in certain circumstances:

1. If the receiver so appointed would not be "an administrative receiver", which is defined for Scotland by s.251(b) of the Insolvency Act 1986 as "a receiver appointed under [Insolvency Act 1986 s.51] in a case where the whole (or substantially the whole) of the company's property is attached by the floating charge",[11] it follows that if the floating charge as created did not extend to "the whole or substantially the whole" of the property of the company or, if, after creation, the holder had released a significant part of that property, a receiver may still be appointed.[12] In practice, where a bank takes a floating charge, it often takes a standard security (i.e. a fixed charge) over the heritable property of the company and, in theory, the holder might release the heritable property leaving him with power to appoint a receiver over the residue who might not be considered to be "an administrative receiver". This however is subject to the terms of para.14(3) of Sch.B1, which states that a person is a holder of a qualifying floating charge "if he holds one or more debentures of the company", secured inter alia by "charges and other forms of security" which together relate to the whole or substantially the whole of the company's property, and at least one of which is a

---

[7] See para.21–2 above.

[8] Section 72A(4)(a) and the Insolvency Act, s.72A (Appointed Date) Order 2003 (SI 2003/2095).

[9] Sch.B1 to the Insolvency Act 1986 (inserted by the Enterprise Act 2002, s.248), para.14(2).

[10] Omitted as not being applicable in Scotland.

[11] Section 51 refers to the general power of the holder of a floating charge in Scotland to appoint or to apply to the court for the appointment of a receiver.

[12] *Scottish & Newcastle Breweries plc v Ascot Inns Ltd (In Receivership)*, 1994 S.L.T. 140; [1993] B.C.C. 634.

qualifying floating charge. Under para.112 of Sch.B1, reference to a charge is reference to a right in security in Scots law, and under the Companies Act 1985, s.744 "debenture" is defined as including any form of security constituting a charge on the assets of the company. It follows that the holder of a floating charge in such a situation could only effect the appointment of a receiver who would not be an administrative receiver by releasing sufficient property from all forms of security held by him. This does not, however, eliminate the possibility of avoiding the prohibition contained in s.72A, by the device of having two wholly-owned subsidiaries of the lender, one of whom holds a standard security over the heritable property of the company and the other holds a floating charge over the remainder of the company's property. In those circumstances, it is considered that the holder of the floating charge could appoint a receiver who would not be an administrative receiver, and the parent company could realise the security held by each of its subsidiaries under the rules applicable in each case and without reference to the reforms introduced by the Enterprise Act 2002.

2. It should also be noted that the definition in Sch.B1, para.14(2)(d), only applies where the floating charge instrument "purports" to empower the holder of a floating charge in Scotland to appoint a receiver; the draftsman of this provision has overlooked the fact that under the Insolvency Act 1986, s.52 there is a statutory right to appoint a receiver or to apply to the court for such an appointment, which does not require to be referred to in the instrument creating the floating charge. Therefore, if that instrument avoids any reference to the power of the holder to appoint a receiver, it would appear to fall outwith the definition of a "qualifying floating charge" provided, of course, it also avoids provisions referred to in para.14(2)(a) or (b).

As noted elsewhere[13] the holder of a "qualifying floating charge" is entitled under the Insolvency Act 1986, Sch.B1, para.15, himself to appoint an administrator. In due course, when the number of floating charges created on or after September 15, 2003, increases, administration will inevitably become the dominant process through which the holder of a floating charge will realise his security.

Other Restrictions on the Appointment of a Receiver. In addition to the restrictions on the appointment of an administrative receiver introduced by the Enterprise Act 2002, a receiver may not be appointed while a moratorium is in force pursuant to Pt I, Sch.A1 of the Insolvency Act 1986.[14] Schedule A1 applies only to a "small company" as defined in the **30–7A**

[13] paras 14–44 *et seq.*

[14] Sch.A1, para.12(1). This refers in terms to an "administrative receiver" but because it also prohibits any steps to enforce a security, this necessarily includes the appointment of a receiver in respect of a part only of the company's property.

Companies Act 1985, s.247(3).[15] The moratorium is effective from the time the directors apply to the court seeking approval of a voluntary arrangement with the company's creditors, until the requisite meetings of the members and creditors to consider the proposed arrangement have been held, subject to a maximum period of 28 days, unless that period is extended for a further period of up to two months.[16]

An interim moratorium preventing steps being taken to enforce any security against the company's property without the consent of the court applies while an application to the court for the appointment of an administrator is pending, or once notice of intention to make such an appointment has been lodged in court by the holder of a qualifying floating charge, or by the company or by its directors.[17] Although this would prevent the appointment of a receiver in respect of part only of the company's property, it remains possible to appoint an administrative receiver.[18] Once a company is in administration, no administrative receiver may be appointed, and no receiver may be appointed over part only of the company's property without the permission of the court.[19]

B. The Floating Charge

30–8 **Creation.**[20] Since only the holder of a floating charge can appoint a receiver, the validity of any such appointment necessarily depends on the existence of a valid floating charge. The 1961 Act prescribed a form of charge, but since 1972 no particular formula has been necessary to create a floating charge in Scots law. It is not necessary (though usual) to include the terms "floating charge" in the deed, so long as it is in effect a charge "over all or any part of the property (including uncalled capital) which may from time to time be comprised in its property and undertaking" (Companies Act 1985, s.462(i)). The term "charge" is not defined, except by necessary inference from the wording of s.462(1), which refers to a charge as being created "for the purpose of securing any debt or other obligation (including a cautionary obligation)[21] incurred or to be incurred by, or binding upon, the company or any other person". The term is, therefore, synonymous with "security", and is employed in Scots law only because of its historical significance in English practice. The essential "floating" character of the security is that the subjects over which it subsists are not, in principle, fixed and identified, but are such assets of the company to which it is in right from time to time (or such of them as are within the scope of

---

[15] *ibid.*, para.3 (which imposes further conditions).
[16] *ibid.*, paras 8 and 32.
[17] Insolvency Act 1986, Sch.B1, para.44.
[18] *ibid.*, para.44(7).
[19] *ibid.*, para.43.
[20] The Bankruptcy and Diligence, etc. (Scotland) Bill currently (March 2006) before the Scottish Parliament proposes to amend Scots law on floating charges, inter alia by providing that a floating charge may be created only by its registration in the Register of Floating Charges (to be established pursuant to the Bill).
[21] The Scots Law term for "guarantee".

the charge, if it is limited to part of the company's property), and the company is free to dispose of and acquire such assets until the charge "crystallises". There is no limit on the property which may competently be charged, and no implied restriction on the company's power to deal with it prior to crystallisation (although the holder may impose such a restriction contractually). Because of the requirements to constitute a fixed charge under Scots law, the question in English law[22] of whether such restrictions so derogate from the "floating" character as to convert the security into a "fixed" charge, do not arise.

A floating charge may be created under the law of Scotland by "any incorporated company, whether a company within the meaning of (the Companies Act 1985) or not" (Companies Act, s.462(1)). Therefore, in addition to companies registered under the 1985 Act and its predecessors, a company incorporated in Great Britain by Royal Charter or by Act of Parliament, or an oversea company having corporate status (whether registered under Pt XXIII of the 1985 Act or not), may grant a floating charge and may be subject to the appointment of a receiver. **30–9**

Other entities which may grant a floating charge recognised by Scots law are:

(1) A European Interest Grouping whose "official address" is in Scotland.[23]

(2) An Open-Ended Investment Company incorporated under the relevant regulations.[24]

(3) A Limited Liability Partnership.[25]

(4) A society registered in Scotland under the Industrial & Provident Societies Act 1987.[26]

For the position of foreign companies, see paras 30–11, 30–13, below.

Until July 31, 1990, a floating charge had to be a document executed under the seal of the company containing an acknowledgement of debt or other obligation and purporting to create a dloating charge (Companies Act 1985, s.462(2)). Alternatively, it could be such a document executed on its behalf by an attorney duly authorised in writing under the company's seal (s.462(3)). Although it was not clear precisely what, in Scots law, was **30–10**

---

[22] See *Re Brightlife Ltd* [1987] Ch. 200; *National Westminster Bank Plc v Spectrum Plus* [2005] B.C.C. 694; [2005] 2 B.C.L.C. 26 (HL).

[23] European Economic Interest Grouping Regulations 1989 (SI 1989/638) paras 18, 19 and Sch.4.

[24] The Open-Ended Investment Companies (Investment Companies with Variable Capital) Regulations 1996 (SI 1996/2827, reg.3(1)).

[25] Companies Act 1985, s.462 as applied to limited liability partnerships by the Limited Liability Partnerships (Scotland) Regulations 2001 (SI 2001/128), reg.3 and Sch.1.

[26] Industrial & Provident Societies Act 1967, s.3 (as substituted by the Companies Consolidation (Consequential Provisions) Act 1985, s.26). It is thought that such a society registered in England and Wales cannot grant a floating charge; see para.20–24, above.

meant by "execution under seal", this was generally understood to mean execution as a probative deed under s.36(3) of the 1985 Act (as it then stood), i.e. sealed and signed by two directors, or by one director and the secretary of the company. Scots law would also regard as "probative" a deed which was sealed and signed by one person duly authorised by the company in the presence of two witnesses, such authority not necessarily having to comply with s.462(3), and this method was not excluded by s.462.

The Companies Act 1989, s.130(3) and Sch.17, para.8, repealed ss.36(3), 462(2) and (3) and substituted a requirement that a floating charge had to be in a written instrument "which is presumed under section 36B to be subscribed by the company". This referred to the new s.36B(3), under which a document was "presumed to have been subscribed by a company", if it bore to have been subscribed on its behalf by a director or by its secretary or by a duly authorised person, together with either a single witness or its common seal.

Section 130(3) of the 1989 Act, and the consequential amendments in Sch.17, were brought into force on July 31, 1990. They were severely criticised and, in the event, substantially amended by s.72 of the Law Reform (Miscellandous Provisions) (Scotland) Act 1990, which came into force on December 1, 1990. Section 72(1) of the 1990 Act replaced the version of s.36B in the 1989 Act with a new s.36B and Sch.8, para.33(6) repealed s.462(2) (as amended by the 1989 Act). The replacement for s.36B was (by s.36B(1)) deemed to have effective as from July 31, 1990, but the repeal of s.462(2) was effective only from December 1, 1990. Section 462(3) was not reinstated.

The effect of these changes was that a floating charge executed in the manner prescribed by the 1990 Act on or after July 31, 1990 was to be regarded as validly executed, whether or not it complied with the provisions of the 1989 Act which became effective on that date. The formalities of execution enacted by the 1989 Act, however, were only available in the period July 31, 1990, to November 30, 1990 (inclusive).

30–11 Section 72 of the 1990 Act was, in its turn, repealed by the Requirements of Writing (Scotland) Act 1995, effective August 1, 1995, which also enacted a further version of the Companies Act 1985, s.36B (Sch.4, para.51). Under the 1995 Act a floating charge is validly executed by a Company incorporated under the Companies Acts, if it is signed on its behalf by a director, the Secretary or a person duly authorised to sign on its behalf (Sch.2, para.3(1)). If it also bears to have been signed by a single witness to that signature it is presumed to have been subscribed by the Company, and that presumption also arises if it bears to have been signed by two directors, one director and the secretary, or two duly authorised persons, without witnesses (Sch.2, para.3(1)). Sealing is not required.

In the case of Companies incorporated outwith Great Britain, the Foreign Companies (Execution of Documents) Regulations 1994 (SI 1994/950, effective May 16, 1994), para.6, provided that a floating charge by a foreign company was to be subscribed by a single person duly authorised under the law of its country of incorporation. Since that is the effect of the

1995 Act in relation to British Companies, reg.6 of the 1994 Regulations was repealed by the Foreign Companies (Execution of Documents) (Amendment) Regulations 1995, (SI 1995/1729), effective August 1, 1995.

Under the 1995 Act, ss.7 and 8, documents are to be signed on the last page of the substantive text. Schedules, plans and other annexations do not have to be executed, provided they are referred to in this text and bear appropriate identification, except that a plan or other annexation describing land must be signed on each page.

With the repeal (by the 1990 Act) of s.462(2) there ceased to be any specific requirement that a floating charge had to be in writing. It is, however, a necessary inference from s.410(5) of the 1985 Act (which defines the date of creation of a floating charge as the date of its execution by the company) that there must be a written instrument creating a floating charge.

A floating charge under the 1961 Act could not, it was believed, be **30–12** amended. Under s.7 of the 1972 Act (now s.466 of the Companies Act 1985), an "Instrument of Alteration" is competent, without restriction. In the Companies Act and the Insolvency Act, and in this Chapter, all references to an instrument of charge include a charge as altered.

An instrument of alteration rquires to be registered if it restricts the creation of any prior or *pari passu* charge, varies the order of ranking of charges, releases property from a floating charge or increases the amount secured by a floating charge. Failure to register an instrument increasing the amount secured by a floating charge potentially invalid to that extent, as with an unregistered charge (s.466(4) and (5)). The Companies Act 1989, s.140(8) provides for the repeal of s.466(4) and (5)), but this has never been brought into effect, it is understood that a decision has been taken not to bring into force Pt IV of the 1989 Act, to which s.140(8) relates, at least in its present form. An instrument of alteration should be executed by or on behalf of the parties to the floating charge or their successors in title, or in accordance with any specific provisions in the charge or any ancillary document. Section 466(2) also provides for its execution by or on behalf of debenture-holders. In the case of a company (not only the granter of the charge), s.466(2)(a) originally required execution "in writing under its common seal", but this was repealed by the Companies Act 1989, Sch.17, para.9, which substituted a reference to the general rules regarding the execution of documents and made no specific provision for a company. This change was not affected by the Law Reform (Miscellaneous Provisions) (Scotland) Act 1990, s.70 or the Requirements of Writing (Scotland) Act 1995 (discussed above).

The date of creation of the charge by a company registered in Scotland is **30–13** the date it is executed by the company (Companies Act 1985, s.410(5)(a)). This appears to apply, even if the instrument has to be executed by other parties to become effective. There is no statutory definition of the time of creation which applies to floating charges created by any other company (e.g. an unregistered, English or foreign company), and this must therefore be a question of fact in each case. In the context of receivership, the date of creation (before or after December 29, 1986), may affect a charge's validity on general grounds (see para.30–50).

30–14 A floating charge may be assigned by the original holder, which preserves the ranking of the charge if, for example, there is a change of banker or other lender. Although the assignation must be intimated to the company (if it is not a party), and entered in its register of charges, there is no requirement to register it with the Registrar of Companies.[27]

30–15 **The floating charge: registration.** The Companies Act 1985, s.410(2) (as amended by the Insolvency Act 1985) provides that "Every charge created by a company, being a charge to which this section applies, is, so far as any security on the company's property or any part of it is conferred by the charge, void against the liquidator or administrator and any creditor of the company", unless the prescribed form and certified copy charge are delivered to the Registrar of Companies within 21 days of the date of creation of the charge. Charges registrable under this section include any floating charge. Floating charges are deemed to have been created on the date of execution by the company (s.410(5)(a)).[28] Section 410 applies to a company incorporated and registered in Scotland (s.410(5)), or to a foreign company charging property in Scotland which has "a place of business" (not necessarily a "principal place of business") in Scotland (s.424(1)). Presentation of the documents for registration of a floating charge under s.410 is a pre-requisite of its validity, and therefore of the appointment of a receiver by its holder. The court may extend the time for registration (s.420) (see further para.30–62). If, however, the particulars are duly presented but the registrar (wrongly) refuses to register them, the section is satisfied.[29] The registrar's certificate of registration is conclusive evidence that the charge has been duly registered.[30] The registrar's certificate is conclusive evidence that the charge has been duly registered, even if it was issued in error.[30a]

30–15A **Ranking of Floating and Other Charges.** It is always open to creditors to agree among themselves how their respective securities shall rank, irrespective of the statutory provisions considered below. The company is normally a party to any such ranking agreement, although that is not essential to make it legally effective. So far as floating charges are concerned, such a ranking agreement may be contained in the charging instrument itself or in a separate document (Companies Act 1985, s.464(1)(b)), or it may be contained in an instrument of alteration under s.466 of the same Act. The holders of any charge adversely affected must consent. A ranking agreement involving a floating charge is, in principle, registerable at Companies

---

[27] *Libertas-Kommerz GmbH v Johnson*, 1978 S.L.T. 222.
[28] *A.I.B. Finance Ltd v Bank of Scotland*, 1995 S.L.T. 2.
[29] *Nv Slavenburgh's v Intercontinental Natural Resources Ltd* etc. [1980] 1 All E.R. 955.
[30] *R. v Registrar of Companies, Ex p. Central Bank of India* [1986] 1 All E.R. 105 (C.A.).
[30a] Section 418(2)(c); *Ali v Top Marques Car Rental Ltd, The Times*, February 10, 2006.

House under s.466(4), but failure to register does not affect the validity of the document, unless there is an increase in the sum or other obligation secured, or additional properties are brought within the scope of the floating charge. Where relevant, application may be made to the court to extend the time for registration (Companies Act 1985, s.466(4) and (5) applying ss.410(2), (3) and 420). A ranking provision cannot, however, confer priority on a charge which is itself void for want of registration or on other grounds.[31]

Whether or not there is a ranking agreement, a fixed security arising by operation of law has priority over a floating charge (Companies Act 1985, s.464(2)).

If there is no ranking agreement (or to the extent that such an agreement does not apply) and if there is no "negative pledge" clause (discussed below) the statutory ranking provisions of s.464[32] will apply, namely:

1. a fixed security constituted as a real right before a floating charge has crystallised has priority over the floating charge;
2. floating charges rank with one another according to the time of registration under ss.410–424 of the Act;
3. floating charges which have been received by the Registrar of Companies by the same postal delivery rank equally.

"Negative Pledge" Clauses. Section 464(1)(a) permits a floating charge (and by extension any instrument of alteration; s.466(6)) to include a provision prohibiting or restricting the creation of any fixed security or any other floating charge having priority over or ranking *pari passu* with the floating charge. Such "negative pledges" are common practice. For this purpose the statutory rules for determining when a charge is "created", contained in s.410(5), apply. A floating charge is created when it is executed by the company granting the charge; a fixed security is created when the creditor's right has been constituted a real right. Thus, if a company grants a standard security and before that security has been recorded in the property register, the company executes a floating charge containing a "negative pledge", the floating charge has priority s.464(1A)), (confirming the decision in *A.I.B. Finance Ltd v Bank of Scotland,* 1995 S.L.T. 2; 1993 S.C. 588). **30–15B**

Restriction of Security. If the holder of a registered floating charge receives intimation in writing of the subsequent registration of another floating charge over the same property or any part thereof, the preference in ranking of the first floating charge is restricted to security for the holder's present advances, any future advances which he may be required to make in **30–15C**

---

[31] *Bank of Scotland v T A Neilson & Co,* 1991 S.L.T. 8.

[32] Section 464 was amended by the Companies Act 1989, s.140(2)–(6) effective July 3, 1995; SI 1995/1352. The amendments have the effect of clarifying the provisions of the Act in accordance with the decisions of the court referred to in this paragraph.

terms of the charge or any ancillary document, interest due or to become due on all such advances, and any expenses or outlays which may reasonably be incurred by him (s.464(5)). Where the charge secures a contingent liability (other than a liability for further advances), such intimation restricts the sum secured to the maximum sum to which that liability may amount (s.464(5)(e), added by the Companies Act 1989, s.140(6), effective July 3, 1995 (SI 1995/1352)).

C. Appointment of Receiver

30–16 **Competence of appointment.** Section 51(1) of the Insolvency Act 1986 (originally s.11(1) of the 1972 Act) states that "it is competent under the law of Scotland for the holder of a floating charge over all or any part of the property (including uncalled capital), which may from time to time be comprised in the property and undertaking of an incorporated company (whether a company within the meaning of the Companies Act or not) which the Court of Session has jurisdiction to wind up, to appoint a receiver of such part of the property as is subject to the charge". This corresponds to the definition of a floating charge in the Companies Act 1985, s.462(1). Section 51(2) provides that such a holder may apply to the court for an appointment.

30–17 Subject to the EC Regulation on Insolvency Proceedings, which may deprive the Scottish courts of jurisdiction[32a] the Court of Session has jurisdiction to wind up any company registered in Scotland,[33] and any unregistered company where Pt V of the Insolvency Act 1986 confers jurisdiction.[34] In addition, the relevant regulations allow a limited liability partnership registered in Scotland, and a European Economic Interest Grouping whose "office address" is in Scotland, to grant a floating charge, under which the holder may appoint (or may apply to the court for the appointment) of a receiver on the same basis as in the case of a Scottish company.[35] Although (as noted above at para.30–9) a society registered in Scotland under the Industrial and Provident Societies Act (1967) may grant a floating charge, there is no provision in that Act for the holder to appoint a receiver, and to enforce his security he would be required to petition for the winding up of the company.[36]

The recognition in Scots law of a receiver appointed elsewhere in Great Britain is dealt with in s.72 (discussed below in para.30–101). For unregistered and foreign companies, see para.30–132.

[32a] See Ch.28.

[33] Insolvency Act 1986, s.120(1); see also Companies Act 1985, s.735, applied by the Insolvency Act 1986, s.251.

[34] *Re International Bulk Commodities Ltd* [1992] B.C.C. 463; [1993] Ch. 77. The charge and the appointment would have to comply with Scots law.

[35] The Limited Liability Partnerships (Scotland) Regulations 2001 (SI 2001/128) and the European Economic Interest Grouping Regulations 1989 (SI 1989/638).

[36] *Re Devon & Somerset Farmers Ltd* [1993] B.C.C. 410; [1994] Ch. 57.

Circumstances justifying appointment. The statutory grounds for appointing a receiver by the holder of the charge (s.52(1) of the Insolvency Act 1986) are: 30–18

(i) the expiry of 21 days after a demand for payment of all or part of the sum secured, without such payment;

(ii) the expiry of a period of two months during the whole of which interest due and payable has been in arrears;

(iii) the making of an order or the passing of a resolution for winding up; or

(iv) the appointment of a receiver by virtue of any other floating charge created by the company.

These grounds apply "in so far as not otherwise provided for by the instrument", so that it is open to the company and the charge-holder to restrict the operation of s.52, and exclude or qualify one or more of the statutory grounds of appointment. The instrument may also (and commonly does) specify additional grounds. If the instrument specifies a particular procedure, e.g. for "calling up" the sum secured, as a preliminary to appointment, that must be strictly adhered to.[37]

The company can seek an order suspending the appointment, if there are grounds for holding that it was unjustified, but it will be difficult for the company to obtain an interim suspension and interdict, the balance of convenience normally favouring the charge-holder.[38]

Section 52(2) allows the court to appoint a receiver on the application of the holder of a floating charge on any of the grounds specified in the instrument of charge, or on those specified in s.52(1), or where the court is satisfied that the position of the holder is likely to be prejudiced if no such appointment is made. Appointment by the court is unlikely in practice, but might be required if the holder's power to appoint has been restricted in the charge, or if some doubt exists about the validity of an appointment by the holder in the particular circumstances. The right to apply to the court may itself be restricted by the instrument of charge. In theory, therefore, a floating charge might effectively exclude the right to appoint a receiver by limiting the holder's powers under both s.52(1) and (2).

Receivers and administrative receivers. Before 1986, there was no distinction in Scots Law between a receiver of part only of the property of the company and one who would, in England, be termed a "receiver and manager", because he controlled all (or substantially all) its property. The Insolvency Act 1986, s.251 introduced this distinction (as between a receiver and an "administrative receiver") to Scotland. Although the same term is used in both jurisdictions, to similar purpose, the Scottish definition 30–19

---

[37] *Elwick Bay Shipping Co Ltd v Royal Bank of Scotland,* 1982 S.L.T. 62.
[38] *Toynar Ltd v Whitbread & Co Ltd,* 1988 S.C.L.R. 35.

differs in detail from that which applies in England. In Scotland an "administrative receiver" is one appointed by (or on behalf of) the holder of a floating charge "where the whole (or substantially the whole) of the company's property is attached by the floating charge". It is therefore necessary to establish whether the charge has attached, or would attach, (on the appointment, or on liquidation) to the whole or substantially the whole of the company's property, which is clearly a question of fact.[39] It must attach by virtue of one charge only; a receiver appointed by a holder of several charges, separately charging parts of the property, will not be an "administrative receiver", even though the effect is to give the receiver control of the entire undertaking.

The importance of this distinction lies in the special provisions of the Insolvency Act 1986, which apply only to an "administrative receiver", of which the most significant are:

(i) an administrative receiver must be an "insolvency practitioner", but this does not apply to a non-administrative receiver (s.388);

(ii) the restrictions on the appointment of a receiver introduced by the Enterprise Act 2002 (discussed in para.30–7) only apply to an administrative receiver;

(iii) only an administrative receiver or the holder of a charge conferring the right to appoint an administrative receiver has to be notified that an application has been made for an administration order (Sch.B1, para.12(2)), or that the holder of a floating charge, the company or its directors intend to appoint an administrator (Sch.B1, paras 15 and 26);

(iv) only an administrative receiver requires to vacate office if the court makes an administration order, or may be required to do so if an administrator is appointed otherwise (Sch.B1, para.41);

(v) only an administrative receiver can safeguard the supply of public utilities, etc. under s.233;

(vi) only an administrative receiver is required to submit a report under the Company Directors Disqualification Act 1986;

(vii) only an administrative receiver has power to seek an order for delivery of property, to examine directors and others and to enforce their duty to co-operate under ss.234–236.

In general, however, the Insolvency Act applies equally to receivers of all or part of the undertaking.

30–20 **Appointment by charge-holder.** The holder of the floating charge may (subject to the restrictions noted above) appoint a receiver by instrument of appointment, whether or not power to appoint is expressly reserved in the

---

[39] *Scottish & Newcastle Breweries Plc v Ascot Inns Ltd,* 1994 S.L.T. 1140; [1993] B.C.C. 634 (where assets had been released from an "all assets" charge).

instrument of charge. The holder of a charge created under the 1961 Act was explicitly granted such a power by the 1972 Act (s.11(1)). There is no prescribed style. The right to appoint is, if the grounds for doing so exist and the statutory restrictions do not apply, absolute, and cannot be opposed by the company, its liquidators or other creditors.[40]

Under the provisions in force from August 1, 1995 (the Requirements of Writing (Scotland) Act 1995), an instrument of appointment by an individual is to be subscribed by him or on his behalf, and in the case of a company it is to be subscribed by a director, the company secretary or a duly authorised person. No witness is required.

The holders of a charge securing a series of debentures may resolve in general meeting to authorise the execution of an instrument of appointment (s.53(4)), unless the charge or debentures make provision for the appointment by any person or body (see s.70(2) of the Insolvency Act 1986).

An instrument of appointment does not attract stamp duty.[41]

Acceptance of charge-holder's appointment. The Insolvency Act 1986 (s.53(6)) introduced the requirement that a receiver appointed by instrument of appointment by the holder of the charge must formally accept office. He must do so "before the end of the business day next following that on which the instrument of appointment is received by him or on his behalf" (s.53(6)(a)). "Business Day" is defined as any day, other than a Saturday, a Sunday, Christmas Day, Good Friday or a day which is a bank holiday in any part of Great Britain (s.251; r.0.2(1)). He must intimate his acceptance to the holder of the charge or his agent within the same period (r.3.1(1)). Rule 3.1(1) makes it clear that the acceptance and intimation thereof to the holder must be by the receiver personally, but need not be in writing. **30–21**

A docquet must be endorsed on the instrument of appointment, stating the day and time it was received by or on behalf of the receiver, as soon as possible after its receipt, and signed by him or on his behalf. This determines the effective date and time of the appointment (s.53(6)(b); r.3.1(2)).[42]

The receiver in person must also endorse a written docquet of acceptance on the instrument of appointment, and send a copy of the endorsed instrument to the charge-holder or his agent as soon as possible (r.3.1(1) and (3)). Where joint receivers are appointed, separate docquets of receipt and acceptance are required, but their appointment takes effect on the day and time the instrument of appointment is received by the last of them (reg.5(b)). If two or more joint receivers endorse one copy of the instrument, the duty of sending it to the holder falls on whoever last endorses his acceptance (r.3.1(4)). (For registration and other publication requirements, see para.30–23.)

---

[40] *Re Potters Oil Ltd (No.2)* [1986] 1 All E.R. 890.

[41] Finance Act 1985, s.85(1) and Sch.24, exempting such instruments from 50p, deed duty as from March 19, 1985.

[42] *Secretary of State for Trade and Industry v Houston,* 1994 S.L.T. 775; 1994 S.C.L.R. 209.

Section 53(6)(a) states that the appointment (and consequential crystallisation of the charge) is of no effect, unless it is accepted within the time limit specified. In the case of joint receivers, all must accept within the business day time limit, calculated according to when the instrument of appointment was received by or on behalf of each of them separately (see reg.5(a)). The docquet of receipt is conclusive evidence of that day and time (s.53(6)(b))[43]

30–22 **Appointment by the court.** Although s.14 of the 1972 Act permitted the holder of a floating charge to petition the court for the appointment of a receiver (see now Insolvency Act 1986, s.54), this procedure is rare in practice. "The court" has the normal meaning of the court having jurisdiction to wind up the company (Insolvency Act 1986, s.251, applying Companies Act 1985, s.744). Application for an appointment (and in relation to receivers generally) can therefore be made in all cases to the Court of Session or, if the issued capital does not exceed £120,000, to the Sheriff Court where the registered office is situated (Insolvency Act 1986, s.120). The Sheriff Court does not have jurisdiction if the company does not have a share capital.[44] The Rules of the Court of Session relating to receivers are contained in Pt IV of the Act of Sederunt (Rules of the Court of Session 1994) (SI 1994/1443) as amended by the Act of Sederunt (Rules of the Court of Session Amendment No.5) (Insolvency Proceedings) 2003 (SSI 2003/385). The Rules for the Sheriff Court are contained in the Act of Sederunt (Sheriff Court Company Insolvency Rules) 1986 (SI 1986/2297) as amended by the Act of Sederunt (Sheriff Court Company Insolvency Rules 1986) Amendment 2003 (SSI 2003/388).

30–23 **Registration and publication of appointment.** A copy of the instrument appointing a receiver, certified by or on behalf of the appointor (reg.4) must be filed by the appointer with the Registrar of Companies and the Accountant in Bankruptcy within seven days (Insolvency Act, s.53(1)).[45] If the appointment is by the court, a certified copy of the interlocutor must be filed by the petitioner within seven days or such longer period as the court allows (s.54(3)). The circumstances leading to the appointment are to be specified on the accompanying form as prescribed by the Regulations.[46] The Registrar enters the particulars in the company's register of charges (Insolvency Act, ss.53(5) and 54(4)). There is as yet no fee; the Act provides for a fee to be prescribed for registration, but no regulations to this effect have been made. No sanction (other than a default fine) attaches to failure to register. On appointment, the receiver must notify the company, and he must (unless excused by the court) notify creditors within 28 days (s.65(1)). These requirements apply only on the first appointment

---

[43] *Secretary of State for Trade and Industry v Houston,* above.

[44] *Pearce v Cannon, Petitioners,* 1991 S.C.L.R. 861 (Sh. Ct.).

[45] The reference to the Accountant in Bankruptcy was inserted by virtue of the Scotland Act 1998, Sch.8, para.23.

[46] Form I (Scot) where the appointment is by the holder; Form 2 (Scot) where the appointment is by the court. These forms were amended by SI 1999/1820.

of a receiver under the charge, unless the first receiver has not completed them (s.65(2)), and they apply even if the receiver has previously been appointed liquidator (s.65(3)). All invoices, orders and letters on behalf of the company must state that it is in receivership (s.64). There is no requirement to advertise in the Gazette or newspapers, and the appointment of a receiver does not require to be "officially notified" under ss.42 and 711 of the Companies Act 1985.

Appointment of receiver on behalf of debenture holders. The definition of the "holder" of a floating charge entitled to appoint a receiver is extended (Insolvency Act 1986, s.70(2)) to cater for the situation where a floating charge secures a debenture or series of debentures, without specifying trustees or other persons as "the holder" for the purposes of the Act. If the instrument contains specific provisions for a receiver to be appointed by a specified person or body, that person or body is to be regarded as "the holder of the charge" for all purposes connected with the Insolvency Act, Rules and Regulations. If there is no such nomination, the trustees for debenture holders (if any) are to be regarded as "the holder". If there are no trustees or a defined "holder", a majority of debenture holders is to be regarded as "the holder". That majority is defined as either a majority in nominal value of those present or represented and voting at a meeting of debenture holders (provided that at least one third in nominal value of the outstanding debentures or series is present), or alternatively, if there is no such meeting, the holders of at least one-half in nominal value of the outstanding debentures. **30–24**

Notwithstanding the definition, which clarifies the position for the purposes of appointing a receiver, the application of other references in the Act, Rules and Regulations to "the holder of the charge" would give rise to a number of practical difficulties, if the instrument of charge does not define who this is to be. It would be preferable if, for example, the Act or Rules were amended so that the holders of a series of debentures to whom this situation applied were required, when resolving to appoint a receiver, at the same time to nominate a person or body who is to be regarded as "the holder of the charge" for all necessary purposes thereafter.

Joint receivers, etc. It is competent to appoint joint receivers, who must act jointly, unless the instrument of appointment provides otherwise (Insolvency Act 1986, s.51(6)).[47] Their appointment takes effect from the time the last joint receiver to accept office receives the instrument (or his copy) (reg.5(a)). It is also possible for a single person to be appointed receiver by virtue of several charges (s.56(7)). In such circumstances, he is not necessarily an "administrative receiver". (See para.30–19, above.) By use of this device, it would be possible to create two or more charges over part of the undertaking (but effectively comprising the whole), and then appoint as receiver under each charge someone who was not an "insolvency practitioner". However, under the Insolvency Act 1986, Sch.B1, para.14 (inserted **30–25**

[47] The normal practice is to appoint joint receivers with power to act separately.

by the Enterprise Act 2002), the holder of such charges is prevented from appointing a receiver if the charges extend to the whole property of the company, and if at least one is a floating charge.

30–26 **Appointment of receivers by several charge-holders.** If there are several floating charges created by one company, several receivers may be appointed with claims on its assets. The appointment of a receiver by one holder does not have the effect of "crystallising" any other charge, so "multiple" appointments are necessary (unless the company is wound up). A single insolvency practitioner may, of course, be appointed receiver on behalf of the holders of several charges, which might create difficulty for him if the assets charged, or his powers in respect of such assets, differ in each case; that might constitute sufficient reason for him declining one of the appointments, to avoid being placed in a conflict of interest. In practice, however, as the assets charged and the powers granted are more or less standard, he will be concerned simply with the ranking of the charges for the purposes of payment. It would be prudent, however, to obtain the consent of all the charge-holders before accepting such an appointment.

30–27 Where several receivers are appointed, they take precedence in accordance with the ranking of the charge by virtue of which they have been appointed, to the exclusion of any other receiver (Insolvency Act 1986, s.56(1)). If the charges rank equally, and separate receivers are appointed by each holder, the receivers are deemed to have been appointed as joint receivers (s.56(2)). The consequences of a joint appointment will follow, including the requirement that they must act jointly, unless the respective instruments of appointment otherwise provide (s.56(3); see para.30–25). If a receiver has been appointed under a charge having a lower ranking, and subsequently a receiver is appointed by a charge having a prior ranking, the powers of the lower ranking receiver are suspended as from the date of the prior ranking appointment, so far as may be necessary for the prior ranking appointee to exercise his powers in relation to the property charged. If for any reason the floating charge having priority ceases to attach, for example by satisfaction of the charge-holder's claim, or by the receiver ceasing to act and no replacement being appointed, the suspended powers of the postponed appointee revive (s.56(4)). Where a receiver's powers have been suspended under these provisions, he is entitled to retain property and documents of the company, until he receives an indemnity (with a maximum value equivalent to the property which is subject to the postponed charge) in respect of any expenses, charges and liabilities which he may have incurred in the performance of his functions (s.56(5)). The suspension of the powers of a receiver does not cause the charge under which he has been appointed to refloat (s.56(6) and see para.30–76, below). If the prior ranking receiver's charge does not extend to the whole assets and undertaking of the company, the powers of the postponed receiver remain effective in respect of any part that is excluded from the prior charge.

Any contract which the receiver whose powers have been suspended has entered into in the performance of his functions while in office, continues in force subject to its terms, notwithstanding the suspension (Insolvency Act 1986, s.57(7)). The personal liability of a receiver whose powers are suspended (unless excluded) continues, notwithstanding the suspension (s.57(2)). Since he is entitled to an indemnity out of the property subject to his charge in respect of any such personal liability (s.57(3)), he will be entitled to retain property in respect thereof until he receives a valid indemnity from the receiver superseding him under s.56(5).

Where the receiver having priority has completed the distribution of monies to the holder and other persons having prior claims under Insolvency Act 1986, s.60(1)(i), any balance remaining is to be paid to those having right thereto including any other receiver (s.60(2)). A postponed receiver whose powers are suspended is, therefore, entitled to an accounting from the receiver having priority.

D. Effect of Appointment

Crystallisation of the charge. On the appointment of a receiver, "the floating charge by virtue of which he was appointed attaches to the property then subject to the charge; and such attachment has effect as if the charge was a fixed security over the property to which it has attached" (Insolvency Act 1986, s.53(7) (appointment by the holder) and s.54(6) (appointment by the court)). This has come to be known as "crystallisation" of the charge. Only the charge by virtue of which he was appointed crystallises, not any other charge. **30–28**

Crystallisation of the charge also occurs when a company goes into liquidation (Companies Act 1985, s.463(1), as amended by the Companies Act 1989, s.140(1)). In s.463(1) (as amended), the words used to describe crystallisation are: "Where a company goes into liquidation within the meaning of s.247(2) of the Insolvency Act 1986, a floating charge created by the company attaches to the property then comprised in the company's property and undertaking or, as the case may be, in part of that property and undertaking".[48] In this case, all floating charges crystallise. Crystallisation also occurs if an administrator files a notice under the Insolvency Act 1986, Sch.B1, para.115 (Form 2.32B (Scot)) to the effect that he has no funds to distribute to unsecured creditors other than the "prescribed part", and this applies to all floating charges.

Since crystallisation is an automatic process, it is not possible to appoint a receiver in respect of part only of the property charged. Section 51(1) and (2) of the Insolvency Act 1986 provide that a receiver may competently be appointed "of *such part* of the property as is subject to the charge" (not of part of the property which is subject to the charge).

---

[48] As to the possibility of a competition between a receiver and a subsequent liquidator deriving from the wording of these sections, see paras 30–29—30–35. The amendment of s.463(1) by the Companies Act 1989, s.40(1) became effective on July 3, 1995 (SI 1995/1352). Previously, s.463(1) provided that crystallisation occurred on the commencement of winding up. The Insolvency Act 1986, s.247(2) provides that a company goes into liquidation on the earlier date of a resolution for voluntary winding up or a winding up-order by the court.

Crystallisation on the appointment of a receiver by the charge-holder is, however, subject to timeous acceptance of office by the receiver under s.53(6)(a) (see para.26A–21).

There is no transfer of title to heritage or other property, which remains vested in the company. That is why the statutes describe crystallisation "as if" there were a fixed security which would in many cases involve a transfer of title.[49] This "statutory metaphor", designed to relate the concept of crystallisation to familiar features of Scottish law on security rights and insolvency, has, in the event, caused some confusion.

30–29 **Assets attached.** The assets which are attached by the charge on crystallisation are determined by the terms of the instrument of charge. Although ss.53(7) and 54(6) of the Insolvency Act 1986 (and their statutory predecessors) provide that, on the appointment of a receiver, the charge "attaches to the property *then* subject to charge", it is not the property which is in the possession of the company at that time which limits the scope of the charge, but the terms of the instrument itself, which may be habile to include assets acquired by the company after crystallisation. The usual formula in the charge, paraphrasing s.462(1) of the Companies Act 1985, is "the whole of the property (including uncalled capital) which is or may be while this instrument is in force comprised in the property and undertaking of the company" (commonly called an "all assets charge"). It was held in *Ross v Taylor*[50] that a floating charge in this form attaches assets acquired by the company after crystallisation, for the benefit of the charge-holder.

The decision of the House of Lords in *Sharp v Thomson*[51] determined that the "property" which is attached on crystallisation is that in which the company retains a beneficial interest. This case concerned a contract for the sale of a dwellinghouse, where the purchasers had taken delivery of a Disposition and had paid the price. Before the purchaser's title had been recorded, the selling company went into receivership. The Court of Session approached the problem on the basis that "property" in s.462 (and the floating charge) meant having a real right and thus fell to be construed in accordance with the general rule of Scots law that a purchaser did not have a real right until his title had entered the Register. The House of Lords (the three English Law Lords concurring with their two Scottish colleagues) rejected this view and construed s.462 as standing apart from these general rules.

30–30 Notwithstanding the decision in *Ross v Taylor,*[52] however, doubt remains whether assets recovered by the receiver from third parties are attached for the benefit of the charge-holder, if the basis of recovery was, in effect, the reduction of a fraudulent preference, gratuitous alienation or extortionate credit transaction, or the reduction of incomplete diligence. There is also

---

[49] *Forth & Clyde Construction Co Ltd v Trinity Timber & Plywood Co Ltd,* 1984 S.L.T.

[50] 1985 S.L.T. 387.

[51] 1997 S.L.T. 636, HL: the Court of Session decisions are reported 1994 S.L.T. 1068 and 1995 S.L.T. 837.

[52] fn.50, above.

the question of whether the charge is limited by a subsequent liquidation, after which further assets acquired by the company would not be attached. In addition, property which is in the possession of the company, and prima facie part of its undertaking attached by the charge, may be subject to a valid retention of title or trust in favour of a third party.

A receiver has no power to reduce a transaction as a fraudulent or unfair preference, gratuitous alienation or extortionate credit transaction. The power to do so is reserved to a liquidator, or (since the Insolvency Act 1986) an administrator. The receiver may, however, persuade the creditor to restore property to the company under threat of instituting winding up proceedings. That, in effect, is what appears to have occurred in *Ross v Taylor.* A receiver could by similar threats persuade the holder of an incomplete diligence to give up such rights as he may have. He would, or course, have to be prepared to carry out his threat within the appropriate period. **30–31**

It seems clear, on the basis of the present law, that if a receiver succeeds in recovering property from a creditor by such means, the benefit will flow to the charge-holder. However, the receiver will require to apply such property in the first instance to satisfying the preferential and pre-preferential claims which rank ahead of the holder of the charge. He is entitled to utilise the proceeds of recovery from a third party in the first instance for such purposes. If the proceeds of recovery were held to be for the benefit of the general creditors, rather than the holder of the charge, the effect in practice would be the same, because the receiver has the right to recoup from the fund available for general creditors any payment that he has made to satisfy preferential and pre-preferential debts (s.59(3)). The question would, however, become of practical importance if the assets recovered from third parties in this way exceeded the receiver's liability for such debts, and the question would arise whether the surplus would be payable to the charge-holder or the general creditors (or the liquidator on their behalf). Assuming the existence of an all-assets charge, on the basis of *Ross v Taylor,* assets recovered by the receiver from the date of his appointment, at least down to the commencement of winding up, would fall into his hands for the benefit of the charge-holder.

In *Ross v Taylor,*[53] the court refused to follow the English authorities, of which the leading case is *Re Yagerphone Ltd*,[54] partly because the terms of the debenture in point there were different from the instrument of charge under consideration in *Ross v Taylor,* but also because reduction of a fraudulent preference and the destination of the proceeds were not in issue. That, however, is necessarily the position, so long as the receiver has no power himself to reduce fraudulent or unfair preferences; the same applies to gratuitous alientations, extortionate credit transactions and incomplete diligence. The Scottish Law Commission[55] has raised the policy question of **30–31A**

---

[53] 1985 S.L.T. 387.
[54] [1935] Ch. 392.
[55] Consultative Memorandum No.72, "Floating Charges and Receivers", October 1986.

whether the proceeds of such action (or threatened action) by a receiver should benefit the charge-holder or the general body of creditors.

30–32 In *Ross v Taylor,*[56] the further question was raised of what (if any) limitation on the receiver's right to *acquirenda* arose on the liquidation of the company. The court held that there was, in effect, a second stage crystallisation of the charge, the effect of which was determined by the Companies Act 1985, s.463(1). In the terms in force at the time, this provided that at the commencement of the winding up, the charge "attaches to the property then comprised in the company's property and undertaking".[57] As was pointed out in *Ross v Taylor,* the reference to property "then comprised" in its property and undertaking is critical. If the charge crystallises on winding up, what is attached in terms of s.463(1) is the property actually in the possession of the company at that time (so far as within the ambit of the charge). There is, however, nothing to prevent the holder, notwithstanding the existence of the liquidation, from appointing a receiver subsequent to the liquidation, and if the charge is in terms habile to bring *acquirenda* within its ambit, property acquired by the company after that appointment will accrue for the benefit of the charge-holder. This appears to be the position, whether the liquidation preceded or followed the appointment of the receiver. The Lord President[58] noted that the floating charge in question, relating to the whole assets of the company, present and future, while it remained in force, remained in force until at least some time after the commencement of the winding up of the company. After referring to the different language used in the relevant sections (now s.53(7) of the Insolvency Act and s.463(1) of the Companies Act), he expressed the view that:

> "there is nothing in the language of [s.53(7)] to prevent full force being given to the words of the instrument. Any property which comes into the company's hands after the appointment of a receiver will be attached and be available, if need be, for realisation by a receiver."

It seems, therefore, to be clear that if the liquidator is appointed after the receiver on a charge in such terms, *acquirenda* continue to benefit the charge-holder to the exclusion of general creditors, notwithstanding the terms of s.463(1).

---

[56] 1985 S.L.T. 387.

[57] The amendment of s.463(1) discussed above, substituting reference to the company going into liquidation for the commencement of winding up, does not affect the issues raised by *Ross v Taylor.* Where a company is wound up by the court (and is not already in liquidation), the effect of the amendment is to postpone the (second) crystallisation occurring under s.463(1) from the date the petition was presented (the "commencment of liquidation" under the Insolvency Act 1986, s.129) to the date of the order. In a voluntary winding up, the date of the resolution is both the date the company goes into liquidation and the commencement of its winding up.

[58] 1985 S.L.T. 387.

Ross v Taylor was, of course, a case where the receiver was appointed first. The second question raised for the opinion of court was whether, if the goods which the receiver had recovered were not to be regarded as attached by the charge, **30–33**

> "on the liquidation of the company, would the floating charge under which the receiver was appointed re-crystallise, to the effect that any *acquirenda,* since the date of his appointment . . . ingathered by the receiver fall within the assets covered by the floating charge".

In response, the court stated:

> "although we are not now required to answer this question, we would have had no hesitation in answering it in the affirmative".

In its opinion subsequently, however, the court indicated that its reason for answering this question at all was to refute the argument that, having appointed a receiver, the holder of the charge is denied any benefit that might accrue from what is now s.463(1) of the Companies Act. The court's position was that, if it was necessary to hold that the charge had "re-crystallised" on the commencement of the winding up, in order to attach *acquirenda* accruing after the receiver's appointment (but before the liquidation), that was an additional ground for finding in favour of the receiver and the charge-holder on the facts of the case. There is no suggestion that if there is a second crystallisation on the commencement of winding up, *acquirenda* after that date are not within the charge; indeed, the opinion of the court on the first question (quoted above) suggests that such *acquirenda* would be attached.

An additional consideration arises in the context of reduction of incomplete diligences. On crystallisation of a charge, no diligence which has not been made "completely effectual" can prevail against the receiver (see para.30–40 and 30–41). If however the diligence is "effectually complete", the receiver cannot reduce it, nor can he recover for the benefit of the charge-holder any money or assets that may have been paid to the executing creditor. On the other hand, if the company went into liquidation within 60 days, the liquidator could reduce completed diligence and recover the proceeds thereof under the Insolvency Act 1986, s.185.[59] If, therefore, the receiver on appointment finds that creditors have completed diligence within 60 days, he can secure recovery, either by petitioning for the liquidation of the company, or by threatening to do so, in the same way that he can "persuade" creditors to repay what he regards as a fraudulent or unfair preference, etc. As the Scottish Law Commission has noted in a consultative memorandum on the questions discussed in this paragraph,[60] it **30–34**

---

[59] See *Palmer's Company Law* (25th (Looseleaf) ed.), paras 15.699–15.700.
[60] S.L.C. Consultative Memorandum No.72, "Floating Charges and Receivers", October 1986, para.2.58.

is unsatisfactory that a receiver should be compelled to put the company into liquidation, simply to reduce diligences; but, under the present law, that remains the position.

30–35 The view that the charge-holder's rights are not affected by the appointment of a liquidator, and any possible limitation on his rights to *acquirenda*, following "re-crystallisation" under s.463(1) of the Companies Act, is supported by the decision in *Manley, Petitioner,*[61] where Lord Kincraig[62] held that "whether the receiver is appointed before or after the commencement of the liquidation, his rights take precedence over the rights of the liquidator, and he is entitled to take control of the property of the company in order to satisfy the debt of the holder of the floating charge".

30–36 The receiver's rights over property in the possession of the company are, however, subject to the rights of any person who has effectually executed diligence over such property (see para.30–40), or who holds a fixed security or a floating charge having priority over or ranking *pari passu* with the floating charge by virtue of which he was appointed (Insolvency Act 1986, s.55(3)). In addition, the receiver's rights are subject to any trust which has been validly constituted, according to Scots law, over property in the possession of the company, or which is the subject of an effective retention of title condition under the Sale of Goods Act 1979, ss.17 or 19. Such a clause must be given effect according to its terms and, to that extent, the property in question (if still identifiable) is not the property of the purchaser and does not fall within a floating charge granted by the purchaser.[63] If the clause is regarded as an attempt to create a security, as distinct from a simple retention of title under the Sale of Goods Act, it will be ineffective against a receiver.[64] It is of course possible for property in the hands of a company to be impressed with trust obligations, and so fall outwith the assets attached by the charge, but any such trust has to be constituted by a method recognised in Scots law. It is possible for a company to constitute itself trustee for a creditor in respect of assets in its own hands by an appropriate declaration in an agreement with, or intimated to, the creditor.[65]

30–37 **Effect of appointment on subsisting contracts.** Section 57(4) of the Insolvency Act 1986 (formerly s.17(4) of the 1972 Act) provides that any contract entered into by the company prior to the date of appointment of a receiver continues in force (subject to its terms), notwithstanding the

---

[61] 1985 S.L.T. 42.

[62] 1985 S.L.T. 42, 43/44.

[63] *Armour v Thyssen Edelstahlwerke AG* [1991] 2 A.C. 339; 1990 S.L.T. 891 (HL).

[64] *Armour v Thyssen Edelstahlwerke AG,* above.

[65] *Tay Valley Joinery Ltd v C.F. Financial Services Ltd,* 1987 S.L.T. 209; also *Turnbull v Liquidator of Scottish County Investment Co Ltd,* 1939 S.C. 5; *Smith v Liquidators of James Birrell Ltd,* 1968 S.L.T. 174. *Style Financial Services Ltd v Bank of Scotland (No.1),* 1996 S.L.T. 421; *Balfour Beatty Ltd v Britannia Life Ltd,* 1997 S.L.T. 10. A trust by a company declaring itself to hold its property in trust must be constituted in writing: Requirements of Writing (Scotland) Act 1995, s.1(2)(iii).

appointment, and the receiver does not by virtue only of his appointment incur personal liability. The receiver can insist upon performance; but, if the contract requires an element of performance by the company which is still outstanding (e.g. payment), the receiver cannot enforce the contract, without incurring liability for performance of the company's obligations.[66] Although not liable for local rates,[67] a receiver may be subject to statutory duties imposed on "the occupier" of company premises.[68] Contracts of employment are, however, in a special position (see para.30–39, below).

Even if there is no specific provision in the contract, however, it may be affected by the appointment. The contract may be repudiated by the receiver, or the company may cease to be able to perform, as a result of the receiver's actions or other consequences of his appointment (e.g. the dismissal of employees). This would leave the third party with a ranking for damages against the company, probably a worthless remedy. Attempts have been made by third parties thus affected to obtain an order for specific implement against the receiver. This will be refused, if performance is impossible or compels the receiver to accept personal liability. Even if performance is possible, however, the powers and duties of the receiver in Scotland must over-ride his inherited obligations under a pre-receivership contract. The receiver's statutory powers include power which, either in its present form "to carry on the business of the company *or any part* of it" (Insolvency Act 1986, Sch.2, para.14), or, as previously, "to carry on the business of the company so far as he thinks it desirable to do so" (Companies Act 1985, s.471(1)(o)), necessarily implies a discretion to discontinue all or part of the business and contracts associated therewith. It is clear from the judgment in *MacLeod,*[69] that Lord Stott regarded an action of specific implement against a receiver as misconceived; such proceedings, if competent at all, should be against the company. Further, if specific implement would interfere with the receiver's powers and discretion in regard to the property attached, it must be inconsistent with the Scottish statutory provisions to grant such an order. The considerations of English property law underlying *Freevale Ltd v Metrostore Holdings Ltd*[70] have no application in Scotland, notwithstanding the careful consideration of *MacLeod* in that decision.

In many contracts, it is provided that the appointment of a receiver will entitle the other party to determine the contract and claim damages. This may frustrate the receiver's efforts to realise the value of the company as a going concern. In the case of a commercial (non-agricultural) lease, however, the receiver may be able to persuade the court, under s.5 of the Law Reform (Miscellaneous Provisions) (Scotland) Act 1985, (effective **30–38**

---

[66] *Graham & Co v United Turkey Red Co,* 1922 S.C. 533.

[67] *Ratford v Nortonavon DC* [1987] Q.B. 357; *Re Atlantic Computer Systems Ltd* [1990] B.C.C. 859; [1990] Ch. 505; *McKillop (Receiver of Rowan Leisure Ltd), Petitioner,* 1995 S.L.T. 216; [1994] B.C.C. 677.

[68] *Lord Advocate, Petitioner,* 1990 S.C.L.R. 794; *McKillop, Petitioner* (fn.67, above).

[69] *MacLeod v Alexander Sutherland Ltd,* 1977 S.L.T. (Notes) 44.

[70] [1984] Ch. 199.

January 1, 1986), that the landlord should not be allowed to irritate the lease on receivership, even if its terms so provide, provided that rent is maintained; s.4 of that Act obliges the landlord to give at least 14 days written notice to pay rent, on pain of irritancy.

An administrative receiver (but not a receiver of part only of the property) can safeguard the continuing supply of gas, electricity, water and telecommunications to the company under the Insolvency Act 1986, s.233.[71] The supplier may require the receiver's personal guarantee for post-appointment charges, but cannot make the supply conditional on payment for supplies to the company before the date of appointment.

30–39 **Contracts of employment.** Nothing in the 1972 Act (s.17) suggested that the appointment of a receiver terminated any contract of employment, or that such contracts were to be treated in any way different to pre-existing contracts in general. A receiver in Scotland, whether appointed by the charge-holder or the court, has always been the agent of the company (1972 Act, s.17(1); Companies Act, s.473(1); Insolvency Act, s.57(1)), and, in that respect, in a similar position to a receiver appointed "out of court" in England; in English law, only the appointment of a receiver by the court automatically operated as a dismissal of the company's employees.[72] In certain circumstances, especially in the case of an executive or managing director, it can be argued that the appointment of a receiver operates as a basis for the employee to claim constructive dismissal, since he is no longer able to discharge his functions.[73] In general, however, such contracts continued in force as between the company and the employee, and the receiver incurred no personal liability, unless he entered into a new contract on his own responsibility.

The 1986 Act amended the position in two respects. First, by an amendment to what was s.17(2) (1986 Act s.57(2)), a receiver is made personally liable "on any contract of employment adopted by him". Secondly, under what is now s.57(5), a receiver is not to be taken as having adopted such a contract by reason of anything done or omitted to be done within 14 days after his appointment. For some time it was thought that a receiver could avoid personal liability by writing to the employees (within the 14-day period) stating that their employment was being continued but without personal liability.[74] This, however, was held to be ineffective by the House of Lords,[75] which held that the mere continuation of employment amounted to "adoption" of the employee's contract. Personal liability was, however, restricted to liabilities incurred during the receiver's tenure of

---

[71] Section 233 applies only to public utility suppliers, as defined in s.233(3) (as amended). Supplies from private sources are excluded from s.233.

[72] *Nicoll v Cutts* [1985] P.C.C. 311.

[73] *Re Mack Trucks (Britain) Ltd* [1967] 1 All E.R. 977, 982; *Griffiths v Secretary of State for Social Services* [1974] Q.B. 468.

[74] Known as a "Specialised Mouldings" letter after an unreported case of this name (Harman J., February 13, 1987).

[75] *Powdrill v Watson (Re Paramount Airways Ltd)* [1995] A.C. 394. *Jamieson, Petitioner,* 1997 S.L.T. 821 and *Lindop v Stuart Noble & Sons Ltd,* 1998 S.C.L.R. 684; [1999] B.C.C. 616 aff'd [2000] B.C.C. 747; 1999 GWD 23–1112 confirmed that this decision applies in Scotland.

office. In addition to wages or salary and pension contributions this included a proportion of holiday pay accruing during any period of notice, or damages for failure to give such notice.

In order to limit the impact of this decision to the wages, etc. actually due in respect of employment during a receiver's tenure of office, s.57 was amended by the Insolvency Act 1994 (amending s.57(2) and inserting s.57(1A) and (2A)–(2D)) to the effect that a receiver's personal liability in respect of a contract of employment adopted by him on or after March 15, 1994 (the date of commencement of the 1994 Act) is limited to "qualifying liabilities". These are defined as wages or salary and pension contributions due after adoption and while the receiver is in office. They include payments due in respect of holidays and sickness absence accruing in that period.[76]

Statutory liabilities under the employment protection legislation or contractual payments due in respect of redundancy or compensation for loss of employment arising in respect of pre-receivership contracts are not "wages or salary" and are therefore not "qualifying liabilities", nor are they among the "expenses and liabilities" of a receiver entitled to rank ahead of the receiver's expenses and preferential creditors in the order of ranking prescribed by the Insolvency Act 1986, s.60.[76a]

The receiver and diligence. Diligence commenced against property of a company before the creation by it of a floating charge is effective against the charge-holder because the assets charged are already subject to the effects of the diligence in question.[77] If diligence has been fully completed prior to crystallisation, to the point where the assets attached have ceased to be the property of the company, they are incapable of being attached by the charge.[78] If diligence commenced after crystallisation, the diligence has no effect.[79] If crystallisation occurs on the appointment of a receiver, property which is the subject of prior incomplete diligence is not available to the holder of the charge, if the diligence has been "effectually executed" prior to the receiver's appointment (Insolvency Act 1986, s.55(3)(a)). The precise point in the diligence process where it has become "effectually executed" depends on the particular diligence in question. An inhibition laid against a company's heritable property is not "effectually executed" until decree of adjudication has been granted, in terms of which title to the property passes to the inhibitor.[80] An arrestment of moveable property on **30–40**

---

[76] *Powdrill v Watson* (above) was decided on the provisions equivalent to s.57 in relation to administration and English receivership and the 1994 Act made similar amendments in respect of these proceedings. However, while the English provisions on receivership (Insolvency Act 1986, s.44) apply only to administrative receivers, s.57 applies to receivers in Scotland generally. For a more detailed discussion, see paras 23–2—23–12, above.

[76a] *Lindop v Stuart Noble & Sons Ltd* [2000] B.C.C. 747; *Re Allders Department Stores* [2005] B.C.C. 289.

[77] *Iona Hotels Ltd v Craig,* 1991 S.L.T. 11; *Murray v Long,* 1992 S.L.T. 292.

[78] *Iona Hotels Ltd,* above. This also applies to sums consigned in court as a condition of the recall of diligence laid before crystallisation; *Hawking v Hafton House Ltd,* 1990 S.L.T. 496.

[79] *Forth & Clyde Construction Ltd v Trinity Timber & Plywood Ltd,* 1984 S.L.T. 94.

[80] *Armour and Mycroft, Petitioners,* 1983 S.L.T. 453; *Taymech Ltd v Rush & Tompkins Ltd,* 1990 S.L.T. 681.

the dependence of an action or in execution of a decree (or equivalent) requires to be followed by an action of furthcoming and is not "effectually executed" until decree on that action is granted.[81] Arrestment of corporeal moveables in the hands of a third party is only "effectually exercised" when decree granting warrant to sell has been granted and the sale has taken place.[82] The former diligence of poinding corporeal moveables in the possession of the debtor in execution of a decree has been replaced by "attachment",[83] but in both cases this must be completed by a sale of the goods in question. In relation to poinding, it has been held that the diligence is "effectually executed" only when the sale has taken place,[84] and this must also apply to "attachment". Arrestment to found jurisdiction against a defender ("*ad fundandam jurisdictionem*") does not render the property arrested "litigious" and does not give priority against the charge-holder or any creditor.[85] However, a receiver will not be able to sell heritage with "clear searches" unless he either settles with the inhibitor, or obtains a court order under s.61 (see para.30–97), and the purchaser may in any event be justified in refusing to accept the title, even if he is not affected by the inhibition.[86]

It appears that the invalidity of ineffectual diligence is to be regarded as a consequence of crystallisation of a floating charge granted by a non-Scottish company, assuming that the law of the company's domicile includes such an effect. This would follow from the decision in *Gordon Anderson (Plant) Ltd v Campsie Construction Ltd*[87] where it was held that crystallisation of an English charge, before diligence had been "effectually completed", had thc same result as if the charge had been granted by a Scottish company.

30–41 If crystallisation occurs in terms of the Companies Act 1985, s.463, on the company going into liquidation (i.e. on the earlier of a resolution to wind up voluntarily or a winding-up order of the court—Insolvency Act 1986, s.247(2)) the rights of the charge-holder are subject to "effectually executed diligence" and the other consequences of crystallisation on diligence (or the lack of them) discussed above. However, a liquidator (but not a receiver) has power to cut down diligence executed within 60 days prior to the "commencement of the winding-up" and recover any assets paid over in respect of arrestment, poinding or attachment, but not inhibition (Insolvency Act 1986, s.185, applying the Bankruptcy (Scotland) Act 1985, s.37(1)–(6)). In this context, the "commencement" is the earlier of the date of the court order (s.185(3)) or the date of the resolution to wind up (Insolvency Act 1986, s.86). A receiver may be able to recover assets paid to the creditor executing diligence by threatening to put the company into

---

[81] *Lord Advocate v Royal Bank of Scotland,* 1976 S.L.T. 130; 1977 S.C. 155; 1978 S.L.T. 38.
[82] *ibid.*
[83] Debt Arrangement and Attachment (Scotland) Act 2002.
[84] *Lord Advocate v Royal Bank of Scotland Ltd,* above.
[85] *Fraser-Johnston Engineering, Co v Jeffs,* 1920 S.C. 222.
[86] *Dryburgh v Gordon,* 1896 24 R. 1.
[87] 1977 S.L.T. 7; see also *Taymech v Rush v Tompkins,* above.

liquidation (see para.30–34). A creditor whose diligence is cut down is entitled to recover his expenses from the assets sold by the liquidator (except in the case of inhibition) (Bankruptcy (Scotland) Act 1985, s.37(5), as applied by s.185).

Effect of receivership on delictual liabilities. In principle, a third party with a claim in delict against the company at the date a receiver is appointed has merely an ordinary ranking as a creditor. If the company is insured in respect of such a claim, however, the injured party has a direct claim against the insurers by virtue of the Third Parties (Rights Against Insurers) Act 1930 (as amended by the Insolvency Acts 1985 and 1986). **30–42**

Directors' continuing functions. The appointment of a receiver suspends the powers of the directors in respect of the assets to which the charge attaches; but it does not relieve them of other duties such as the preparation of statutory accounts. The receiver must give the directors sufficient information to enable them to prepare such accounts.[88] **30–43**

The receiver must also give the directors such information as they may reasonably require to enable them to pursue a *bona fide* attempt to redeem the debt secured by the charge, including information about assets which still remain in his hands.[89]

It has been held in England[90] that the directors can raise proceedings in name of the company in relation to attached assets without the consent of the receiver, and might have a duty to do so, especially if the claim lies against the charge-holder. This contradicts opinions expressed in a Scottish case,[91] which was decided at the same time. The English approach seems preferable in principle and, although the point remains technically undecided, it has been preferred in a subsequent Scottish case.[92] There has also been a Scottish decision[93] allowing the directors to defend proceedings in the name of the company, where the receiver declined to do so. In either situation, of course, the directors risk being found personally liable in expenses.

The directors remain in office during the receivership, and they remain subject to the legal obligations imposed on them, subject to the extent that the company's assets have been removed from their *defacto* control. They have to maintain accounting records under s.221 of the Companies Act 1985.[94] The statutory duty to prepare annual accounts (s.227) and a director's report (s.225), and to lay copies of the accounts and reports before an annual meeting of members (s.241), to hold an annual general meeting (s.366) and to file an annual return, all continue, at least in theory.

---

[88] *Smiths Ltd v Middleton* [1979] 3 All E.R. 842.

[89] *Gomba Holdings (UK) Ltd, etc.* [1986] 1 W.L.R. 1301; (1986) 2 B.C.C. 99, 102.

[90] *Newhart Developments Ltd v Co-operative Commercial Bank Ltd,* [1978] Q.B. 814.

[91] *Imperial Hotel (Aberdeen) Ltd v Vaux Breweries Ltd,* 1978 S.L.T. 113.

[92] *Shanks v Central Regional Council,* 1987 S.L.T. 410; 1988 S.L.T. 212.

[93] *Hastings Black Construction Ltd v AIR (Air Conditioning and Refrigeration Ltd)* (1984) (Sh. Ct.) unreported; see *Greene & Fletcher, The Law and Practice of Receivership in Scotland* (Butterworths) paras 2.22–2.23.

[94] *Smiths Ltd v Middleton,* above.

The provisions of the Articles relating to retiral by rotation (if any) remain effective.

The directors are required to assist an administrative receiver and may be the subject of an order to recover property, books and other records, or an examination by order of the court to provide relevant information (Insolvency Act 1986, ss.234–237). The directors may take proceedings in the name of the company to restrain the improper disclosure of confidential or privileged information given to the receiver.[95]

E. The Office Holder

30–44 **Qualification for appointment.** Only an individual (or several individuals jointly) may be appointed as a receiver. Undischarged bankrupts, firms or partnerships, and corporations cannot be appointed (Insolvency Act 1986, s.51(3)–(5)). Persons who have been disqualified from acting as directors, etc. under the Company Directors Disqualification Act 1986 cannot be appointed as receivers. These restrictions apply to all forms of receivership, and were in force prior to the 1986 legislation. As from December 29, 1986, (see ss.388–390 of that Act), however, only a duly authorised insolvency practitioner may act as an "administrative receiver". A person who is an undischarged bankrupt, or who is the subject of a disqualification order under the 1986 Act, or who is a patient within the meaning of the Mental Health Acts, is automatically disqualified from being an insolvency practitioner (Insolvency Act 1986, s.390(4)).

30–45 **Caution.** Prior to the 1986 Act, there was no requirement imposed on a receiver to find caution for the performance of his duties and the proper custody of the assets in his control. The 1986 Act (s.390(3)) introduced such a requirement, but only in respect of "insolvency practitioners", and thus in respect of "administrative receivers" only, and not receivers generally. Caution is now governed by the Insolvency Practitioners Regulations 2005 (SI 2005/524, effective March 8, 2005) which require an insolvency practitioner appointed to act as an administrative receiver to have in force a Bond in the approved form in accordance with Sch.2 of those Regulations. There are two elements: (a) a "general penalty sum" of £250,000, and (b) a "specific penalty sum" at least equal to the value of the assets of the company under the control of the receiver (subject to a minimum of £5,000 and a maximum of £5,000,000). The practitioner is required to prepare a "cover schedule" in respect of each appointment. The Bond is to be retained by the practitioner's authorising body, and the practitioner is obliged to submit to that body the cover schedule giving details of the specific penalty sum for each appointment held. The principal copy of the cover schedule relating to the company is to be kept in the Sederunt Book for the proceedings.

---

[95] *Sutton v GE Capital Commercial Finance Ltd,* [2004] EWCA Civ 315; [2004] 2 B.C.L.C. 662 CA; see also para.23–12A.

Rule 7.28(1) of the Insolvency (Scotland) Rules 1986 imposes on the person making the appointment (i.e. the holder of the charge, or the court) the duty of satisfying himself that the receiver has found caution; of necessity, this can only refer to the general bond of £250,000. The court rules simply require any petition for the appointment of a receiver to aver "that he is qualified to act as a receiver"; but this must include reference to caution, if relevant.

The Regulations require the receiver to increase the amount of caution, if he finds the original estimate to be under-stated (subject to the maximum of £5,000,000). If a committee of creditors has been established, one of its duties is to keep the amount of caution under review (r.7.28(2)). There is no provision for reducing the amount of caution, or for its upward review by anyone other than the receiver himself, if there is no committee, in the Rules; this is, however, within the power of the court to give directions under s.63(1).

The cost of "the insolvency practitioner's caution" forms part of the expenses of the proceedings (r.7.28(3)).

It is not clear whether this includes the cost of his general bond, as well as the certificate of specific penalty, but there seems no reason in principle why it, or a due proportion thereof, should not be payable as the expenses of all the insolvency proceedings in which the practitioner is acting.

Remuneration. The Insolvency Act 1986, s.58 provides that the receiver's **30–46** remuneration is to be agreed between him and the holder of the charge. If it is not agreed, or is disputed by the receiver, the holder of the charge or any other secured creditor, the company (presumably the directors) or its liquidator, it may be fixed by the Auditor of the Court of Session. Section 58(2) also gives the receiver (or the chargeholder) the right to review before the Auditor of Court remuneration already agreed between them under s.58(1). Section 60 of the Insolvency Act 1986 gives the receiver a right to receive payment for his liabilities, expenses and remuneration in priority to the preferential creditors and the charge-holder, subject to any variation in "any instrument". The instrument of appointment (or the charge if incorporated therein) may adversely affect the receiver's ranking. If the company has insufficient funds to meet his claim, there is no automatic right to be paid by the charge-holder.[96] A receiver is, therefore, at risk in accepting office that the assets will not suffice to meet his remuneration and expenses; in cases of doubt, he should obtain an indemnity from the charge-holder before undertaking (or continuing) the receivership.

F. Effect of Invalid Appointment

General. The appointment of a receiver may be attacked on a number of **30–47** grounds:

---

[96] *Hill Samuel Ltd v Laing,* 1988 S.L.T. 454; [1988] B.C.C. 9; aff'd 1989 S.L.T. 760; [1991] B.C.C. 665.

(i) *Instrument of charge alleged to be invalid or ineffective,* for one of the following reasons:

(a) a defect relating to the original instrument of charge, arising from s.462 of the Companies Act 1985 and having the result that no valid floating charge was ever created, such as:
   (i) that it was not created by "an incorporated company", or
   (ii) that it was not "for the purpose of securing any debt or other obligation", or
   (iii) that it was not validly executed, or
   (iv) that it did not effectively create a "floating" charge;

(b) that the floating charge is invalid under ss.242 (gratuitous alienations), 243 (unfair preferences), 244 (extortionate credit transactions) or 245 of the Insolvency Act 1986, or is at common law a gratuitous alienation or a fraudulent preference.

(c) that the obligation secured by the charge has been satisfied or is ineffective.

(ii) *Want of registration*

(d) failure to have the charge registered (or duly presented for registration) under s.410 of the Companies Act 1985.

(iii) *Defective appointment alleged to be invalid or ineffective,* for one of the following reasons:

(e) that there were no proper grounds which entitled the holder of the charge to make the appointment;
(f) that the instrument of appointment is defective in execution or form under s.53 of the Insolvency Act 1986;
(g) that the receiver did not accept office within the statutory time limit of one business day (Insolvency Act 1986, s.53(6));
(h) that the receiver is not duly qualified to act.

The effect of such defects (or alleged defects) in the charge or the appointment differs according to the circumstances.

30–48 **Instrument of charge alleged to be invalid or ineffective.** The formal requirements of a floating charge are discussed in paras 30–8—30–11. If the instrument of charge is defective, such that no valid floating charge was ever created, the receiver has no right or title to act, and is personally liable for any loss to the company. He cannot bind the company as its statutory agent, and any contract with third parties which purports to bind the company is void. He is personally liable to any third party who has acted in good faith, even if the contract provides (under Insolvency Act 1986, s.57(2)) that the receiver is not to incur personal liability.

If the obligation secured by the charge has been satisfied, or is itself null and void, there is no basis upon which the receiver can be appointed. The consequences of a purported appointment in such circumstances are the same as if the instrument of charge was defective. A charge created after the commencement of winding up by the court is void, unless the court directs otherwise, under the Insolvency Act 1986, s.127.[97]

If the charge is open to challenge as a fraudulent preference, gratuitous alienation, etc. at common law or by statute, the charge remains valid, until successfully challenged by the liquidator or administrator or (at common law) a creditor. The same result follows if the appointment is open to attack on the basis that the circumstances did not permit the charge-holder to appoint a receiver, or if the obligation which the charge purported to secure was itself a nullity; in these situations, a challenge by the company, as well as by a liquidator or creditor, is possible. The acts of the receiver however, prior to a successful challenge on the grounds discussed in this paragraph, remain valid. **30–49**

Floating Charge Invalid by Statute or at Common Law

(a) The Companies Act 1985, s.617. Before the introduction of the floating charge to Scotland, floating charges granted by English companies were invalidated, or limited, by s.322 of the Companies Act 1948 (consolidated as s.617(1) and (2) of the Companies Act 1985). The 1961 Act (s.7(c)) applied the provisions of s.322 to Scotland, by the expedient of adding to the definition section of the 1948 Act a definition of "floating charge" to include a charge created by a Scottish company under the 1961 Act. Section 322 (as it then stood) provided simply that a floating charge created within 12 months of the commencement of winding up (and from December 29, 1986, also within 12 months of an administration order) was invalid, unless it was proved that the company was solvent immediately after its creation, except as to the amount of any cash paid to the company at the time of the charge, or subsequently and "in consideration for" the charge (together with interest at five per cent.). So far as English law was concerned, s.322, in effect, extended the period for challenging a floating charge as a "fraudulent preference" (on a slightly different basis) from six months (under s.320 of the 1948 Act; s.615 of the 1985 Act) to 12 months. In Scotland, however, the granting of a security by a company could be challenged as a fraudulent preference or gratuitous alienation at common law (without limit of time), or by statute. Section 322 (as applied by the 1961 Act) did not exclude the possibility of such a challenge in Scotland. Section 8 of the 1972 Act, however, added a new sub-s.(3) to s.322 (consolidated as s.617(3) of the Companies Act 1985), which excluded any challenge to a floating charge in Scotland otherwise than under the section, and this remained the position until the Insolvency Act 1986 (see below). **30–50**

A floating charge created before December 29, 1986 is not affected by the Insolvency Act, and is challengeable only on the grounds available before the 1986 Act came into force, that is, a fundamental invalidity affecting the instrument of charge itself, lack of registration in the Register

[97] *Site Preparations Ltd v Buchan Development Co Ltd,* 1983 S.L.T. 317.

of Charges, or the Companies Act 1985, s.617 (Insolvency Act 1986, Sch.11, para.9).

30–51 **(b) Insolvency Act 1986, s.245 (as amended).** Under the provisions of s.245 (as amended by the Enterprise Act 2002),[98] a floating charge created "at a relevant time" is invalid except as provided in s.245(2) and (4) (discussed below). The "relevant time" is defined in s.245(3). If the charge is in favour of a person "connected with" the company,[99] it is the period of two years ending with the "onset of insolvency" and if the charge is in favour of any other person it is the period of 12 months ending with the onset of insolvency. It also includes the period between the making of an application for an administration order and the granting of an order, and the period between notice of intention to appoint an administrator under Sch.B1, paras 14 or 22 being lodged in court and the appointment being made. The "onset of insolvency" is defined (s.245(5)) as the commencement of winding up (i.e. the date of a resolution to wind up voluntarily or, if earlier, that of a winding-up order) or, in the case of administration, the date the application for an administration order is filed, the date notice of intention to appoint under paras 14 or 22 is lodged in court, or the date on which the administrator is appointed, as the case may be.

Section 245(3)(a), which lays down the two-year rule, is specifically limited to a charge "which is created in favour of a person who is connected with the company". The section overlooks the possibility of the charge being assigned, and it would appear possible, therefore, for a charge to be created in favour of someone who is not "connected with" the company, and then assigned to a "connection", without invoking the two-year rule.

If the charge is not in favour of a person connected with the company, s.245(4) provides that the charge is not to be challengeable unless the company is, at the time it was created, unable to pay its debts within the meaning of s.123 of the Insolvency Act, or becomes unable to pay its debts within the meaning of that section in consequence of the transaction under which the charge was created. It is for the challenger to establish that the company was "unable to pay its debts" at the relevant time.

If s.245 applies, under s.245(2) the charge is invalid, except to the extent of:

(i) the value of so much of the consideration for its creation as consists of money paid or goods or services supplied to the company, at the same time as or after the creation of the charge;

(ii) the value of so much of that consideration as consists of the discharge or reduction, at the same time as, or after, the creation of the charge, of any debt of the company; and

---

[98] Enterprise Act 2002, Sch.17, effective September 15, 2003 (Enterprise Act 2002 (Commencement No.4 and Transitional Provisions and Savings) Order (SI 2003/2093)).

[99] Persons "connected with" the company are its directors, shadow directors or "associates" of the company or any director or shadow director (Insolvency Act 1986, s.249). "Associate" is widely defined in s.435 of the Act.

(iii) such interest as is payable on the amounts under (i) or (ii) pursuant to any agreement under which the money was paid, the goods or services were supplied, or the debt was discharged or reduced.

Goods or services are included, together with payments made to creditors of the company, provided that these were part of "the consideration for the creation of the charge". Section 245 has removed the difficulty in the former law (s.617 of the Companies Act 1985) associated with payments made by the holder of the charge in favour of creditors.[1] Such payments to creditors of the company by the holder of the charge are protected by s.245. As regards interest, the holder is able to claim his contractual rate, and is not limited to the statutory rate of five per cent which previously applied. Section 245 applies to "money", whereas s.617 applied only to "cash", although this was interpreted to include the honouring of cheques by a bank.[2]

Under s.245(2)(a) and (b) protection only extends to money or other consideration paid, etc. "at the same time as, or after, the creation of the charge". This wording (unlike the terms of the predecessors of s.245) excludes money, etc. paid before the charge was created, although it has been suggested (on doubtful grounds) that an interval "so short that it can be regarded as minimal" would be acceptable.[3]

Section 245(6) is an anti-avoidance provision, which requires that the value of goods and services protected by s.245 be limited to reasonable market terms.

Section 245 does not explicitly address the criticism voiced in the Cork **30–52**
Report,[4] that the protection of subsequent advances, together with the rule in *Clayton's case,* gave an unfair advantage to a bank taking security by way of floating charge from a company already in overdraft. Such a security would be, in principle, a fraudulent/unfair preference. Using the rule in *Clayton's case,* however, the bank could apply credits received after the creation of the charge against pre-charge indebtedness, until only post-charge debits protected by s.245 remained.

If a charge is vulnerable to attack under s.245, the receiver's appointment is valid until the court upholds the challenge. Even then, the charge is not invalidated, but only limited to the amounts secured by s.245(2), and the receiver is entitled to exercise his powers over the assets attached by the charge until such time as the restricted amount secured has been paid off.

If the receiver has succeeded in paying off the amount secured before an **30–53**
administrator or liquidator has been appointed, the payments cannot be recovered under s.245, even if they exceed the protected amounts.[5] This case, curiously, concerned a Scottish company in liquidation and receivership, which should, therefore, have been argued before a Scottish court. It

---

[1] *Libertas-Kommerz GmbH v Johnson,* 1978 S.L.T. 222.
[2] *Re Yeovil Glove Co Ltd* [1965] Ch. 148.
[3] *Re Shoe Lace Ltd* [1993] B.C.C. 609, 620 (CA).
[4] "Insolvency Law and Practice", Cmnd. 8558 (July 1982) paras 1560–1562.
[5] *Mace Builders (Glasgow) Ltd v Lunn* [1986] Ch. 459, aff'd [1987] Ch. 191.

proceeded upon the false assumption that the laws of Scotland and of England regarding the reduction of fraudulent preferences (before the Insolvency Act) were the same, which may have been strictly correct for the limited purposes of the decision. On the facts in *Mace,* however, the payments to the charge-holder were open to attack in Scotland as a fraudulent preference at common law. While the legislation then applicable (Companies Act 1985, s.617) protected the charge from challenge as a fraudulent preference, which is not the case with s.245, the liquidator or administrator could still have recovered the payments made to the charge-holder as a fraudulent or unfair preference under statute or at common law, if the relevant conditions were satisfied.[6] Such a claim, however, would not affect the position of the receiver, who would have vacated office.

30–54 **(c) Gratuitous alienations.** A charge created before December 29, 1986 cannot be attacked as a "gratuitous alienation" by virtue of the Companies Act 1985, s.617(3). With the repeal of that section, however, the possibility of a challenge on this basis, in respect of charges granted after that date, is now open. Further, a charge granted before November 17, 1972 (when s.617(3) came into effect) may be open to challenge on a similar basis.

The basis for challenge at common law is that the consideration for the alienation was less than full value, and that the company was insolvent at the time, or become insolvent as a result. The test of insolvency is whether the liabilities of the company exceeded its assets ("absolute insolvency"). The challenge may be by the liquidator, administrator or any creditor, but the onus of proof lies with the challenger. The Bankruptcy Act 1621, c.18 of the Scottish Parliament, which reversed this onus if the alienation was in favour of a "conjunct and confident person", has been repealed, and is not available for a challenge at common law of a charge created after December 29, 1986.[7] The common law basis of challenge is expressly preserved by the statutory rules on "gratuitous alienation" (Insolvency Act 1986, s.242(7)).[8]

30–55 Section 242 of the Insolvency Act consolidates reforms which were first introduced by the Bankruptcy (Scotland) Act 1985, Sch.7, para.20, and were brought into effect on April 1, 1986. A transaction may be challenged as a gratuitous alienation under the Act, only after commencement of winding up or administration. The challenge may be by the liquidator or administrator. In a liquidation (but not an administration), a creditor may challenge, whether his debt arose before or after the commencement of the winding up. The Act applies to any transfer of property or discharge of any claim or right, whatever the date, provided it became completely effectual on a "relevant day". The term "completely effectual", which is not defined in any of the legislation, presumably means when the transferee completes his

---

[6] *Re Parkes Garage (Swadlincote) Ltd* [1929] 1 Ch. 139.

[7] See further *Goudy on Bankruptcy* (4th edn.) Ch.III; Scottish Law Commission Report on Bankruptcy, etc. (No.68, February 25, 1982) paras 12.1–12.12.

[8] *Bank of Scotland, Petitions,* 1988 S.L.T. 282 (aff'd 1988 S.L.T. 690); *Stuart Eves Ltd (in liq.) v Smiths Gore,* 1993 S.L.T. 1274.

real right to the property in question. A "relevant day" is a day not earlier than two years before the commencement of winding up (or administration as the case may be), except where the beneficiary of the transaction is an "associate" of the company, when the period is extended to five years. The definition of "associate" for the purposes of s.242 is that contained in the Bankruptcy (Scotland) Act 1985, s.74, as extended to companies by the Bankruptcy (Scotland) Regulations 1985.[9] The Bankruptcy Act definition is close to, but not identical with, the similar definition in the Insolvency Act, s.435(2).

Although s.242 was effective on April 1, 1986, as noted above it cannot be used in respect of any floating charge created prior to December 29, 1986 (see para.30–50).

It is a defence to a challenge under s.242 if the holder of the charge **30–56** proves that at the time of, or at any time after, the alienation the company's assets were greater than its liabilities. It is also a defence that the consideration was adequate. A reasonable gift is protected, provided that it was "a birthday, Christmas or other conventional gift" to any person or a gift for charitable purpose to a person who is not an associate of the company; in this case "associate" has the meaning in s.435. "Charitable purpose" is given a wide interpretation (s.242(5)). As a result of s.242(4)(a), an alienation made at a time when the company was insolvent, provided it is proved that it became solvent (in the "absolute" sense) at any subsequent date, is not subject to attack under the Act. As this argument is not available against a challenge at common law, s.242 would appear to have increased the attraction of using the common law basis of challenge.

While it is difficult to envisage circumstances in which a floating charge **30–57** might in itself be interpreted as a "gratuitous alienation", there is no doubt that the Insolvency Act contemplates the possibility. Schedule B1, para.39 (like it predecessor s.9(3)) provides inter alia that the holder of a charge entitled to appoint an administrative receiver cannot prevent an administrator being appointed if the security is challengeable under s.242 or any rule of law in Scotland (i.e. at common law). Section 244(5) implies that an "extortionate credit transaction" is a gratuitous alienation, but s.242 is not limited (as is s.244) to transactions within three years of liquidation, etc. The release of a security by the company is an "alienation".[10]

Section 242(4) provides that if the court reduces a transaction as a **30–58** gratuitous alienation, it may order restoration of property to the company, which would permit recovery from the holder of the charge of the proceeds of realisation by any receiver whom he has appointed[11] but this is without prejudice to rights acquired in good faith and for value from the receiver. Although s.242(4) refers to reduction or restoration or other redress a

---

[9] SI 1985/1925, para.11.
[10] *Rankin and Meek,* 1995 S.L.T. 526.
[11] *Mace Buildings (Glasgow) Ltd v Lunn* [1986] Ch. 459; [1987] Ch. 191.

remedy other than reduction may only be granted if restoration is impossible.[12]

30–59 **(d) Fraudulent or unfair preferences.** As in the case of gratuitous alienations, a floating charge may only be attacked as a fraudulent or unfair preference at common law or by statute, if it was created on or after December 29, 1986. In addition, possibly, a floating charge created before November 17, 1972 may be open to challenge on this basis.

At common law, any transaction by which a creditor obtains a preference over other creditors directly or indirectly from the company is reducible at the instance of any creditor who can show prejudice, or the liquidator. The challenger has to show that the preference was voluntary, that the liabilities of the company exceeded its assets (i.e. "absolute insolvency"), and that the company was aware of its insolvency. The burden of proof, at common law, lies with the challenger. The statutory presumption in his favour provided by the Bankruptcy Act 1696, c. 5 (of the Scottish Parliament) was repealed on April 1, 1986, and is, accordingly, not available to a challenge at common law of a floating charge.

An involuntary transaction is not a preference at common law. If the company undertakes to grant a security at a time when its obligation could not be impugned, the subsequent granting of the security at any time up to the commencement of winding up cannot be challenged.[13] A *"novum debitum"*, where the company grants security in respect of some fair and present consideration, is not a preference.[14] A security for a new loan or a substituted security for an existing loan is protected by this rule. The provision of the new consideration and the granting of the security do not require to be simultaneous, provided they are *unico contextu.*[15]

30–59A The statutory basis for challenging a preference was amended with effect from April 1, 1986 by the Bankruptcy (Scotland) Act 1985, Sch.7, para.20. These provisions are now consolidated as the Insolvency Act 1986, s.243. The common law rules are expressly preserved (s.243(6)). As with gratuitous alienations, the Act explicitly envisages the possibility of a challenge to a floating charge under these provisions and at common law (Insolvency Act 1986, s.9(3)). As noted above, however, s.243 can only be used to challenge a floating charge created on or after December 29, 1986.

An "unfair preference" open to challenge under the section is any transaction which creates a preference in favour of a creditor to the prejudice of the general body of creditors, and which was created not

---

[12] *Short's Trustee v Chung,* 1991 S.L.T. 472. *Cay's Trustee v Cay,* 1999 S.L.T. 321; *Baillie Marshall Ltd (in liq.) v Avian Communication Ltd,* 2002 S.L.T. 189; *Nottay's Trustee v Nottay,* 2001 S.L.T. 769; *Short's Trustee v The Registers of Scotland,* 1994 S.L.T. 65; 1996 S.L.T. 166 (HL); *Short's Trustee v Chung (No.2),* 1998 S.L.T. 200, aff'd 1999 S.L.T. 751; 1999 S.C. 50.

[13] *T v L,* 1970 S.L.T. 243; *Turnbull v Liquidator of Scottish County Investment Co Ltd,* 1939 S.C. 5; *Bank of Scotland, Petitioners,* 1988 S.L.T. 282, aff'd 1988 S.L.T. 590

[14] *Nordic Travel Ltd v Scotprint* [1980] S.L.T. 189; 1980 S.C. 1.

[15] *Thomas Montgomery & Sons v Gallacher,* 1982 S.L.T. 138; *Renton & Gray's Trustees v Dickison,* 1880 7 R. 971; *Roy's Trustees v Colville and Drysdale,* 1903, 5 S. 769; *T v L,* above; *Nicoll v Steelpress,* 1993 S.L.T. 533.

earlier than six months before the commencement of the winding up or the making of an administration order (s.243(1)). A preference is made on the day on which it became "completely effectual" (s.243(3)), and this phrase, as under s.242, is undefined, but is presumed to mean the day on which the real right in favour of the transferee, etc. was completed. The challenge under the Act can be at the instance of the liquidator or the administrator, and also (in the case of a liquidation only) of any creditor by virtue of a debt incurred on or before the commencement of the winding up (including an assignee) (s.243(4)).

There are a number of defences, of which only one is directly relevant to the holder of a floating charge. The section does not apply to a transaction whereby the parties undertake reciprocal obligations (whether the performance by the parties of their respective obligations occurs at the same time, or at different times), unless the transaction was collusive, with the purposes of prejudicing the general body of creditors (s.243(2)(c)). This would protect a *novum debitum,* on a similar basis to the protection afforded at common law.

The effective date in determining whether a preference is reducible **30–60** under s.243 is the date on which it is made "completely effectual" (i.e. the funds are completely removed from the control of the company),[16] a floating charge which is created within the six month period is open to challenge under s.243 (in contrast to the common law rule) notwithstanding that it may be in implement of a prior obligation.

Under s.243(5), (like s.242), the reduction of the charge as an unfair preference may be accompanied by an order to restore property alienated by the company (for the benefit of the general body of creditors) or other redress. However, as with s.243 damages or other remedy should only be granted if restoration is impossible.[17] This would appear to make it possible for the court to require payment of the proceeds of realisation by a receiver appointed on the charge;[18] but s.243(5) preserves the right of any third party acquired in good faith and for value.

(e) Extortionate credit transactions. The Insolvency Act 1986, s.244 **30–61** provides for the reduction of a transaction, if it is for the provision of credit on "extortionate" terms. It applies in the same circumstances as s.238, i.e. when the company goes into liquidation or administration, and the challenge to the transaction can be made by the liquidator or the administrator as the case may be.

Section 244 applies to any transaction to which the company "is or has been a party", so long as it obtained credit thereby. It applies to a transaction entered into in the period of three years ending with the date the company enters administration or (as the case may be) the commencement of liquidation. It can, therefore, apply to a transaction where the

---

[16] *Short's Trustee v Chung,* etc. (para.30–58, fn.12, above.

[17] *Craiglow Developments Ltd v Wilson,* 1998 S.L.T. 1046; [1998] B.C.C. 530.

[18] *cf. Mace Builders (Glasgow) Ltd v Lunn,* above.

company has ceased to be a party, e.g. if the company has repaid the advance provided on the extortionate terms.

The definition of "extortionate" is if, having regard to the risk assumed by the person providing the credit, the terms require grossly exorbitant payment or are otherwise in gross contravention of ordinary principles of fair dealing (s.244(3)). The onus lies with the lender to prove the contrary.

The court can set aside the transaction or vary its terms, including the terms of the security provided, and require repayment to the administrator or liquidator of any sums paid by the company. The court can require the surrender of security and provide for an accounting.

30–62 **Charge not registered.** If the charge was not duly presented for registration under s.410 of the Companies Act 1985, the appointment of a receiver is not automatically invalid. Section 410 (as amended by the Insolvency Act 1985) provides only that the unregistered charge is "void against the liquidator or administrator and any creditor of the company", and that any money secured is immediately repayable. The charge remains valid until challenged by the liquidator, administrator or any creditor, and can form the basis for the appointment of a receiver.[19] Late registration under s.420 of the Companies Act 1985 would, in any event, cure such a defect even after a receiver has been appointed, provided the charge-holder applies as soon as he discovers the defect.[20] The appointment of a liquidator would not necessarily prevent late registration.[21] Accordingly, the reference in s.410 to the charge being "void against the liquidator and any creditor", can only be interpreted procedurally.

30–63 **Instrument of appointment alleged to be invalid.** The Insolvency Act 1986, s.53 does not indicate the effect of a defect in the instrument of appointment; but s.63(2) of the Act implies that this renders the appointment invalid. If the receiver has failed to accept office before the end of the business day following that on which he received the instrument of appointment, s.53(6) provides that the appointment is to be "of no effect", so that the charge cannot crystallise. Since, however, acceptance may be oral, the evidence of such a defect may not be readily available, unless it is apparent from the written docquet endorsed on the instrument (s.53(6)(b)) or the Form 1 (Scot) filed with the Registrar of Companies and the Accountant in Bankruptcy (Receivers (Scotland) Regulations 1986, para.4). If tainted by such a defect, the appointment is invalid and the receiver is personally liable for his acts, on the same basis as if the original charge was invalid.

30–64 **Lack of qualification.** The appointment of a person who is not an insolvency practitioner to be an administrative receiver is valid, and is effective to crystallise the charge. The person appointed is, however, guilty

---

[19] *Burston Finance Ltd v Speirway Ltd* [1974] 3 All E.R. 735.
[20] *Victoria Housing Estates Ltd v Ashpurton Estates Ltd* [1982] 3 All E.R. 665.
[21] *Re R M Arnold & Co Ltd* [1984] B.C.L.C. 535.

of a criminal offence under s.389 of the Insolvency Act 1986 if he acts in that capacity. If he finds himself in this position, he should formally vacate the office to enable a duly qualified successor to be appointed. The same applies to the appointment of any other disqualified person.

Statutory relief for accepting invalid appointment. Section 63(2) of the Insolvency Act 1986 provides that: **30–65**

> "Where the appointment of a person as a receiver by the holder of a floating charge is discovered to be invalid (whether by virtue of the invalidity of the instrument or otherwise), the court may order the holder of the floating charge to indemnify the person appointed against any liability which arises solely by reasons of the invalidity of the appointment".

In its original form (as s.23(2) of the 1972 Act, s.479 of the Companies Act 1985), the equivalent provision gave the person purportedly appointed a right to indemnity at the discretion of the court, only if the floating charge "is discovered to be invalid". The revised law clearly extends the protection to defects relating to the instrument of appointment, but it is still uncertain whether every possible ground of attack is within the Act. It applies only to the appointment by the holder of a floating charge, not to an appointment by the court. A defect which might invalidate the appointment if made by the court, therefore, cannot be the basis for an application under s.63(2); for example, if there is not a valid "floating charge" upon which the appointment could have been made.

The Act does not provide any criteria upon which the court might exercise its discretion, and there have been no reported cases on the former provisions or on the 1986 Act to offer guidance. Presumably, the court will treat each case on its merits, and refuse or limit the indemnity only where the receiver himself has occasioned the defect, e.g. by late acceptance, or has continued to act when he knew or ought to have known of its existence.

Invalid appointments and third parties. Section 55(4) of the 1986 Act provides that "a person dealing with a receiver in good faith and for value is not concerned to enquire whether the receiver is acting within his powers". Third parties, therefore, have to concern themselves with whether the receiver's appointment is valid, and whether there are other receivers appointed to act jointly. Where there are joint receivers, acting separately, third parties have also to satisfy themselves that this is authorised by the terms of their appointment. **30–66**

A third party transacting with a receiver invalidly appointed has no automatic right of recourse against the holder of the charge. If he suffers loss, his primary remedy is against the receiver personally; but if the holder was to any extent responsible for effecting an invalid appointment, the holder also may be liable in damages.

G. Cessation of Office

30–67 The 1972 Act required a receiver appointed by the court to obtain leave of the court before resigning (1972, s.22(2); Companies Act 1985, s.478(2)). This requirement no longer applies to receivers appointed after December 29, 1986.

Under the 1986 Act, s.62, and the Regulations, a receiver may resign by notice in writing of at least seven days. Such notice must be given to the holder of the charge under which he has been appointed, the holder of any other floating charge, any other receiver, the members of the committee of creditors (if any) and the company or, if it is in liquidation, its liquidator (Insolvency Act 1986, s.62(1) and reg.6). The notice must specify the date it is to take effect (1986 Regulations, para.6). Within 14 days of his resignation taking effect, the receiver must notify the Registrar of Companies and the Accountant in Bankruptcy (1986 Act, s.62(5) (as amended)). The prescribed form is Form 3 (Scot) in the 1986 Regulations (as amended).

Because "refloating of the charge" (see below) may follow if a receiver is not replaced, a receiver may be liable in damages if he fails to give proper notice to those entitled to receive it, particularly the holder of the charge, under s.62 and reg.6.

30–68 **Death of receiver.** If a receiver dies, the holder of the charge by virtue of which he was appointed must give notice forthwith of his becoming aware of the death to the Registrar of Companies and the Accountant in Bankruptcy, to the members of the creditors' committee (if any) to the company or, if it is in liquidation, the liquidator, and to the holder of any other floating charge and any receiver appointed by him (Insolvency Rules 1986, r.3.10 (as amended); Form 3.3 (Scot)). In view of the risk of refloating if no replacement has been appointed within one month, it is therefore important for the holder of the charge to keep sufficient contact with the activities of the receiver to ensure that he is aware of his death, if it occurs, as quickly as possible.

30–69 **Removal of a receiver.** A receiver may be removed by order of the court (Insolvency Act 1986, s.62(3); see also r.74.19 of the Rules of the Court of Session and Sh.Ct.R. 17), whether he was originally appointed by the court or by the holder of the charge. Although the Act refers only to an application by the holder of the charge for removal, it is suggested that the Court of Session could entertain an application for removal by any other interested party, such as the company or a creditor, by virtue of its *nobile officium.*[22] The holder of the charge must give notice to the Registrar of

---

[22] *Toynar Ltd v Whitbread & Co Ltd,* 1988 S.C.L.R. 35, though not strictly in point, shows the court entertaining an application by the company for suspension and interdict of the appointment; the action was directed against the charge holder, and an interim order was refused.

Companies and the Accountant in Bankruptcy of the order removing the receiver within 14 days (Insolvency Act 1986, s.62(5); Form 3 (Scot) prescribed by the 1986 Regulations). The notice is entered in the company's register of charges.

Vacation of Office

(a) Loss of qualification. As noted above, an "administrative receiver" must be a duly qualified "insolvency practitioner". If the receiver ceases to hold the appropriate qualification, he must forthwith vacate office. Within 14 days, the receiver must give notice to the Registrar for entry in the Register of Charges. He must also give notice to the holder of the charge under which he was appointed, the members of the creditors' committee (if any), the company, or, if it is in liquidation, the liquidator, and the holder of any other floating charge and any receiver appointed by him, and to the Accountant in Bankruptcy (Insolvency Act 1986, s.62(5) (as amended); Insolvency Rules 1986, r.3.11 (as amended); the Form is prescribed by the 1986 Regulations, Form 3 (Scot)). **30–70**

(b) Completion of receivership. From the wording of the Insolvency (Scotland) Rules 1986, r.3.11, it is clear that a receiver who has completed the receivership does not resign but vacates office. The Rules require him to give notice in the same form and to the same persons as would be required if he vacated office on ceasing to be duly qualified (see (a), above); but, of course, in these circumstances the Rules apply whether he is "an administrative receiver" or otherwise. **30–71**

There is no provision in the Act or the Rules to define when a receiver has completed his duties otherwise than, obviously, by complete satisfaction of the charge-holders' claim. If the receiver decides that, although the charge-holders' claim has not been fully satisfied, he cannot realise any further assets, it appears to be open to the receiver either to resign or to intimate that he is vacating office on completion of the receivership. If the holder of the charge disagrees, it is open to him to appoint a successor.

(c) Vacation on adminstration. The Insolvency Act 1986, Sch.B1, para.41(1) provides that, on the making of an administration order, any administrative receiver shall vacate office. He is required to notify the Registrar of Companies and the Accountant in Bankruptcy within 14 days (s.62(5) (as amended); Form 3 (Scot) in the 1986 Regulations). An administrator cannot be appointed by the holder of a floating charge, by the company or by its directors if an administrative receiver is in office (Sch.B1, paras 17(b) and 25(c)), but this does not apply if the receiver is not "administrative". A receiver of part only of the company's property remains in office, unless and until the administrator requires him to vacate (Sch.B1, para.41(2)). The receiver's remuneration and expenses, together with any indemnity to which he is entitled out of the assets of the company, become a charge on the property which was in his custody or control, in priority to **30–72**

the security of the charge-holder. Payment is, however, in the hands of the administrator, and the receiver cannot enforce his indemnity without the consent of the administrator or the court (Sch.B1, paras 41(3)(a) and (4) and 43)). The indemnity to which he is entitled is defined in s.62(4) (see below). The receiver is released from any obligation to meet preferential debts under s.59 (Sch.B1, para.41(3)(b)).

30–73 **(d) Indemnity to a receiver who has vacated office.** The Insolvency Act 1986, s.62(4) provides that when a receiver vacates office his remuneration, and any expenses properly incurred by him and any indemnity to which he is entitled out of the property of the company, shall be paid out of the assets subject to the floating charge. In terms of s.60(1), such sums are payable after sums due to the holders of fixed or *pari passu* securities, the holders of effectual diligence and creditors of the receivership, but ahead of any payment to preferential creditors. The reference to "any indemnity to which he is entitled" relates to s.57(2) and (3), under which a receiver who incurs personal liability for contracts entered into in the course of his duties is entitled to be indemnified out of the property in respect of which he was appointed.

30–74 Before the 1986 Act, the receiver's right of indemnity was more general (1972 Act, s.22(4); Companies Act 1948, s.478(4)). It applied in any circumstances "where a receiver ceases to act as such". The 1986 provision (both in its original form in s.11 and now in Sch.B1, para.41), however, only applies where he "vacates office". The only circumstances where the Act and the Rules refer to vacation of office are if he ceases to be qualified to act as an insolvency practitioner in relation to the company (s.62(2)), and on the completion of the receivership (1986, r.3.11). Section 62(3), however, provides that, "subject to the next sub-section", a receiver may be removed by the court. The next sub-section is, of course, s.62(4), which confers a right of indemnity on a receiver who "vacates office", described above. Accordingly, it appears to be the intention of the Act that a receiver who is removed by the court is entitled to the same indemnity in respect of his remuneration, expenses and liability out of the property subject to the charge as a receiver who vacates office. There is nothing in the Act to suggest that the court can impose conditions upon the removal order, such as to limit that right of indemnity.

30–75 No right of indemnity is conferred by s.62 on a receiver who resigns. Section 60(1)(d), however, accords to the receiver a priority in respect of his remuneration, expenses and liabilities, in terms which infer that these rights subsist, notwithstanding his resignation. It is, however, unfortunate that the Act has not clarified the position and removed the possibility of a receiver who has resigned being placed in a worse position than one who has been removed by the court or vacated office.

Refloating of Charge

If on the expiry of one month, following the removal of a receiver or his ceasing to act, no other receiver has been appointed, the floating charge by virtue of which he was appointed "refloats". It will cease to attach to the property previously subject to the charge, and again subsist as a floating charge over such assets as remain within its scope. The directors of the company resume control (or if there is a postponed receiver in office, his suspended powers revive). If the company is in liquidation, control of the assets subject to the charge passes to the liquidator. If an administration order has been granted in respect of the company, for the purpose of calculating the period of one month, the period during which that order has been in force is to be ignored (Insolvency Act 1986, s.62(6)). Refloating in terms of the Act is automatic, and those whose rights may be affected thereby should therefore ensure that they become aware of the event which has caused the receiver to cease acting, whether or not formal notice as required by the Act and Rules has been given by him or by the holder of the charge. **30–76**

H. Powers of Receiver

General and statutory powers. In contrast to the position in England, where (until 1986) a receiver's powers depended solely on the debenture deed or the equitable jurisdiction of the courts, receivers in Scotland have always had extensive statutory powers (subject to any express limitation in the instrument of charge). It was, of course, necessary to provide such powers in 1972, when the holders of charges created under the 1961 Act were given the right to appoint a receiver, since their instruments of charge could not have contained any such provision. **30–77**

The receiver has, in relation to the property attached, such powers (if any) as are conferred by the instrument creating the charge (Insolvency Act 1986, s.55(1)). In addition, he has the powers specified in Sch.2 to the 1986 Act, "in so far as these are not inconsistent with any provision contained in that instrument" (s.55(2)). These provisions (but not Sch.2) are in substance identical to the former law (1972 Act, s.15(1); Companies Act 1985, s.471(1)) and make it clear that a receiver's powers may be added to or limited only by the instrument of charge (or any instrument of alteration), i.e. they are conferred by the company in creating the charge itself. It is not open to the holder of the charge (or the court) to modify his powers in the instrument of appointment.

The receiver can act only in relation to the property covered by the charge. He has no right or title to intromit with property over which the charge has not crystallised, and does so at his personal risk. **30–78**

In 1986, the opportunity was taken to modify and improve the recitation of powers, as given in s.471(1) of the Companies Act 1985, in some cases simply to remove archaic terminology (e.g. power (11)). Problems, however, remain (as discussed below). The list as now contained in Sch.2 of the 1986 Act is as follows, the amendments from s.471(1) being emphasised:

1. to take possession of, collect and get in the property from the company or a liquidator thereof[23] or any other person, and for that purpose to take such proceedings as may seem to him expedient;
2. to sell, feu, hire out or otherwise dispose of the property by public roup or private bargain, and with or without advertisement;
3. to *raise or* borrow money and grant security therefor over the property;
4. to appoint a solicitor or accountant or other professionally qualified person to assist him in the performance of his functions;
5. to bring or defend any action or other legal proceedings in the name and on behalf of the company;
6. to refer to arbitration all questions affecting the company;
7. to effect and maintain insurances in respect of the business and property of the company;
8. to use the company's seal (but see para.30–79 below);
9. to do all acts and to execute in the name and on behalf of the coinpany any deed, receipt or other document;
10. to draw, accept, make and endorse any bill of exchange or promissory note in the name and on behalf of the company;
11. to appoint any agent to do any business which he is unable to do himself, or which can more conveniently be donc by an agent and to employ and *dismiss employees.* (The original words were "discharge servants": the change has no legal significance);
12. *to do all such things (including the carrying out of works) as may be necessary for the realisation of the property.* (The original wording of this power was "to have carried out to the best advantage any work on the property of the company and in general to do all such other things as may be necessary for the realisation of the property". The change improves the wording and may remove a suggestion that if works were not done to "best advantage", the receiver was acting ultra vires);
13. to make any payment which is necessary or incidental to the performance of his functions;
14. to carry on the business of the company *or any part of it.* (The original wording, instead of "or any part of it", was "so far as he thinks it desirable to do so");

---

[23] *Manley, Petitioner,* 1985 S.L.T. 42.

15. to grant *or accept a surrender of a lease or tenancy of any of the property and to take a lease or tenancy* of any property required or convenient for the business of the company. (The original version referred to power "to input and output tenants", and did not mention "tenancy");
16. *to make any arrangements or compromise on behalf of the coinpany;*
17. *to call up any uncalled capital of the company;*
18. *to establish subsidiaries of the company;*
19. *to transfer to subsidiaries of the company the business of the company or any part of it and any of the property;*
20. to rank and claim in the bankruptcy, insolvency, sequestration or liquidation of any person or company indebted to the company, and to receive dividends and to accede to trust deeds for creditors of any such person; (There is no specific reference to power to accede to a voluntary arrangement under the insolvency Act 1986, s.1, but this must be competent under power (23));
21. to present or defend a petition for the winding up of the company;
22. *to change the situation of the company's registered office.* (A new power of obvious practical advantage to the receiver. However, the transfer of the records and registered address to the receiver's premises may increase the difficulty of the directors in discharging their continuing responsibilities);
23. to do all other things incidental to the exercise of the powers mentioned in s.55(1) (i.e. in the charge), or above.

The statutory powers in Sch.2 apply to any receiver appointed on or after **30–79** December 29, 1986, regardless of the date of the charge. Receivers appointed earlier have the powers in the former law. (See Insolvency Act 1986, Sch.11, para.3).

The statutory powers of a receiver are seldom modified in the instrument of charge (unless special circumstances exist). It is understood that institutions sometimes seek to clarify powers 16 (to include specifically a compromise with the charge-holder), and 17 (to ensure that a portion of uncalled capital maybe called up, not necessarily the whole). If uncalled capital is charged, however, this is subject to ss.120 and 124 of the Companies Act 1985 ("reserve liability" and "reserve capital").

The use of a common seal became unnecessary fron July 31, 1990, under the Companies Act 1989, s.130(3). Under the Requirements of Writing (Scotland) Act a document signed on behalf of the company by a receiver need not be witnessed unless it is to enter the property register or be registered for preservation in the Books of Council and Session, or if it is desired to benefit from the presumption that it has been duly signed. The consent of the liquidator (if any) is not required, since the receiver's powers take precedence.[24] In a disposition, the receiver should grant warrandice

---

[24] *Manley, Petitioner,* above.

from his own facts and deeds only, and expressly exclude personal liability (pursuant to s.57(2)).

30–80 An administrative receiver may obtain a court order to deliver property, or to examine persons in possession of assets or information, and is entitled to co-operation from directors and others under the Insolvency Act 1986, ss.234–236. The powers of a receiver must be exercised for the purpose of assisting him in his functions in that capacity, and not to further the interests of the charge-holder in collateral matters. Confidential or privileged information which the receiver obtains (whether under the statutory powers of ss.234–237 or otherwise) cannot be disclosed to the charge-holder, without either the permission of the person entitled to preserve confidentiality or the sanction of the court, if the purpose of that disclosure is to assist the charge-holder in pursuing a claim against a third party, such a guarantor of the debt secured by the charge. The directors of the company retain sufficient *locus* to take proceedings in the name of the company to restrain improper disclosure.[25]

Proceedings by Receiver

30–81 **(a) Power to bring actions.** Powers 1 and 5 both confer power to institute proceedings. Power 1 authorises a receiver "to take possession of, collect and get in the property" (which has been attached) "from the company, or a liquidator thereof or any other person, and for that purpose to take such proceedings as may seem to him expedient". Power 5 authorises him "to bring or defend any action or other legal proceedings in the name and on behalf of the company" (in relation to the property attached by the charge). The relationship between these powers, where they appear to overlap, has been the cause of much debate and confusion, not assisted by contradictory judicial decisions. It is regrettable that, when the list of powers was revised in 1986, the opportunity to clear up the confusion was not taken; indeed, the difficulty was "exported" to English receivers (and administrators in both countries) by Sch.1 of the 1986 Act.

30–82 It is clear that power 1 allows the receiver to take action in his own name and capacity to obtain possession or control of any asset or property which is attached by the charge. Equally, power 5 allows him to act in the name of the company as pursuer or defender in any proceedings which involve it in either capacity. In some situations, however, both powers are, prima facie, available. This is most apparent where the receiver seeks to recover a debt due to the company (although not necessarily confined to such a situation). Power 5 is clearly available to the receiver, but power 1 seems to apply also.

30–83 In *McPhail v Lothian Regional Council,*[26] it was held by Lord Grieve that both powers are available; and if the receiver sues in his own capacity under power 1, the defender cannot plead a defence, such as compensation (set-

---

[25] *First Tokyo Index Trust Ltd v Gould,* 1993 GWD 36–2298; *Sutton v GE Capital Commercial Finance Ltd* [2004] EWCA Civ 315; [2004] 2 B.C.L.C. 662 CA.

[26] 1981 S.L.T. 173; 1981 S.C. 109.

off), which would be available against the company, or the receiver suing in its name under power 5. This decision has been criticised on both counts (and not followed), but has not yet been overruled by higher authority. In *Taylor, Petitioner*[27] Lord Ross disapproved of the reasoning of his colleague, and held that power 1 was not available to sue for a debt (although it could be used to procure an assignation of the right to sue to the receiver), and that a defender could plead against the receiver any defence which was available against the company. This view has since been followed by Lord Kincraig, in *McPhail v Cunninghame District Council,*[28] and by Lord Prosser in *Myles J Callaghan Ltd v City of Glasgow District Council.*[29] In the latter, it was pointed out that, by what is now s.57(4) of the Insolvency Act 1986, contracts entered into by the company continue in force after a receiver has been appointed, and in terms of what is now s.57(1), the receiver is deemed to be the agent of the company in relation to the property which is attached. Also, in *Forth and Clyde Construction Co Ltd v Trinity Timber and Plywood Co Ltd,*[30] the Lord President observed that title to sue for a debt remained with the company, notwithstanding that crystallisation operated "as if" there had been the assignation and intimation necessary to constitute the charge as a fixed security.

In *Callaghan,*[31] after reviewing the previous decisions, Lord Prosser **30–84** concluded that power 1 was inappropriate for actions to vindicate the rights of the company, and should be confined to possessory remedies at the instance of the receiver. In the case before him, however, Lord Prosser was confronted by an action in which the pursuers were designated as "Myles J. Callaghan Ltd. (in Receivership) and Stuart Matthew Fraser, CA, the Receiver thereof", with no indication whether power 1 or power 5 was actually being invoked. While criticising this customary designation, as inconsistent with his view that power 5 only should have been used, and that the receiver should not have been referred to as a pursuer, he did not uphold the defenders' plea to the competency of the action thus raised. He "interpreted" it as being an action raised in the name of the company by the receiver under power 5. It may be that the views of Lord Prosser in *Callaghan* represent what is now the preferred construction of power 1; nevertheless, the statute does allow a receiver to bring proceedings in his own name for the recovery of property, and (in the absence of a specific prohibition) there is nothing improper in his doing so, even where power 5 might be more logical.

(b) Compensation (or set-off). Compensation (or set-off) is the right of a **30–85** defender to answer a claim (by the receiver) for payment (in whole or in part) on the basis that the pursuer (the company) is indebted to him. It has to be pleaded, and is not mandatory in Scots law. In the normal course, it

---

[27] 1982 S.L.T. 172.
[28] 1985 S.L.T. 149.
[29] 1987 S.C.L.R. 627; 1988 S.L.T. 227.
[30] 1984 S.L.T. 94, 97.
[31] fn.29, above.

can only be pled if both claim and counter-claim are liquid (or arise from the same contract), and both parties are creditor and debtor in the same capacity ("*concursus debiti et crediti*") e.g. both parties are pursuing claims due to them personally, even if the defender has acquired the debt due by the company by assignation from another creditor. The *concursus,* would be broken if, e.g. the claim was personal but the pursuer's debt was due by him as trustee. This rule is, however, modified in bankruptcy in two respects:

(i) illiquid claims can be compensated; and

(ii) claims acquired by assignation after bankruptcy cannot be compensated.

Modification (i) applies to insolvent receivership.[32] Modification (ii) is justified on grounds of public policy to prevent debtors of a bankrupt estate purchasing claims cheaply and then pleading compensation in respect of their own debts, to the prejudice of the general body of creditors. The rule certainly applies after sequestration (or its equivalent), and might also apply after notour bankruptcy, if the debtor acted *mala fides* or with notice of his creditor's bankruptcy.[33] In *Taylor, Petitioner,*[34] it was argued that similar principles should be applied in receivership. Lord Ross refused to do so, justifying his decision as follows:[35]

> "I am not satisfied that compensation should be disallowed for reasons of equity or public policy. The normal rules of compensation are plain (Gloag on *Contract* (2nd ed.) pp.644–645)). I see no ground for introducing into the law any fresh exception based on alleged public policy. There may well be reasons for certain exceptions in the case of bankruptcy or insolvency, but I see no ground for extending them to cases of receivership. As already pointed out, receivership is different to liquidation or bankruptcy, and there is no reason why the same rules should apply to these different situations".

With due respect for Lord Ross's reluctance to extend a rule based solely on "public policy", his reasons do not seem to be sufficient to justify his refusal to do so. Of course, it is right that "receivership" is different to bankruptcy and liquidation, and does not necessarily imply insolvency (though it usually does). If the company is insolvent, whether it is in receivership, liquidation, administration or the subject of a voluntary

---

[32] *William London & Son Ltd v Cunninghame District Council,* 1985 S.L.T. 149. Compensation applies to debts due to and by the Crown under the provisions of the Crown Proceedings Act 1947, s.35(2) as applied to Scotland by s.50 of that Act. Compensation is excluded in respect of taxes, duties or penalties due to or by the company; however, compensation is allowed in relation to VAT by virtue of the Finance Act 1994, s.47. In respect of all other claims due to or by different government departments, the Crown is treated as a single entity and compensation is allowed, subject to the leave of the court. See further Palmer's Company Law, paras 15.675 *et seq.*

[33] See *Goudy Bankruptcy,* 4th ed., pp.554–556.

[34] 1982 S.L.T. 172.

[35] 1982 S.L.T. 172, 176.

arrangement, the public policy considerations enunciated by *Goudy*[36] are equally relevant; indeed *Goudy* indicates that the rule might apply, even if no formal bankruptcy process has commenced. Lord Ross himself accepts that the rule is applicable in cases of insolvency. Receivership is a new concept (so far as the Scots law of insolvency is concerned), but it is not in itself sufficient reason for refusing to apply to it sound principles of general relevance.[37]

The Inner House in *Forth & Clyde Construction Co Ltd v Trinity Timber & Plywood Co Ltd*[38] moreover held that crystallisation effectively assigned charged book debts to the receiver, "as if" there had in fact been assignation to him duly intimated. It follows that the *concursus debiti et crediti* is broken because, although the receiver would sue for such debts in the name of the company as its deemed agent (Insolvency Act 1986, s.57(1), and would be using power 5), he is to be treated as its assignee in the capacity of representative of the charge-holder, and a claim acquired from a third party after crystallisation could not, therefore, be compensated against a claim by the receiver. This was conceded by the defenders in *McPhail v Cunninghame District Council.*[39] **30–86**

The Scottish Law Commission has recommended legislation to put this matter beyond doubt.[40]

In respect of counterclaims which subsisted at the time of crystallisation, receivers have sought to resist compensation which would otherwise have been available, on an argument, which was advanced in *Taylor,*[41] based on the statutory result of crystallisation, which is that a charge over debts due to the company takes effect "as if the charge was a fixed security over the property" (Insolvency Act 1986, ss.53(1) and 54(6); Companies Act 1985, s.463(2); the equivalent sections in the earlier Acts were in similar terms). In the case of a debt, such a fixed security would take the form of a duly intimated assignation. On the appointment of a receiver, the argument ran, he is deemed to have taken a fixed security over the debt which cannot be "devalued" by compensation. This argument, however, was rejected as unsound, because the property over which the charge subsisted was not the debt itself, but the *jus crediti* represented by the debt, subject to any defences pleadable against the company which must also, therefore, be pleadable against the receiver.[42] **30–87**

In *Myles J Callaghan Ltd v Glasgow District Council,*[43] Lord Ross's decision in *Taylor* on this point was followed; but a further attempt was made to argue that compensation could not be pled against a receiver as **30–88**

---

36 fn.33, above.
37 See further, Patrick, "Set-off and Receivership", 1988 J.L.S.S. 357, 392.
38 1985 S.L.T. 94.
39 1985 S.L.T. 149.
40 Consultative Memorandum No.72, "Floating Charges and Receivers" (October 1986), para.2–76.
41 1982 S.L.T. 172.
42 See *Taylor,* above.
43 1988 S.L.T. 227.

deemed assignee, on the basis that this was not one of the rights "saved" from the effect of crystallisation by what is now s.55(3) of the Insolvency Act 1986 (or s.463(1) of the Companies Act 1985), protecting holders of effectually executed diligence or prior securities. This also failed on the same grounds, that the receiver was open to any defence that could have been maintained against the company, and his position "as if" he were the holder of a fixed security was not completely analogous to an actual assignee.

30–89 Compensation can also be in question where the claim by the receiver arises *after* his appointment, and the debtor seeks to compensate a debt due by the company to him at the date of crystallisation. There appears to be no Scottish decision in point; but the Scottish Law Commission Memorandum[44] suggests that Scots Law should follow the English decision in *Rother Iron Works Ltd v Canterbury Precision Engineers Ltd*,[45] in holding that if a post-crystallisation debt arose from the receiver continuing the same contract from which the pre-crystallisation debt arose, there should be compensation, but not if the receiver had entered into a new contract.[46]

30–90 Special rules apply where the Crown is a party and compensation is sought (Crown Proceedings Act 1947, s.50(2)). Taxes and related debts due to the Crown cannot be met by a plea of compensation. A decree in absence against the Crown cannot be given effect, without leave of the court. Claims due to and by the same government department can be compensated; but if different departments are involved the leave of the Court is required.[47]

30–91 **(c) Power to defend proceedings and winding up petitions.** Statutory power 5 also authorises the receiver to defend proceedings in the name of the company, or to continue with its defence of an action already raised.[48] Even if the outcome of such proceedings does not affect the charge-holder's position, it is still necessary for the receiver to consider what steps should be taken to protect the company and its ordinary creditors, or any guarantors of its obligations, who may be prejudiced if the action is not defended (see further, para.30–98). The receiver should (if he is not to defend on behalf of the company) invite the directors to defend on the basis of their residual powers, or petition for a liquidation order under power 12 so that the liquidator (acting for the creditors generally) can decide whether to defend the proceedings.

In addition to general power 5, power 12 authorises the receiver to defend a petition for winding up. While a creditor petitioning on the

---

[44] See fn.40, above, at para.2.78.

[45] [1974] Q.B. 1.

[46] See also W A Wilson, "The Nature of Receivership", 1984 S.L.T. (News) 106.

[47] *Smith v Lord Advocate (No.2)*; *Secretary of State for Trade and Industry v Frid (Re West End Networks Ltd)* [2004] B.C.C. 525; [2004] 2 B.C.L.C. 1 (HL) (where the Crown claim arose by way of subrogation in respect of payments to employees of an insolvent company); 1980 S.L.T. 105.

[48] Including a petition for recall of diligence; *Iona Hotels Ltd v Craig* 1991 S.L.T. 11.

ground of the company's inability to pay its debts is prima facie entitled to a winding up order, the receiver may provide an effective answer by demonstrating that no assets will emerge to meet the claims of ordinary creditors. This will not, however, prevent the court ordering intimation and service of the petition.[49] If a liquidator is eventually appointed, of course, the receiver's powers are theoretically unaffected;[50] but there may be an indirect effect damaging to his position, e.g. if valuable contracts terminate on the granting of a winding up order. In such circumstances, the receiver should be able to persuade the court that granting the order will be to the disadvantage of the charge-holder and ordinary creditors, and have the petition at least sisted until the receivership is complete.

(d) Expenses. A receiver suing in his own name (under power 1) is liable personally for expenses if unsuccessful. If he sues or defends under power 5, any award of expenses will be against the company, but, as *dominus litis,* he could be made personally liable (if necessary by a separate action) if the company fails to satisfy the award.[51] In the light of his personal liability, there should, therefore, be no question of the receiver being required to find caution for expenses under the Companies Act 1985, s.726(2), unless he himself is unlikely to be able to meet them.[52] The expenses of unsuccessful proceedings are expenses of the receivership (r.7.31). **30–92**

Carrying on the business. The introduction of receivership to Scotland in 1972 was justified, inter alia, on the basis that it provided the opportunity (which was seldom, if ever, possible in an insolvent liquidation) to carry on the business of the company, which might be preserved and sold on as a going concern to the benefit of the charge-holder, other creditors and the employees (or even the shareholders). On occasion, this has happened for the company as a whole; but more often the receiver has been able to identify viable parts of its business for sale as separate units. There developed the practice of "hiving down" such parts into a subsidiary company (or companies) formed by the receiver, whose shares he then sold. Although the legitimacy of this practice was never seriously doubted, and was implicitly recognised by the Transfer of Undertakings (Protection of Employment) Regulations 1981,[53] it was thought desirable to add specific authority to the statutory list of powers. The amendment to power 14, and the addition of powers 18 and 19, are the result. The value of a hive-down to the receiver has diminished as a result of restrictions on carrying forward losses for tax purposes, which are not now available if the company is insolvent.[54] **30–93**

---

[49] *Foxhall & Gyle (Nurseries) Ltd, Petitioners,* 1978 S.L.T. (Notes) 29).

[50] *Manley, Petitioner,* 1985 S.L.T. 42.

[51] Maclaren on *Expenses,* pp.147–149, 151; *Myles J. Callaghan Ltd v City of Glasgow District Council,* 1987 S.C.L.R. 627, 630; 1988 S.L.T. 227.

[52] *Stewart v Steen,* 1987 S.L.T. (Sh.Ct.) 60.

[53] (SI 1981/1794). The 1981 Regulations have been replaced by the Transfer of Undertakings (Protection of Employment) Regulations 2006 (SI 2006/246) effective April 6, 2006. The point made in the text is not affected.

[54] Finance Act 1986, s.42 and Sch.10. (See now Income and Corporation Taxes Act 1988, ss.343 and 344.)

There is, however, a doubt about what is meant by carrying on "the business of the company" (power 14, and previously power (o) in s.15(1) of the 1972 Act, s.471(1) of the Companies Act 1985). Does this mean only that business which the company was actually carrying on when the receiver was appointed (or part thereof)? That would be too restrictive, since the company may have been forced (or have chosen) to abandon activities which the receiver could revive and sell advantageously. It would also be wrong to draw any analogy from the power of a liquidator to carry on the business of the company; since that is expressly limited to doing so "so far as may be necessary for its beneficial winding up" (see now Insolvency Act 1986, Sch.4, para.5), and has been restrictively interpreted by the courts, so as to exclude carrying on the business to enhance the value of its shares,[55] which is, of course, precisely why a receiver would wish to carry on the business. What is more doubtful is whether the receiver's statutory powers entitle him to embark on a new activity which would be *intra vires* the company, i.e. authorised by its objects, but which it had not chosen to attempt. There seems to be no reason why this should not be competent, and this may be a legitimate inference from his other powers, such as 12, 18, 19 and 23. The clear inference from power 14, however, is that the receiver is at liberty to abandon any part of the business of the company at his discretion, and cannot be compelled by specific implement to continue contracts which interfere with his decision (see further, paras 30–37—30–38).

30–94 **Contracts entered into by receiver: personal liability.** "A receiver is deemed to be the agent of the company in relation to such property as is attached by the floating charge" (Insolvency Act 1986, s.57(1)). The receiver's statutory agency is not affected by the liquidation of the company, in contrast to the position in England, where the agency of an administrative receiver terminates on liquidation (Insolvency Act 1986, s.44(1)(a)). In the exercise of his powers, therefore, he acts on behalf of the company and not in any personal capacity. This is not consistent with power 1 in Sch.2 to the Act, as it has been interpreted (see pp.516–518), which is regarded as conferring on him a personal right to take proceedings for recovery of property belonging to the company. Further, unlike agents in the general law, a receiver is presumed to incur personal liability on any contract entered into by him in the performance of his functions, unless the contract otherwise provides (s.57(2)). Such liability may be to the charge-holder who appointed him.[56] Exclusion need not be express; an implied term is sufficient.[57] There is an apparent inconsistency between s.57(1), in terms of which a receiver is *deemed* to be the company's agent and therefore, under the law of agency not personally liable for contracts entered into on behalf of the company, and s.57(2), under which he is to be

---

[55] *Re Wreck Recovery and Salvage Co* (1880) 15 Ch.D. 353, C.A.
[56] *Manley, Petitioner,* 1985 S.L.T. 42.
[57] *Hill Samuel Ltd v Laing,* 1988 S.L.T. 452; (1988) B.C.C. 9; aff'd. 1989 S.L.T. 760; [1991] B.C.C. 665.

personally liable on any contract "entered into by him in the performance of his functions except in so far as the contract otherwise provides" (modified in relation to employment contracts). (In practice, receivers avoid the impact of s.57(2) by excluding personal liability.[58]) It is suggested that the correct interpretation of s.57(1) is that it is worded so as to emphasise that the receiver's agency (qualified inter alia by s.57(2)) is restricted to such property as is attached, and that he is not a general agent for the company (an academic point in the case of "all-assets" charge). The receiver is, however, indemnified out of the property under his control (and limited to its value), not by the holder of the charge, in respect of any liability arising from s.57(2) (s.57(3)). This statutory indemnity is without prejudice to any other right of indemnity to which he may be entitled, e.g. by contract from the charge-holder, and a receiver cannot escape personal liability for ultra vires acts (s.57(6)). The receiver's claim for indemnity ranks after the rights of fixed charge creditors ranking prior to or *pari passu* with the charge, the holders of effectual diligence, and creditors of the receiver personally (Insolvency Act 1986, s.60(1)(a)–(c)) (For the position of a receiver whose powers are suspended by the appointment of a receiver on a prior charge, see para.30–27).

Section 57(1) raises a presumption that, in continuing with a contract entered into before his appointment, the receiver is acting as agent for the company and is not acting on his own account. It is not clear, however, what will rebut this presumption. In *Inverness District Council v Highland Universal Fabrications Ltd,*[59] it was suggested (obiter) that the receiver must be shown to have acted solely in his own interests, and without regard to the interests of the charge-holder or the company, a situation which presupposes misconduct on his part. **30–95**

Neither the receiver nor (after the appointment of a receiver) the charge-holder can be liable for "wrongful trading" under s.214 of the Insolvency Act. Section 214 applies only to directors or "shadow directors", and the definition of a shadow direction is "a person in accordance with whose directions or instructions the directors of the company are accustomed to act" (Companies Act 1985, s.741(2)). A receiver, acting on his own authority, or the charge-holder "directing" him, fall outwith this definition. However, a receiver may be liable for "fraudulent trading" under the Insolvency Act 1986, s.213, if he excludes personal liability for debts he knows will not be paid.[60] He will not be exposed to such liability if he merely continues the company's occupation of premises knowing that rent and rates will only have an unsecured ranking and are unlikely to be paid.[61] **30–96**

Securities over charged assets. If property within the charge is burdened with a prior or *pari passu* security, or effectually executed diligence, the receiver will require the consent of the creditor concerned to dispose of the **30–97**

---

[58] Such an exclusion extends to claims based on negligence in the performance of the contract; *Stewart v Engel* [2000] B.C.C. 741.

[59] 1986 S.L.T. 556.

[60] *Leyland DAF Ltd v Automotive Products Plc,* etc. [1996] B.C.C. 389.

[61] *Re Sobam BV* [1996] B.C.C. 531; *McKillop, Petitioner,* 1995 S.L.T. 216.

property, and his co-operation in discharging the security or diligence; alternatively, the receiver can obtain authority to sell from the court (Insolvency Act 1986, s.61).

The court's power is discretionary, and it may impose such conditions as it thinks fit (s.61(2)). The court order is to be filed with the registrar of companies within 14 days (s.61(6)). The receiver's conveyance, etc. and completion of the disponee's title (or equivalent), has the effect of disburdening the property from the security or diligence (s.61(8)). The creditor, if not paid in full, retains his ranking in the winding up of the company (s.61(9)).

Before 1986, the court was unable to sanction the sale of an asset subject to a prior security, unless it had been met or satisfied in full (Companies Act 1985, s.477). Under the 1986 Act (s.61(3)–(5)), however, the court can authorise a sale, if satisfied that this is likely to be the most advantageous method of realisation. The net proceeds must be applied towards the secured creditor's claim. If the court is persuaded that a sale by the receiver is going to prove less beneficial (to the creditor) than an open market sale, the receiver can obtain his order on agreeing to make good the deficiency. This is likely to be attractive only if the receiver is selling the burdened asset along with other assets, or the business as a going concern. These conditions (like s.477 before them) do not affect the court's power to authorise a sale, where the burden is a *pari passu* security or an effectually completed diligence.

The requirements of s.61 cannot be used to protect ineffectual diligence such as an inhibition (alone); but if the receiver contracts to sell with "clear searches", he may be obliged to satisfy the inhibitor or obtain an order under s.61 to fulfil the contract.[62]

If (as seems to be correct, notwithstanding *Cumbernauld Development Corp v Mustone),*[63] a landlord's hypothec should be regarded as a right in security, s.61 can be used to obtain a discharge from such a claim.[64]

It is unsettled whether rent payable to a company in receivership by a tenant of subjects burdened with a standard security properly belongs to the receiver, or to the standard security creditor. It appears that, in practice, the receiver concedes the issue for reasons of expediency.

30–98 **General duties of receiver.** Neither the 1972 Act nor the 1986 amendments contain any statement of the general duties of a receiver in Scotland, such as is given for a liquidator (ss.107 and 143 of the 1986 Act), the supervisor of a voluntary arrangement (s.1 of the Act) or an administrator (s.17 of the Act). It is an inescapable inference from the context in which he is appointed, however, that his primary duty is to the holder of the charge by virtue of which he has been appointed.[65] Nevertheless, he cannot avoid a

---

[62] *Armour and Mycroft, Petitioners,* 1983 S.L.T. 453. *Taymech Ltd v Rush and Tompkins Ltd,* 1990 S.L.T. 681; *Iona Hotels Ltd v Craig,* 1991 S.L.T. 11.

[63] 1983 S.L.T. (Sh.Ct.) 55.

[64] This view was upheld in *Grampian Regional Council v Drill Stem (Inspection Services) Ltd,* etc. 1994 S.C.L.R. (Sh.Ct.) 36.

[65] See *Re Pearl Maintenance Services Ltd* [1995] B.C.C. 657.

degree of responsibility to other creditors and the company's shareholders or others, who will inevitably be affected by his actings. He has protection against summary removal by the charge-holder (s.62(3) of the 1986 Act, see para.30–69), and he can obtain guidance on any point of difficulty, or approval for a particular act, not only from the company, its directors or any individual who may be affected, but also from the creditors' committee (if any) or the court (s.63(1)). The Lord President in *Forth & Clyde Construction Co Ltd v Trinity Timber & Plywood Co Ltd*[66] confirmed that a receiver can choose how to go about the realisation of the property to satisfy the charge-holder at his discretion, and he is not affected by common law rules, which require a "catholic" creditor in possession (i.e. one in control of all the assets of a bankrupt) to have regard in deciding what assets to realise to the interests of a "secondary" creditor, whose (postponed) security extends to certain assets only; the receiver can realise such assets for the benefit of the charge-holder, even if that is to the prejudice of another creditor.

He must, however, "exercise care to see that he does not realise company assets for less than the value they might reasonably be expected to obtain". In that respect, he is in no different position to any secured creditor in possession, and he will be liable in damages to any person (the company, a creditor or a guarantor of the company's obligations), who suffers loss by virtue of his negligence regardless of the powers conferred on him by the security holder.[67] He is not, however, bound by the procedure which may be required of a heritable creditor, e.g. under the Conveyancing and Feudal Reform Act 1970, s.25.[68] Similar considerations arise where the receiver has to decide whether to defend proceedings against the company which do not affect the charge-holder (see para.30–91). A claim against the receiver for loss suffered by the company would be in the name of the company (authorised by the directors or members), not by the directors or shareholders personally.[69] An administrative receiver (but not any other receiver *qua* receiver) can be made liable to compensate the company for "misfeasance" under the Insolvency Act, s.212. A receiver may also be liable for negligence if he fails to take due care of property of third parties in his custody.

Protection of third parties. Section 55(4) of the Insolvency Act 1986 **30–99**
provides that "a person dealing with a receiver in good faith and for value is not concerned to enquire whether the receiver is acting within his powers". The previous wording (s.15(3) of the 1972 Act, s.471(3) of the

---

66 1984 S.L.T. 94, 97.

67 *Rimmer v Thomas Usher & Sons Ltd,* 1967 S.L.T. 7; *Standard Chartered Bank Ltd v Walker,* [1982] 1 W.L.R. 1410; *Lord Advocate v Maritime Fruit Carriers Co Ltd,* 1983 S.L.T. 357; *American Express International Banking Corp v Hurley* [1985] 3 All E.R. 564, 569; *Macrae v Henderson,* 1989 S.L.T. 423; *Larsen's Executrix v Henderson,* 1990 S.L.T. 498.

68 The English case of *Downsview Nominees Ltd v First City Corp Ltd* [1993] A.C. 295 (excluding a general duty of care) is not good law in Scotland; see the cases cited in fn.69 above.

69 *Newhart Developments Ltd v Co-operative Commercial Bank Ltd* [1978] Q.B. 814; *Watts v Midland Bank plc* [1986] B.C.L.C. 15.

Companies Act 1985) was significantly different: "A person transacting with a receiver shall not be concerned to enquire whether any event has happened to authorise the receiver to act". The change does not affect a person dealing with a (sole) receiver appointed before December 29, 1986 (see Insolvency Act 1986, Sch.11, para.3); so it remains necessary for third parties to ascertain the date of the receiver's appointment to determine which version is applicable. It is the date of the appointment of the receiver currently in office which is relevant, not the date of crystallisation of the charge (unless there are joint receivers where the first appointment was made before December 29, 1986) (see para.30–6).

Section 55(4) clearly only protects third parties against an allegation that the receiver was acting ultra vires. The onus of proving that he dealt with the receiver "in good faith and for value" lies with the third party. A third party with actual knowledge of a limitation of the receiver's powers is, presumably, acting in bad faith. Section 55(4) merely excuses third parties from the need to make inquiries, e.g. as to whether the "statutory powers" have all been granted, or even if a receiver acting beyond the powers expressed in Sch.2 had been granted the necessary extension. Section 55(4), however, does not extend to questions of the validity of the appointment or whether the property which is the subject of the transaction in fact falls within the charge under which the receiver purports to act.

If the receiver's action is intra vires, so far as a third party is concerned, it may still be an abuse of the receiver's powers. For example, he may be selling property at less than market value. A third party cannot be in good faith if this is done collusively, but even if the receiver is innocent, and the true value is known only to the third party, the onus of proving his good faith could not be satisfied.

30–100 If a transaction is successfully challenged, it is not clear from the Act whether it is void or merely voidable. This has important implications for those (other than the person dealing with the receiver) who derive rights from the transaction, e.g. subsequent purchasers. It would be unfortunate if the rules formerly (i.e. prior to the Companies Act 1989 amendments) applicable to ultra vires acts of the company were applied; and the better view would be that, as the agent of the company his ultra vires acts are voidable only.

30–101 **Powers of English or Northern Ireland receivers in Scotland and vice versa.**[70] A receiver appointed in either part of Great Britain, by virtue of a floating charge by a company, may exercise his powers in the other part of Great Britain "so far as their exercise is not inconsistent with the law applicable there" (Insolvency Act, s.72(1)). For this purpose, "receiver" includes "a manager and a person who is appointed both receiver and manager" (s.72(2)). There is no formal definition of the terms "manager" and "receiver and manager"; but the reference is obviously to persons appointed in England and Wales, under Ch.1 of Pt III of the Act, to a

---

[70] For other jurisdictions, see para.30–132.

position equivalent to a receiver in Scotland. The appointment of a receiver in England causes the floating charge to crystallise as it does in Scotland, but crystallisation may occur in English law on other events which are outwith the "cross-border" scope of s.72. An English receiver's powers have customarily been defined by the debenture (charge) under which he is appointed; but, like a receiver in Scotland, an administrative receiver in England is now presumed to have statutory powers (s.42 and Sch.1), and power to dispose of property which is burdened with a security (s.43), which are, in substance, the same as those of a Scottish receiver. The purpose of s.72 and its predecessor (s.15(4) of the 1972 Act) is to ensure that a receiver appointed under English law can exercise his powers in relation to Scottish property.[71] Except in regard to unusual powers conferred on the receiver by the instrument of charge (or its equivalent), there is unlikely to be any conflict between them and the *lex situs* which would inhibit a receiver operating in the "other" jurisdiction. The law under which he operates, however, remains that of the company's place of registration.

The original equivalent of s.72 was s.15(4) of the 1972 Act. This, in effect, gave an English receiver power to deal with property situated in Scotland, so far as his powers were not inconsistent with Scots law. It did not give equivalent powers to a Scottish receiver in respect of property in England. This was amended by the Administration of Justice Act 1977, s.7, which repealed s.15(4) and substituted a provision in the same terms as s.72 (1986), but referring to "the United Kingdom" (not "Great Britain"). Section 7 of the 1977 Act has not been repealed (although the Table of Derivations annexed to the Companies Act 1985 claims, misleadingly, that s.724 derives from it), so that, in relation to Northern Ireland, the "cross-border" powers of receivers still derive from the 1977 Act.

It is, however, doubtful whether s.72 is anything more than a statement ("for the avoidance of doubt" perhaps) of the obvious generality that someone appointed to administer an estate in a foreign jurisdiction may exercise his powers over property in Scotland, unless prevented from doing so by Scots law.

Since the 1961 Act first enacted that "it shall be competent under the law of Scotland for an incorporated company (whether a company within the meaning of the Act of 1948 or not) . . . to create . . . a floating charge", it has ceased to be a valid objection that the title of such a person to intromit with the assets in Scotland derives from a form of security not to be recognised or given effect in Scots law.

The Receiver and the Creditors

Statement of affairs. Section 66(1) provides that a receiver "shall" require some or all of the persons mentioned in s.66(3) to submit a statement of affairs in the prescribed form forthwith upon his appointment. There is no specific time limit; but since the receiver is required to submit a report **30–102**

---

[71] *Gordon Anderson (Plant) Ltd v Campsie Construction Ltd*, 1997 S.L.T. 7; *Norfolk House Plc (in receivership) v Repsol Petroleum Ltd*, 1992 S.L.T. 235.

within three months of his appointment, based on the information provided (s.67), the Act envisages the receiver taking steps to obtain a statement of affairs very shortly after his appointment. The terms of s.66(1) indicate that it is the receiver's duty to call for a statement of affairs, even if he considers that this is unnecessary; in that respect, his position is different from that of a liquidator appointed by the court, who, in a similar situation, has discretion whether to call for a statement of affairs (Insolvency Act 1986, s.131).

Unlike the situation in England, where only an "administrative receiver" can call for a statement of affairs (see Insolvency Act 1986, s.47), these provisions apply to all receivers in Scotland. This means, curiously, that a receiver of part only of the undertaking can (and must) obtain a statement of affairs relating to the whole property and undertaking; this information will, in such cases, be largely irrelevant. The general powers of the court would, however, permit such a receiver to obtain release from s.66 (see paras 30–128—30–130).

30–103 The persons among whom the receiver may choose to provide a statement of affairs are listed in s.66(3). Primarily, they are the current and former directors and secretaries of the company. In addition, however, the receiver can call for a statement from persons who, within one year prior to his appointment, were involved with the formation of the company, were employees of the company, or were officers or employees of a company which is or was itself a director or secretary of the company in receivership. For the purposes of s.66, "employment" includes a contract for services, so that self-employed persons are also included. In addition to his discretion to choose from among the list of potential providers of a statement of affairs, the receiver has power to release a person called upon to do so from that obligation, and he also has power to extend the time allowed; if the receiver refuses to grant a release or extension, the person concerned may apply to the court (s.66(5)).

In calling for a statement of affairs, the receiver must use the form prescribed by the Rules (r.3.2(1) and Form 3.1 (Scot)), and with the notice he must send a copy of the form of statement prescribed by the Receivers (Scotland) Regulation 1986 (Form 5 (Scot)[72]) for completion; the statement is to provide details of the assets, debts and liabilities of the company, the names and addresses of its creditors, and the particulars of any securities held by such creditors (s.66(3)). The person giving the statement must depone to it by affidavit on the prescribed form, subject to any extensions that may be allowed, within 21 days, beginning with the day after that on which the notice of requirement is received (s.66(4)). A default fine may be incurred for delay (s.66(6)). When received, the statement or statements must be retained in the sederunt book (r.3.2(3)).

---

[72] The Insolvency (Scotland) Amendment Order 2006 (effective April 6, 2006) purports to substitute an amended p.2 of Form 5 (Scot). However, the Order is defective in that it refers to "Form 5 (Scot) set out in Schedule 5 to the 1986 Rules". There is no Form 5 (Scot) in that Schedule. The reference is clearly intended to be to Form 5 (Scot) set out in the Regulations, but the Order does not bear to amend that form.

The receiver may allow a deponent providing a statement of affairs any expenses which the receiver considers to be reasonable, as expenses of the receivership. The receiver's decision can be reviewed by the court. A dispute over the question of expenses does not relieve a deponent of his duty to provide a statement or other information to the receiver (r.3.3).

Although the receiver is required to call upon at least one of those mentioned in s.66(3) to provide a statement, there is nothing to prevent him from releasing that person from the obligation, if he considers that no useful purpose would be served. Further, he is not prevented from making additional calls upon the same person or call for further statements from other persons if he considers that this is necessary.

In addition to providing the receiver with essential information to carry out his functions, the reports he receives under s.66 are to form the basis of his own report under s.67.

Report by receiver. The 1986 Act, s.67 requires the receiver to prepare a report (as discussed below) and provides for a general meeting of unsecured creditors to consider it and whether to appoint a committee of creditors. **30–104**

Like s.66, s.67 is not confined to "administrative receivers", but a receiver of part of the undertaking only might obtain release from the unnecessary burden of compliance from the court under s.63.

Under the 1986 Act, s.67, the receiver's report must be circulated within three months or such longer period as the court may allow. There is no prescribed form for the report, but the report must contain: **30–105**

(i) the events leading up to his appointment, so far as he is aware of them;

(ii) the disposal or proposed disposal by him of any property of the company and the carrying on or proposed carrying on by him of any business of the company;

(iii) the amounts of principal and interest payable to the holder of the floating charge by virtue of which he was appointed and the amounts payable to preferential creditors;

(iv) the amount (if any) likely to be available for the payment of other creditors; and

(v) material relating to the "prescribed part" (discussed below).

As discussed in Ch.29, by virtue of the Enterprise Act 2002, s.176A and the Insolvency Act 1986 (Prescribed Part) Order 2003 (SI 2003/2097) a receiver (whether or not "administrative") appointed by virtue of a floating charge created after September 15, 2003, is (subject to the terms of the Act and Order) required to make a "prescribed part" (calculated in terms of the Order) of the "net property" realised for the benefit of the charge-holder available for distribution to unsecured creditors. The Receivers **30–106**

(Scotland) Regulations, reg.7, were amended by the Enterprise Act 2002 (Consequential Amendments) (Prescribed Part) (Scotland) Order 2003 (SI 2003/2108), effective September 15, 2003) and now require the receiver's report under s.67 to state "to the best of his knowledge and belief" an estimate of the value of the "net property" and of the "prescribed part". The receiver is entitled to omit information which could seriously prejudice the commercial interests of the company, but the report must state that he has done so (reg.7(2)). The report must also state whether and, if so, why the receiver intends to apply to the court for an order under s.176A(5) disapplying s.176A on the grounds that the cost of making a distribution to unsecured creditors would be disproportionate to the benefits (reg.7(3)).

30–107 The report must also include a summary of the statement of affairs (or statements) submitted to the receiver under s.66, and any comments that he may have on such statement (s.67(5)). The receiver may, however, omit from his report any information which, in his opinion, would seriously prejudice the carrying out of his duties (s.67(b)).

A receiver, who is appointed to act jointly with an existing receiver or in place of a receiver who has died or who has ceased to act, is not required to submit a report under s.67, except in the case of a receiver dying or ceasing to act before the report has been completed (ss.65(2) and 67(7)).

Although the provisions relating to the report allow a receiver to comment on the statement or statements of affairs, e.g. as to any discrepancy among them, there is no obligation on him to do so. No obligation is placed upon the receiver to check the accuracy of any information given to him, and forming the basis of his report. Given the relatively short time within which the report must be prepared, this could not reasonably be expected. It would, however, be reasonable to expect a receiver to qualify his report, if he has any doubt as to the accuracy of the information or to indicate (by way of caution) that the report is based on information supplied to him.

30–108 The report must be sent to the Accountant in Bankruptcy,[73] to the holder of the floating charge under which he was appointed, to any trustees for secured creditors of the company, and to all secured creditors so far as he is aware of their addresses. According to the strict wording of the Act (s.67(1)), the receiver is not relieved from the duty to send a copy of the report to trustees for secured creditors if he does not know their addresses but, on the basis that the Act must be interpreted reasonably, he can hardly be expected to attempt circulation of a report to such persons. In theory, of course, the company's register of charges maintained under the Companies Act 1985, s.422 should provide this information. Section 67(9) defines "secured creditor" for this purpose as any creditor who holds a security over property of the company in respect of his debt.

In addition to circulating a copy of his report to secured creditors and others, the receiver must (unless excused under the Act) send a copy to all

---

[73] Substituted for the Registrar of Companies by the Scotland Act 1998, Sch.8, para.23.

unsecured creditors, so far as he is aware of their addresses; alternatively (and in practice more usually), he may publish a notice giving an address where unsecured creditors may obtain a free copy of his report. Such notice does not require to be published in the Edinburgh Gazette, but is to be published in a newspaper circulating in the area where the company has its principal place of business, or in such other newspaper as the receiver thinks most appropriate for bringing it to the notice of unsecured creditors (1986 Regulations, para.7(1)). If the company is in liquidation, the receiver must send his report to the liquidator within seven days of circulating it among secured creditors, and this relieves him from any obligation to send a copy to the unsecured creditors or to convene a meeting of unsecured creditors (see below), if the liquidator is appointed after the receiver, the receiver must submit his report to the liquidator within seven days of its circulation to secured creditors or the liquidator's appointment (whichever occurs later), and again, if he provides a liquidator with a statement within the period of three months after his own appointment, he is excused from circulating his report to unsecured creditors (s.67(4)).

Meetings of creditors. Unless the court otherwise directs, the receiver must **30–109** also convene a meeting of unsecured creditors, giving not less than 14 days notice, and lay a copy of his report under s.67 before the meeting. As a condition of applying to the court for relief from this obligation, the receiver must include within his report a statement of his intention to apply for that direction, and the report must be sent to unsecured creditors; any notice giving them an address for a copy must have been published at least 14 days before the hearing of his application (s.67(3)).

Meetings of creditors: procedure. The procedure for convening and **30–110** conducting a meeting of creditors in a receivership is laid down in Pt 7 of the 1986 Rules, as amended by the Insolvency (Scotland) Amendment Rules 1987 (SI 1987/1921), which took effect on January 11, 1988. The amendments apply to any receivership governed by the original Rules, i.e. where the receivership commenced on or after December 29, 1986. Further amendments (primarily relating to administration) were made by the Insolvency (Scotland) Amendment Rules 2003 (SI 2003/2111, effective September 15, 2003), and by the Insolvency (Scotland) Amendment Rules 2006 (SI 2006/734, effective April 6, 2006). The procedure in receivership is based on that for liquidation, and the relevant Rules are adapted from that procedure. The entitlement of a creditor to vote requires the submission of a claim pursuant to rr.4.15–4.17 (as applied) (r.7.9). The procedure laid down in the Rules may be modified by the court, and the court also has power to cure any defects in procedure under r.7.32.

The meeting must be convened for a "business day". This is defined (r.0.2) as any other day than a Saturday, a Sunday, Christmas Day, Good Friday or a day which is a Bank Holiday in any part of Great Britain. Paradoxically, therefore, a meeting of creditors in a Scottish receivership cannot be held on a day which is a Bank Holiday in England. The meeting is to commence between 10.00 am and 4.00 pm, and in fixing the date, time and place for the meeting, the receiver must "have regard to the convenience of the persons who are to attend" (r.7.2).

30–111 Not less than 14 days' notice must be given of the meeting. The receiver has the option of giving notice in writing to all unsecured creditors known to him or, subject to the approval of the court, by newspaper advertisement only. In considering whether to substitute public advertisement for notice by post, the court is directed to have regard to the cost of the advertisement and the assets available. The inference from the Rule (r.7.3(6)) is that public advertisement will be more expensive but that, of course, will not necessarily be the case. The receiver may also, if he considers it appropriate, publish a newspaper advertisement of the notice as well as giving notice by post to unsecured creditors individually.

In addition to the date, time and place of the meeting, the notice must state the purpose of the meeting (i.e. to consider the report by the receiver and whether to establish a creditors' committee), and who are entitled to attend and vote (i.e. the unsecured creditors). The notice must also indicate, pursuant to r.7.9, whether a creditor wishing to vote may be required to lodge his claim in the prescribed form with the receiver (Form 4.7 (Scot), as amended by the 1987 Amendment Rules[74]) and must explain that voting on resolutions will be by majority in value of those present in person or by proxy, pursuant to r.7.12.

30–112 Rules 7.21–7.23 prescribe in detail the method of giving notice by post, normally by letter sent to the last address of the creditor, either by first or second class post or personally. If posted, the notice is deemed to be received on the second "business day" after the date of posting (first class) or the fourth such day (second class), unless the contrary is proved. The receiver must prepare a Certificate of Posting, which should be endorsed on a copy of the notice and constitutes sufficient evidence that the meeting was convened accordingly, unless the contrary is shown.

A proxy form must be sent with any written notice. The 1987 amendments to the Rules prescribe a form (Form 4.29 (Scot)) which is compulsory in any notice issued after March 1, 1988. Rules 7.14–7.20 contain further provisions with regard to the persons who may be appointed and the duties of the proxy, the effect of which is summarised in the notes on Form 4.29 (Scot). The proxy must be lodged at or before the meeting at which it is to be used (r.7.16(2)).

30–113 Rule 4.15(2) allows the receiver to dispense with the formality of submitting a claim in the prescribed form with supporting vouchers, etc., and, considering the limited purpose of doing so in a receivership, this should be the normal course. If, however, he requires a formal claim, and there is any dispute about its value, the procedure for adjudication is the same as in liquidation procedure under rr.4.15–4.17 with the appropriate

---

[74] The Form inappropriately refers to a claim in the liquidation of the company, but is intended for other proceedings also.

modifications (r.7.9). The Rules in turn apply the relevant provisions of the Bankruptcy (Scotland) Act 1985 with further modifications. The receiver is obliged to adjudicate upon any claim submnitted and either accept or reject it, subject to further rights of appeal in the event of a dispute. In the context of receivership, however, the only purpose of submitting a claim is to entitle the creditor to vote on the question of whether to establish a committee of creditors and who should be nominated for it. The procedure does not affect the position in regard to the creditor's claim against the company, in the event of funds being available.

The receiver will act as chairman of the meeting, but he may appoint his **30–114** employee or another insolvency practitioner to act in his stead (r.7.5). A single creditor present in person or by proxy constitutes a quorum (r.7.7). The chairman may adjourn the meeting under r.7.8, if no creditor appears.

Voting on any resolution is in accordance with the value of claims (r.7.12). The chairman is to make up a report of the proceedings at the meeting listing the creditors present in person or by proxy, the terms of any resolution which is passed and the particulars of those appointed to be members of the creditor's committee (if any). The chairman is to sign a copy of the report and retain it in the sederunt book of the proceedings (r.7.13), and that report is deemed to be suffident evidence ol the matters contained therein (r.7.25).

A meeting is presumed to have been duly convened. even if not all those to whom notice of the meeting should have been given have received it (r.7.24).

Committee of creditors. The Cork Committee[75] proposed that statutory **30–115** authority be given to the formation of a committee of creditors, which had, in practice, been established on an informal basis in some receiverships. This proposal was also designed to some extent as a response to the request that receivers should be "accountable" to the ordinary creditors, a concept which the Cork Report and subsequent legislation, in general, rejected. In some cases, also, receivers found it useful to work with such a committee of creditors, where it was likely that the company could be "rescued", with a surplus emerging to meet unsecured claims, or where it seemed likely that the receivership would evolve into a liqudation in due course, probably with the same insolvency practitioner acting as liquidator.

The statutory basis for the committee of creditors now exists in s.68 of the 1986 Act. Normally, as noted above, the decision to appoint a committee of creditors and the nomination of members on it is taken at the only creditors' meeting in a receivership, held under s.67. In many cases, also, the court will have excused the receiver from holding such a meeting, although the court could order the holding of a meeting of creditors for this purpose at a later stage.

Under s.68, the committee is "to exercise the functions conferred on it by or under this Act". Section 68(2) entitles the committee, on giving not less

---

[75] "Insolvency Law and Practice", (June 1982, Cmnd. 8558, para.481): the recommendation that a committee be obligatory was not accepted.

than seven days notice, "to require the receiver to attend before it at any reasonable time and to furnish it with such information relating to the carrying out by him of his functions as it may reasonably require". Rule 3.5 provides that the committee "shall represent to the receiver the views of the unsecured creditors and shall act in relation to him in such manner as may be agreed from time to time". While the main purpose of the committee is, therefore, to represent the views of the unsecured creditors and discuss the operation of the receivership, r.3.5 envisages the possibility of the receiver entering into a formal arrangement with the committee for specific areas of assistance.

In addition, under r.7.28, if there is a committee of creditors, its duties include keeping under review the amount of the caution to be maintained by the receiver (see para.30–45).

30–116 **Committee of creditors: constitution and proceedings.** Rules 3.4–3.8 deal with the constitution and procedure of the committee, by adopting with appropriate modification the Rules relating to liquidation committees (rr.4.40–4.59A).

There have to be at least three and not more than five members elected at the meeting which resolves to establish the committee. Any creditor whose claim has not been rejected is eligible. Partnerships and bodies corporate may be represented (r.3.4).

The receiver must issue a certificate of due constitution of the committee, and lodge this with the Accountant in Bankruptcy, giving details of the members (Forms 4.20 (Scot) and 4.22 (Scot)—see r.4.42 as applied by r.3.6). A member of the committee can appoint a representative to attend meetings in his place (r.4.48, as applied). A member may resign by notice in writing to the receiver. Membership terminates automatically, if a member goes bankrupt or ceases to be a creditor. A committee member can be removed by majority vote of the unsecured creditors. Membership is lost if a member fails to attend three consecutive meetings, unless he is excused at the last of these (rr.4.49–4.51, as applied). Rule 4.52, as applied, makes provision for the filling of any vacancy on the committee. Changes in the membership require an amended certificate lodged with the Accountant in Bankruptcy by the receiver (Forms 4.20 (Scot) and 4.22 (Scot)).

The first meeting of the creditors' committee is to be held within three months after its establishment, and thereafter as it requires. Not less than seven days notice is to be given of meetings. The receiver or his nominee (his employee or other insolvency practitioner) will act as chairman. A quorum of two members is required and voting is by simple majority. Resolutions may be circulated for signature. The acts of the committee are valid notwithstanding any defect in the appointment, election or qualifications of any member of the committee or any committee member's representative or in the formalities of its establishment (r.4.59A, as applied).

Members of the committee of creditors are entitled to recover, as an expense of the receivership, their reasonable travelling expenses in attending meetings of the committee or otherwise involved in its business; but the receiver may disallow these expenses, if a meeting is convened otherwise than by himself within three months of the previous meeting (see r.3.6(4)). The receiver has no power, however, to reject claims for expenses, if the meetings are held at the instance of the committee itself at longer intervals than three months. If he considers that the committee is involving the receivership in unnecessary expense, he would require to apply to the court for directions under s.63.

If the committee wishes to summon the receiver to attend before it and give information, pursuant to s.68(2), the notice to the receiver must be in writing signed by a majority of the committee or their representatives. It must give him at least seven days notice and be for a "business day" (see para.30–110, below) chosen by the committee. The receiver, however, is entitled to select the time and place of the meeting. For such a meeting, a person other than the receiver may be elected by the committee as chairman (r.3.7).

Creditors' committee: transactions by members. The members of a creditors' committee in a receivership are not subject to the restrictions imposed on a committee of creditors in a liquidation, with respect to dealings between them and the company (see r.4.59). Provided that the transaction is entered into on "normal commercial terms", a member of the committee may deal with the company while the receiver is acting. Any interested party may, however, apply to the court for an order setting aside such a transaction, and the court may order compensation for any loss which the company may have incurred (r.3.8). **30–117**

I. Distribution of Funds and Accounting

Payments by receiver. Payment to the holder of the floating charge under which the receiver was appointed is subject to the rights of the following which, subject to agreed variation, have priority over the holder of the charge and rank in the following order (Insolvency Act 1986, s.60(1)): **30–118**

(i) the claims of the holder of a fixed security over assets subject to the charge which ranks prior to or *pari passu* with the floating charge;

(ii) the claims of all persons holding effectually executed diligence on any part of the property subject to the charge (see paras 30–40—30–41);

(iii) creditors in respect of outlays and liabilities incurred by the receiver or on his behalf;

(iv) the receiver in respect of his own expenses and remuneration, and in respect of such liabilities which he has incurred, and any right of indemnity which he has out of the property of the company; and

(v) the preferential creditors entitled to payment under Insolvency Act 1986, s.59 (see paras 30–120 *et seq.).*

This order of priority may be varied by any instrument relevant to the rights of the creditor concerned (typically, a ranking agreement). Clearly, however, the rights of a particular creditor cannot be postponed without his consent in such instrument.

Unlike the situation in a liquidation, there is no statutory obligation to have the account of the receiver's solicitor taxed before payment.

In the case of a floating charge created after September 15, 2003, a receiver requires to provide a "prescribed part" of net assets realised for distribution to unsecured creditors, unless he obtains a court order dispensing with this requirement (discussed in Ch.29).

30–119 After satisfaction of the foregoing, the receiver pays any monies remaining to the holder of the floating charge under which he was appointed (up to the amount secured). After the prior claims and the charge-holder have received full satisfaction, any balance remaining is to be paid in accordance with their respective rights to any other receiver, the holder of a fixed security postponed to the charge and the company or its liquidator as the case may require (s.60(2)). The expenses incurred by a liquidator appointed prior to the receiver are not the responsibility of the receiver.[76] If the receiver wishes to dispose of an asset which is subject to a security or diligence and he cannot obtain the creditor's consent, he may obtain a court order to permit the disposal under s.61 (discussed in para.30–97).

If there is any dispute as to the person entitled to payment, or where the receiver cannot obtain a receipt or discharge in respect of such payment, he is required to consign the amount due in a bank in the name of the Accountant of Court, for behalf of such persons as may be entitled thereto (s.60(3)). The inference is that the Accountant of Court will not release such funds, until he is satisfied that the claimant is entitled thereto, and has obtained such receipt or discharge as may be required.

30–120 **Preferential creditors.** The claims of preferential creditors (as defined in s.386 and Sch.6 of the Insolvency Act 1986, as amended) have priority over the claims of the holder of the floating charge under which the receiver was appointed, If the company is not being wound up at the time the receiver is appointed, it is his responsibility to establish whether there are any preferential claims and, if so, the amount thereof. In order to limit his liability, the receiver will advertise for claims in the Edinburgh Gazette and a newspaper circulating in the district where the company carries on business. He will not be responsible for any preferential claims, unless these have been brought to his notice, or are otherwise known to him, within six months after such advertisement (Insolvency Act 1986, s.59(1) and (2)). If the company is already in liquidation, notwithstanding s.59(1), the receiver may accept responsibility for paying the preferential claims in order to maintain his priority over the liquidator.[77] If the receiver (e.g. by carrying on the business of the company) dissipates funds which were available for

---

[76] *Manley, Petitioner,* 1985 S.L.T. 42.

[77] *Manley, Petitioner,* 1985 S.L.T. 42. This is consistent with s.60 (see p.536).

preferential claims, he is personally liable.[78] If there are assets available for the ordinary creditors of the company, any payment of preferential creditors which the receiver requires to make may be recovered from such surplus (s.59(3)). If the company is in liquidation when the receiver is appointed, responsibility for meeting the preferential claims lies with the liquidator, and again they have priority to the claims of the charge-holder (Insolvency Act 1986, s.175). The calculation of such claims in the two insolvency procedures may, however, differs, since they are determined by reference to the separate commencement dates of the two procedures (see para.30–123).

Following the abolition of Crown preference by the Enterprise Act 2002, s.251(1)(a) with effect from September 15, 2003, the categories of preferential debts are: **30–121**

(1) Any unpaid remuneration due to an employee, subject to a maximum of four months' pay, and also subject to a maximum sum which is prescribed by Statutory Instrument;

(2) Accrued holiday remuneration (without limit) which is due to employees or former employees;

(3) Sums advanced by a third party to meet payments which would otherwise fall within category (1) or (2);

(4) Any sum due to be paid under the Reserve Forces (Safeguard of Employment) Act 1985, subject to the prescribed maximum;

(5) Levies on the production of coal and steel, and any related surcharge for delay, arising from Arts 49 and 50 of the European Coal and Steel Community Treaty. These were added to the list of preferential debts by the Insolvency (ECSC Levy Debts) Regulations 1987 (SI 1987/2093), which came into effect on January 1, 1988. The preference for such levies, etc. is to be given effect, regardless of the date of commencement of the insolvency proceedings, but shall not affect any declaration or payment of a dividend before January 1, 1988.

Paragraphs 13–15 of Sch.6 extend the definition of remuneration, so as to **30–122** include piece work, commission and various sums due under the Employment Protection legislation, and define "holiday remuneration". Sums not recovered from the receiver as preferential debts may be paid by the Secretary of State. Claims not satisfied by either will receive an ordinary ranking in the liquidation of the company. The preference for wages is not clearly defined as the gross sum due, or the sum net of PAYE, NIC contributions, etc. (subject to the prescribed limit). This practical problem was noted by the Cork Report.[79] The "gross" interpretation seems preferable, on the basis that this gives the same results, whether the payment is to

[78] *Westminster Corp v Haste* [1950] Ch. 442; *IRC v Goldblatt,* etc. [1972] 1 Ch. 498.

[79] "Insolvency Law and Practice", Cmnd. 8558, para.1444.

the employee (with PAYE and NIC deducted and paid to the Revenue) or to a third party (under (3) above), where there is no such deduction.

All payments of preferential claims rank *pari passu* (see Insolvency Act 1986, s.175).

30–123 Section 387(4) of the Insolvency Act 1986 provides that, for the purposes of calculating preferential claims, where necessary, the "relevant date" is the date of the appointment of the receiver. If, however, a liquidator has already been appointed, the preferential claims will fall to be calculated by reference to the date when winding up commenced. Although the receiver will have priority over the liquidator, in respect of the assets subject to the charge, the liquidator will be entitled to withhold such assets as may be required to meet any outstanding preferential claims for which he is responsible under s.175. It is clear from the terms of ss.59 and 175 of the 1986 Act that responsibility for paying the preferential claims lies with whichever insolvency practitioner was first appointed; if the liquidator was appointed first, the receiver has no responsibility under s.59.

30–124 **Annual accounts.** The duty to circulate annual accounts, previously contained in the Companies Act 1985, s.481(2), is now regulated by r.3.9. The receiver must make up accounts of receipts and payments in the prescribed form (Form 3.2 (Scot)) for each period of 12 months, and for the final period of the receivership. The accounts must be submitted within two months of the end of the period for which they are due. The court may extend the time for preparing the accounts from the stipulated period of two months. The receiver must lodge a copy of his annual abstract with the Account in Bankruptcy, and send copies to the holder of the charge under which he was appointed, the members of the creditors' committee (if any) and the company or, if it is in liquidation, its liquidator.

Compliance with r.3.9 does not relieve the receiver of any general obligation to render proper accounts for his intromissions (r.3.9(4)). This may require him to provide the company (or its liquidator) with fuller accounting records than the Rules prescribe.[80]

J. Miscellaneous

30–125 **Books and records.** The receiver must maintain a sederunt book "for the purpose of providing an accurate record of the administration". He must record in it copies of anything which the Act or the Rules require him to record, and make it available for inspection at all reasonable hours by any interested person. If it is maintained in non-documentary form (e.g. computer records), it must be capable of being reproduced in legible form. Entries in the sederunt book are sufficient evidence of the facts stated therein, unless "founded on by the responsible insolvency practitioner in his own interest." The receiver must retain or make arrangements for the

---

[80] *Smiths Ltd v Middleton* [1979] 3 All E.R. 842.

retention of the sederunt book for at least 10 years from ceasing to hold office, unless a further receiver (to whom the records would pass) is appointed (r.7.33, as amended by the Insolvency (Scotland) Amendment Rules 1987 (SI 1987/1921)).

This does not, however, apply to the receiver's personal notes, etc. which remain his property.[81]

The Amendment Rules of 1987 (above) further provide for the ultimate disposal of the sederunt book and other records. If the receivership is succeeded by other insolvency proceedings, the receiver must hand over the records to the insolvency practitioner concerned, within 30 days of being requested to do so, and in any event within six months after the receiver ceased to hold office. If no other insolvency proceedings have commenced in respect of the company within six months after the receivership has terminated, the receiver must obtain directions for the disposal of the records from the creditors' committee (if any), by an extraordinary resolution of the company or from the court (r.7.34).

The book and records of the company itself remain its property, available for consultation by the receiver, who can use his power to require information under s.66, or apply to the court, if access to them is denied. The receiver (if he is given custody of the records) must make them available to the directors (e.g. to enable them to fulfil their statutory duties; see para.30–43), and in any event must have them ready for delivery to the company or its liquidator on completion of the receivership.

Value added tax. A receiver is no longer required to provide a certificate of **30–126** insolvency for recovery of VAT paid by a creditor (Value Added Tax Regulations 1995 (SI 1995/2518, para.167)), but the relevant Rules (rr.3.12–3.14), although no longer operative, have not yet been repealed.

Reports on conduct of directors. What is now the Company Directors **30–127** Disqualification Act 1986[82] was brought into force on April 28, 1986. This Act empowers the Secretary of State to apply to the court for a disqualification order against a director of a company which has become insolvent, whose conduct makes him unfit to be concerned in the management of a company. The appointment of an "administrative receiver" is sufficient evidence of insolvency for this purpose (Disqualification Act, s.6(2)). The order may be sought against any person who is or who has been a director (or shadow director) of the company which became insolvent while he was a director or afterwards.

An administrative receiver is required to report to the Secretary of State on the conduct of the company's current and former (within three years) directors and shadow directors, pursuant to the Insolvent Companies (Reports on Conduct of Directors) (Scotland) Rules 1996 (SI 1996/1910).

---

[81] *Gomba Holdings UK Ltd v Minories Finance* (1987) 3 B.C.C. 643, aff'd [1989] 1 All E.R. 281, CA.

[82] Consolidating ss.295–302 of the Companies Act 1985 and ss.12–14 and 18 of the Insolvency Act 1986.

30–128 **General powers of the court.** The 1986 Act and the Rules give the court certain general powers, in addition to the specific powers referred to elsewhere in this chapter. Under s.63(1), the holder of a floating charge or the receiver may apply to the court for directions in respect of any matter arising in connection with the performance of his duties. While similar provisions existed before the 1986 Act, only the holder of the charge, and not the receiver himself, could apply to the court for directions (1972 Act, s.23(1); Companies Act 1985, s.479(1)). Accordingly, only a receiver can apply to the court under s.63, only if appointed on or after December 29, 1986. Directions cannot, however, be given to any party other than the receiver in question.[83]

The court also has power, under s.63(2) of the 1986 Act, to order the holder of the floating charge to indemnify the receiver against any personal liability arising solely by reason of the invalidity of his appointment. The precise scope of the section is not clear (see further para.30–65). Section 63(2) is in similar terms to the previous provisions (Companies Act 1985, s.479(2) and (3)), so that indemnity on this basis can be sought by a receiver, whenever appointed.

30–129 In addition to the provisions of the Act, the Rules (r.7.32) allow the court to cure procedural defects. This is done by the somewhat clumsy device of "translating" the provisions of the Bankruptcy (Scotland) Act 1985, s.63 into terminology appropriate for receivership. Applying the relevant changes in the terminology, s.63 of the Bankruptcy Act reads as follows:

> "(1) the court may, on the application of any person having an interest:
>
> (a) if there has been a failure to comply with any requirement of the Act or the Rules, make an order waiving any such failure and, so far as practicable, restoring any person prejudiced by the failure to the position he would have been in, but for the failure;
>
> (b) if for any reason anything required or authorised to be done in, or in connection with, the insolvency proceedings cannot be done, make such order as may be necessary to enable that thing to be done.
>
> (2) the court, in an order under sub-section (1) above, may impose such conditions, including conditions as to expenses, as it thinks fit and may:
>
> (a) authorise or dispense with the performance of any act in the insolvency proceedings;
>
> (b) appoint as reponsible insolvency practitioner on the company's estate a person who would be eligible to act as a responsible insolvency practitioner, whether or not in place of an existing practitioner;

---

[83] *Jamieson, Petitioner,* 1997 S.L.T. 821; [1997] B.C.C. 682. By contrast, the equivalent English provision (s.35) is not so limited; *Re Therm-a-Stor Ltd* [1997] B.C.C. 301.

(c) extend or waive any time limit specified in or under the Act or the Rules.

(3) an application under sub-section (1) above:

(a) may at any time be remitted by the Sheriff Court to the Court of Session, *ex proprio motu* or on an application by any person having an interest;
(b) shall be so remitted if the Court of Session so directs on an application by any such person,
(c) if the Sheriff Court or the Court of Session, as the case may be, considers that the remit is desirable because of the importance or complexity of the matter raised by the application.

(4) the responsible insolvency practitioner shall record in the sederunt book the decision of the court under this section".

The "translation" applied is not completely specified by r.7.32, which, however, directs that s.63 of the Bankruptcy Act shall apply, with the modifications specified and any other necessary modifications. "Insolvency proceedings" includes any receivership under the Act and Rules, even if not strictly "insolvent", and whether "administrative" or not (r.0.2(1)). It seems clear, therefore, that any defect in the receivership procedure which derives from a provision of the Insolvency Act 1986 or the 1986 Rules can be cured by an application to the court. The generous width of the provisions of s.63 (as adapted) appear to be sufficient to cover defects in the instrument of appointment and the acceptance by the receiver, as well as defects of procedure arising in the course of the administration of the receivership. The section does not, however, warrant any relief in respect of defects arising under the Companies Act 1985, e.g. lack of registration of the original charge, or under the Receivers (Scotland) Regulations 1986, or any other statutory provisions or subordinate legislation other than those specifically included. This is clearly a defect in the legislation.

Under s.69 of the 1986 Act (as modified by the Scotland Act 1998, **30–130**
s.125(1) and Sch.8, para.21(1)–(3)), the court may order a receiver to rectify certain omissions. If the receiver has failed to file returns, reports, etc. an application for an order to compel him to do so can be made by any creditor or member of the company, by the Registrar of Companies or by the Accountant in Bankruptcy. If the receiver has failed to give a proper accounting for his intromissions to the liquidator of the company, an order may be sought by the liquidator. In either case, there must be a preliminary notification to the receiver of the alleged default, to give him an opportunity to rectify it himself. The court may order expenses against the receiver. These orders are in addition to any penalty that may be imposed for the default in question. Presumably, also, they are without prejudice to any obligation to account to the company or other interested parties, at common law or under the Rules (see r.3.9(4)).

30–131 **Dispositions in a winding up.** There is an apparent conflict between the duties of a receiver to effect distributions and the Insolvency Act 1986, s.127 of which provides that, in a winding up by the court, any disposition of the property of the company made after the commencement of the winding up is void unless the court otherwise directs. Taken literally, this would mean that, once a liquidator has been appointed by the court, the receiver must obtain the authority of the court for any subsequent payment out of the assets in his charge. It appears however that this literal interpretation of s.127 is not justified, and the receiver can distribute the property of the company in accordance with his powers without reference to the court.[84]

30–132 **Unregistered and foreign companies.** The Companies Act, 1985, s.462 provides that Scots law shall recognise floating charges by any company (whether a company within the meaning of the Act or not). A floating charge may, therefore be granted by an "unregistered company", such as a company incorporated by special Act or Royal Charter, a friendly society or a foreign or oversea company. If an oversea company has "a place of business" in Scotland, such a charge must be registered in Scotland (Companies Act 1985, ss.410, 411 and 424). If the Court of Session has jurisdiction to wind up the unregistered or foreign company:

(i) the floating charge must be in an instrument in writing (Companies Act 1985, s.462(4)),[85] and

(ii) a receiver may be appointed by the holder of that charge under the Insolvency Act 1986, s.51(1) or by the court on the holder's application under s.51(1) or by the court on the holder's application under s.51(2).

Such a receiver is subject to the Insolvency Act, and relative Regulations and Rules, in the same manner as a receiver of a company incorporated in Scotland (s.70(1)). Subject to the EC Regulation on Insolvency Proceedings, the Court of Session has jurisdiction to wind up any "unregistered company" which has a principal place of business in Scotland (s.221(3)), and it may also (in certain circumstances) wind up a foreign company which never had a place of business in Scotland.[86] In effect, therefore, for a receiver to be competently appointed to an unregistered or foreign company under Scots law, although both the Companies Act and the Insolvency Act do not expressly so provide, the floating charge has to comply with the Companies Act, s.462 (and be registered, if required by ss.410, 411 and 424), and the receiver has to be appointed under the Insolvency Act ss.51 or 52. There is no room for a "foreign" floating charge

---

[84] *Sowman and Samuel v David Samuel Trust (in liq.)* [1978] 1 All E.R. 616.

[85] The requirement that it be executed under seal (s.462(2)), or by attorney authorised under seal (s.462(3)), was repealed by the Law Reform (Miscellaneous Provisions) (Scotland) Act 1990.

[86] *Re Compania Merabello San Nicholas S.A.* [1983] 1 A.C. 244.

or a "foreign" receiver to be recognised, unless it and the appointment comply with the law applicable in Scotland. This does not, however, apply to companies registered in England and Wales or in Northern Ireland (see para.30–101). The European Council Regulation on Insolvency Proceedings (discussed in Ch.28) does not directly apply to receivership, but if its effect is to prevent the Scottish courts from having jurisdiction to wind up a company (even one registered in Scotland), on the basis that its "centre of main interests" is in another EC Member State (except Denmark), the terms of s.51(1) prevent a receiver being appointed to that company, since they restrict that to a company which the Court of Session has jurisdiction to wind up.

APPENDIX A[1]

PRACTICE STATEMENT—THE FIXING AND APPROVAL OF THE REMUNERATION OF APPOINTEES (2004)

Registrar Baister, Chief Registrar

15 July 2004

PART ONE—GENERAL

1. DEFINITIONS AND INTERPRETATION

1.1 In this Practice Statement:

(1) "appointee" means:

(i) a provisional liquidator appointed under Section 135 of the Insolvency Act;
(ii) a special manager appointed under Section 177 or Section 370 of the Insolvency Act;
(iii) a liquidator appointed by the members of a company or partnership or by the creditors of a company or partnership or by the Secretary of State pursuant to Section 137 of the Insolvency Act, or by the court pursuant to Section 140 of the Insolvency Act;
(iv) an administrator of a company appointed to manage the property, business and affairs of that company under the Insolvency Act or other enactment and to which the provisions of the Insolvency Act are applicable;
(v) a trustee in bankruptcy (other than the Official Receiver) appointed under the Insolvency Act;
(vi) a nominee or supervisor of a voluntary arrangement under Part I or Part VIII of the Insolvency Act;
(vii) a licensed insolvency practitioner appointed by the court pursuant to Section 273 of the Insolvency Act;
(viii) an interim receiver appointed by the court pursuant to Section 286 of the Insolvency Act;

(2) "appointment" means the appointment as an appointee;

(3) "assessor" means a person appointed in accordance with Rule 35.15 of the CPR;

[1] Appendix A does not apply in Scotland.

(4) "CPR" means the Civil Procedure Rules 1998 (as amended);

(5) "the court" means the court exercising jurisdiction in respect of the appointment in accordance with the Insolvency Act and the Insolvency Rules or other relevant enactment and/or applicable rules;

(6) "the guiding principles" means the statements of principle contained in paragraph 3.4;

(7) "Insolvency Act" means the Insolvency Act 1986 (as amended);

(8) "Insolvency Rules" means the Insolvency Rules 1986 (as amended);

(9) "the objective" means the objective stated in paragraph 3.2.

1.2 References to paragraphs are references to paragraphs of this Practice Statement.

2. APPLICABILITY

2.1 This Practice Statement shall, save to the extent and as may otherwise be ordered by the court, apply to all appointees in respect of:

(1) any application to the court by an appointee for the fixing and approval of his remuneration where his remuneration has not otherwise already been fixed and approved;

(2) any application to the court by an appointee for the fixing and approval of his remuneration in circumstances where he considers that the amount of his remuneration as fixed and approved by resolution of the members of the partnership or company or the creditors' committee or the liquidation committee or by resolution of the general body of creditors (as appropriate) is insufficient;

(3) any application by a person who may be permitted to apply under the Insolvency Act, the Insolvency Rules, or otherwise including by reference to the jurisdiction of the court to supervise the conduct of one of its officers and the inherent jurisdiction of the Supreme Court and is dissatisfied with the remuneration of an appointee that has otherwise been fixed and approved on the basis that such remuneration is excessive.

2.2 This Practice Statement shall come into effect on 1 October 2004 and shall apply to all applications for the fixing and approval of the remuneration of an appointee issued after that date.

3. THE OBJECTIVE AND THE GUIDING PRINCIPLES

3.1 This Practice Statement is supplemental to the Insolvency Act, the Insolvency Rules and such other enactments or rules as have been or may be introduced and which are relevant to the fixing and approval of the remuneration of an appointee.

3.2 The objective of this Practice Statement is to ensure that the remuneration of an appointee which is fixed and approved by the court is fair, reasonable and commensurate with the nature and extent of the work properly undertaken by the appointee in any given case and is fixed and approved by reference to a process which is consistent and predictable.

3.3 Set out below are the guiding principles by reference to which applications for the fixing and approval of the remuneration of appointees are to be considered both by applicants, in the preparation and presentation of their application, and by the court which is required to determine such applications.

3.4 The guiding principles are as follows:

(1) "Justification": It is for the appointee who seeks to be remunerated at a particular level and/or in a particular manner to justify his claim and in order to do so the appointee should be prepared to provide full particulars of the basis for and the nature of his claim for remuneration.

(2) "The benefit of the doubt": The corollary of guiding principle (1) is that on any application for the fixing and approval of the remuneration of an appointee, if after considering the evidence before it and after having regard to the guiding principles (in particular guiding principle (3)), the matters contained in paragraph 5.2 (in particular paragraph 5.2(10)) and the matters referred to in paragraph 5.3 (as appropriate) there remains any element of doubt as to the appropriateness, fairness or reasonableness of the amount sought to be fixed and approved (whether arising from a lack of particularity as to the basis for and the nature of the appointee's claim to remuneration or otherwise) such element of doubt should be resolved by the court against the appointee.

(3) "Professional integrity": The court should give weight to the fact that the appointee is a member of a regulated profession (where such is the case) and as such is subject to rules and guidance as to professional conduct and (where such is the case) the fact that the appointee is an officer of the court.

(4) "The value of the service rendered": the remuneration of an appointee should reflect and should be fixed and approved so as to reward the value of the service rendered by the appointee, not simply to reimburse the appointee in respect of time expended and cost incurred.

(5) "Fair and reasonable": the amount of the remuneration to be fixed and approved by the court should be fair and reasonable and represent fair and reasonable remuneration for the work properly undertaken or to be undertaken.

(6) "Proportionality":

(i) "proportionality of information": in considering the nature and extent of the information which should be provided by an appointee in respect of an application for the fixing and approval of his remuneration the court, the appointee and any other parties to the application shall have regard to what is proportionate by reference to the amount of remuneration to be fixed and approved, the nature, complexity and extent of the work to be completed (where the application relates to future remuneration) or that has been completed by the appointee and the value and nature of the assets and liabilities with which the appointee will have to deal or has had to deal;

(ii) "proportionality of remuneration": the amount of remuneration to be fixed and approved by the court should be proportional to the nature, complexity and extent of the work to be completed (where the application relates to future remuneration) or that has been completed by the appointee and the value and nature of the assets and/or potential assets and the liabilities and/or potential liabilities with which the appointee will have to deal or has had to deal, the nature and degree of the responsibility to which the appointee has been subject in any given case, the nature and extent of the risk (if any) assumed by the appointee and the efficiency (in respect of both time and cost) with which the appointee has completed the work undertaken;

(7) "Professional guidance": In respect of an application for the fixing and approval of the remuneration of an appointee, the appointee may have regard to the relevant and current statements of practice promulgated by any relevant regulatory and professional bodies in relation to the fixing and approval of the remuneration of an appointee. In considering an application for the fixing or approval of the remuneration of an appointee, the court may also have regard to such statements of practice and the extent of compliance with such statements of practice by the appointee.

(8) "Impracticability": where the appointee has not, either upon or shortly after the commencement of his appointment, sought to have the basis upon which his remuneration is to be fixed approved by the members of the partnership or the company, the creditors' committee, the liquidation committee or the general body of creditors (as appropriate) and in circumstances where the appointee considers that it will be impracticable to have his remuneration fixed and/or approved in such a manner, he may, as soon as reasonably practicable after his appointment, apply to the court to have the basis upon which he is to be remunerated fixed and for directions as to the manner in which his remuneration is to be approved (which may include provision for payments to be made on account). In circumstances where such an application may be made, to the extent that such an application is not made but the appointee subsequently makes an application to the court for the fixing and approval of the whole or any part of his remuneration, an explanation as to why no earlier application was made shall be provided to the court.

PART TWO—THE FIXING AND APPROVAL OF REMUNERATION

4. DISTRIBUTION OF BUSINESS

4.1 All applications for the fixing and approval of the remuneration of an appointee shall in the first instance (unless otherwise ordered by the court, having regard to the particular circumstances of an application) be made, where the court is the High Court to a Registrar or a District Judge in the appropriate District Registry of the High Court or, where the court is a County Court, a District Judge in the appropriate County Court.
4.2 On the hearing of the application the court shall consider the evidence then available to it and may either summarily determine the application or adjourn it giving such directions as it thinks appropriate. Such directions may include a direction that:

(1) an assessor or a Costs Judge prepare a report to the court in respect of the remuneration which is sought to be fixed and approved; and/or

(2) the application be heard by the Registrar or the District Judge sitting with or without an assessor or a Costs Judge or by a Judge sitting with or without an assessor or a Costs Judge.

4.3 In the usual course an application for the fixing and approval of the remuneration of an appointee should be determined by a Registrar or a District Judge sitting without an assessor or a Costs Judge and without the need for a report from an assessor or a Costs Judge.
4.4 The court may give the directions referred to in paragraphs 4.2(1) and (2) where it considers this to be appropriate having regard to the size and complexity of the case or in the event that the application gives rise to complicated issues of fact or of law. The court ought only to make an order for the involvement of a Costs Judge in circumstances where it considers the involvement of an assessor is (for whatever reason) not appropriate and that the application can only properly be determined by reference to the particular expertise and assistance that can be provided by a Costs Judge.
4.5 A list of suitably qualified persons appointed by the court to act as assessors in respect of applications for the fixing and approval of the remuneration of an appointee is available from the court.
4.6 The reasonable costs of an assessor appointed by the court shall be paid from the assets under the control of the appointee.

5. RELEVANT CRITERIA AND PROCEDURE

5.1 When considering an application for the fixing and approval of the remuneration of an appointee the court shall have regard to the objective, the guiding principles and all relevant circumstances including the matters referred to in paragraph 5.2 and where appropriate paragraph 5.3, each of which should be addressed in the evidence placed before the court.
5.2 On any application for the fixing and approval of the remuneration of an appointee, the appointee should:

(1) Provide a narrative description and explanation of:
   (i) the background to, the relevant circumstances of and the reasons for the appointment;
   (ii) the work undertaken or to be undertaken in respect of the appointment and in respect of which work the remuneration of the appointee is sought to be fixed and approved, which description should be divided, insofar as possible, into individual tasks or categories of task. General descriptions of work, tasks, or categories of task should (insofar as possible) be avoided;
   (iii) the reasons why it is or was considered reasonable and/or necessary and/or beneficial for such work to be conducted, giving details of why particular tasks or categories of task were undertaken and why such tasks or categories of task are to be undertaken or have been undertaken by particular individuals and in a particular manner;
   (iv) the amount of time to be spent or that has been spent in respect of work to be completed or that has been completed and in respect of which the fixing and approval of remuneration is sought and which it is considered is fair, reasonable and proportionate;
   (v) what is likely to be and has been achieved, the benefits that are likely to and have accrued as a consequence of the work that is to be or has been completed, the manner in which the work required in respect of the appointment is progressing and what, in the opinion of the appointee, remains to be achieved.

(2) Provide details sufficient for the court to determine the application by reference to the criteria which is required to be taken into account by reference to the Insolvency Rules and any other applicable enactments or rules relevant to the fixing and approval of the remuneration of an appointee.

(3) Provide a statement of the total number of hours of work undertaken or to be undertaken in respect of which the fixing and approval of remuneration is sought, together with a breakdown of such hours by individual member of staff and individual tasks or categories of tasks to be performed or that have been performed. Details should also be given of:
   (i) the tasks or categories of tasks to be undertaken as a proportion of the total amount of work to be undertaken in respect of which the fixing and approval of remuneration is sought and the tasks or categories of tasks that have been undertaken as a proportion of the total amount of work that has been undertaken in respect of which the fixing and approval of remuneration is sought; and
   (ii) the tasks or categories of task to be completed by individual members of staff or grade of personnel including the

appointee as a proportion of the total amount of work to be completed by all members of staff including the appointee in respect of which the fixing and approval of remuneration is sought, or the tasks or categories of task that have been completed by individual members of staff or grade of personnel as a proportion of the total amount of work that has been completed by all members of staff including the appointee in respect of which the fixing and approval of remuneration is sought.

(4) Provide a statement of the total amount to be charged for the work to be undertaken or that has been undertaken in respect of which the fixing and approval of remuneration is sought which should include:

(i) a breakdown of such amounts by individual member of staff and individual task or categories of task performed;
(ii) details of the time expended and the remuneration charged in respect of each individual task or category of task as a proportion (respectively) of the total time expended and the total remuneration charged.

In respect of an application pursuant to which the amount of the appointee's remuneration is to be fixed and approved on the basis of a percentage of the value of the assets realised and/or distributed, the appointee shall provide (for the purposes of comparison) the same details as are required by this paragraph (4), but on the basis of what would have been charged had he been seeking remuneration on the basis of the time properly spent by him and his staff.

(5) Provide details of each individual to be engaged or who has been engaged in work in respect of the appointment and in respect of which the fixing and approval of remuneration is sought, including details of their relevant experience, training, qualifications and the level of their seniority.

(6) Provide an explanation of:

(i) the steps, if any, to be taken or that have been taken by the appointee to avoid duplication of effort and cost in respect of the work to be completed or that has been completed in respect of which the fixing and approval of the remuneration is sought; and
(ii) the steps to be taken or that have been taken to ensure that the work to be completed or that has been completed is to be or was undertaken by individuals of appropriate experience and seniority relative to the nature of the work to be or that has been undertaken.

(7) Provide details of the individual rates charged by the appointee and members of his staff in respect of the work to be completed or that

has been completed and in respect of which the remuneration is sought to be fixed and approved. Such details should include:

(i) a general explanation of the policy adopted in relation to the fixing or calculation of such rates;

(ii) in relation to charges in respect of secretarial, administrative and cashiering services (and/or such other charges as might also otherwise be regarded as an overhead cost forming a component part of the rates charged by the appointee and members of his staff), an explanation as to why (where this is the case) such costs are to be or have been charged for separately together with confirmation that where such work is to be or has been charged for separately such work will not or has not also been charged for as part of the rates that are to be or have been charged by the appointee and/or members of his staff;

(iii) a description of the manner in which the appointee and members of his staff record the nature of the work they will undertake or have undertaken in respect of which the fixing and approval of remuneration is sought and the manner in which the amount of time spent in carrying out such work is recorded. This explanation should include, in circumstances where time is charged for on the basis of a unit of time a description of such unit and the practice and policy applied in recording time spent by reference to that unit.

As regards sub-paragraphs (i) to (iii) of this paragraph (7) only sub-paragraph (iii) shall apply to applications to which paragraph 5.3 applies.

(8) Where the application for the fixing and approval of remuneration is in respect of a period of time during which the charge out rates of the appointee and/or members of his staff engaged in work in respect of the appointment have increased, provide an explanation of the nature, extent and reason for such increase and the date when such increase took effect. This paragraph (8) does not apply to applications to which paragraph 5.3 applies.

(9) Provide details of any remuneration previously fixed and approved in relation to the appointment (whether by the court or otherwise) including in particular the amounts that were previously sought to be fixed and approved and the amounts that were in fact fixed and approved and the basis upon which such amounts were fixed and approved.

(10) In order that the court may be able to consider the views of those persons which the appointee considers have an interest in the assets that are under his control, provide details of:

(i) what (if any) consultation has taken place between the appointee and those persons and if no such consultation has taken place an explanation should be given as to the reason why; and

(ii) the number and value of the interests of the persons consulted including details of the proportion (by number and by value) of the interests of such persons by reference to the entirety of those persons having an interest in the assets under the control of the appointee.

(11) Provide such other relevant information as the appointee considers, in the circumstances, ought to be provided to the court.

5.3 This paragraph applies to applications where the remuneration of the appointee is to be fixed and approved on the basis of a percentage of the value of the assets realised and/or distributed. On such applications in addition to the matters referred to in paragraph 5.2 (as applicable) the appointee shall:

(1) Provide a full description of the basis of and reasons for his remuneration being sought to be fixed and approved by reference to a percentage of the value of the assets realised and/or distributed.

(2) Provide a full explanation of the basis upon which the percentage rates to be applied to the values of the assets realised and/or distributed have been chosen.

(3) Provide a statement that to the best of the appointee's belief the percentage rates which are sought to be applied are similar to the percentage rates that are applied or have been applied in respect of other appointments of a similar nature.

(4) By reference to the matters contained in paragraph 5.2 (as applicable), provide a comparison of the amount to be charged by reference to a percentage of the value of the assets realised and/or distributed and an estimate of the amount that would otherwise have been charged if the remuneration was to be fixed by reference to the time properly given by him and his staff.

(5) Provide a comparison between the amounts to be charged by reference to a percentage of the value of the assets realised and/or distributed using the percentage rates sought to be fixed and approved by the court and the percentage rates provided for by the scale of fees referred to in Schedule 6 to the Insolvency Rules.

5.4 If and insofar as any of the matters referred to in paragraph 5.2 or 5.3 (as appropriate) are not addressed in the evidence placed before the court on the hearing of an application for the fixing and approval of the remuneration of an appointee an explanation for why this is the case should be included in such evidence.

5.5 Notwithstanding that the expenses and disbursements of the appointee and his staff are not required to be approved by the court on any

application by the appointee for the fixing and approval of his remuneration, a summary of the amount and nature of such expenses and disbursements incurred during the relevant period should be provided as should an explanation of the steps taken by the appointee to subject such expenses and disbursements to critical scrutiny.
5.6 There should be included in the evidence placed before the court by the appointee in respect of any application for the fixing and approval of the remuneration of an appointee the following documents:

(1) A copy of the most recent receipts and payments account;

(2) Copies of any reports by the appointee to the persons having an interest in the assets under his control relevant to the period for which the remuneration sought to be fixed and approved relates;

(3) Schedules or such other representations of the information referred to in paragraphs 5.2 and 5.3 such as are likely to be of assistance to the court in fixing and approving the remuneration of the appointee.

(4) Evidence of consultation with those persons having an interest in the assets under the control of appointee in relation to the fixing and approval of the remuneration of the appointee.

5.7 On any application for the fixing and approval of remuneration of an appointee the court may make an order permitting payments of remuneration to be made on account subject to final approval whether by the court or otherwise.
5.8 Unless otherwise ordered by the court (or as may otherwise be provided for in any enactment or rules of procedure) the costs of and occasioned by an application for the fixing and/or approval of the remuneration of an appointee shall be paid from the assets under the control of the appointee.

APPENDIX B[1]

PRACTICE NOTE ON THE HEARING OF INSOLVENCY PROCEEDINGS

23 May 2005

Practice Note—Proceedings relating to insolvent companies—Proceedings relating to insolvent matters—Matters to be heard by judge—Matters to be heard by registrar or district judge—Matters to consider when deciding whether to adjourn proceedings to the judge.

Statutory provisions referred to
Insolvency Rules 1986 (S.I. 1986/1925), Rule 7.6(2).

Case referred to
Practice Direction: Insolvency Proceedings [1999] B.P.I.R. 441.

1. The following statement was issued by the Vice-Chancellor.

2. This Practice Note supersedes all previous Practice Statements of the Bankruptcy Registrars dealing with jurisdiction and work distribution and the Guidelines issued by the Insolvency Court Users' Committee in November 1988.

3. As a general rule all petitions, claims and applications (except for those listed in paragraph 4 below) should be listed for initial hearing before a registrar or district judge in accordance with Rule 7.6(2) of the Insolvency Rules 1986.

4. The following applications should always be listed before a judge:

   — Proceedings relating to insolvent companies:

      — applications for committal for contempt;
      — applications for an administration order;
      — applications for an injunction;
      — applications for the appointment of a provisional liquidator;
      — interim applications and applications for directions or case management after any proceedings have been referred or adjourned to the judge (except where liberty

[1] Appendix B does not apply in Scotland.

to apply to the registrar or district judge has been given).

- Proceedings relating to insolvent individuals:
  - applications for committal for contempt;
  - applications for an injunction;
  - interim applications and applications for directions or case management after any proceedings have been referred or adjourned to the judge (except where liberty to apply to the registrar or district judge has been given).

5. When deciding whether to hear proceedings themselves or refer or adjourn them to the judge, the registrar or district judge should have regard to the following factors:
   - the likely date and length of the hearing;
   - public interest in the proceedings;
   - the availability in the court which is likely to hear the proceedings of relevant specialist expertise.

6. Litigants and their advisors are reminded that paragraph 17 of the *Practice Direction on Insolvency Proceedings* applies to appeals and that an appeal from a registrar, district judge or County Court judge lies, in the first instance and without permission, to a single judge of the High Court.

INDEX
(all references are to paragraph number)